Sue Krzowski, born in 1949, comes from a working-class family in the Midlands, where she grew up, married and had her two children. She moved to London in 1975, divorced and returned to study as a mature student at Middlesex Polytechnic. After completing a degree in social science, she became a member of The Women's Therapy Centre collective. She trained at the centre and now practices as a psychotherapist there. Since 1979 she has been involved in the administration, organisation and development of the Workshop Programme. She also works with Perspective, an organisation offering training and consultancy from a feminist perspective to women and men working in the caring profession. A special area of her work is with the adult survivors of child sexual abuse.

Pat Land was born in Southampton in 1940, and spent her childhood there and in Sussex. Her adolescence was spent in Canada. She married and returned to the UK at the age of has since lived in London. She has trained and worked as a social worker and psychotherapist. She is divorced and ha adult sons.

SUE KRZOWSKI AND
PAT LAND (EDITORS)

# In Our Experience

Workshops at the Women's Therapy Centre

 The Women's Press

Published by The Women's Press Limited 1988
A member of the Namara Group
34 Great Sutton Street, London EC1V 0DX

British Library Cataloguing in Publication Data

In our experience : workshops at the
   Women's Therapy Centre.
   1. Self-help groups——Great Britain
   2. Women's networks——Great Britain
   I. Krzowski, Sue   II. Land, Pat
   361.8'3       HQ1597

ISBN 0-7043-4065-8

Typeset by AKM Associates (UK) Limited
Ajmal House, Hayes Road, Southall, London
Printed and bound in Great Britain by
Hazell Watson & Viney, Aylesbury, Bucks.

# Contents

# Acknowledgments

We would like to thank Lucy Goodison whose idea this project was; the contributors for their hard work and creativity; The Women's Therapy Centre and The Women's Press for trusting and supporting us to gather this book together. Thanks also to Julia Vellacott for her help in the final stages. We learned a lot from her around her kitchen table. We offer our warm appreciation to all the women who have attended workshops and who continue struggling to grow and change. We hope this record of shared experience will encourage and enable others to do so too.

Sue Krzowski   Pat Land

# Foreword

This book grows out of the bravery and honesty of the many women who have brought their problems and preoccupations to Women's Therapy Centre workshops. Problems with relationships, parents, depression, self-image, stress, agoraphobia. Issues like class, competition, needing to please, body awareness, disability, sexuality, self-assertion. Interests like dance, dreams and massage. The experience of being black or a lesbian in our racist and homophobic society. Problems from childhood, like incest, or from adult life, like coming to terms with abortion and growing old. Over the past ten years the Centre has run workshops on all of these topics. And over the years thousands of women, stepping in from the street, have talked about their fears, hopes, distresses and conflicts; sometimes for a day, sometimes over a series of meetings. They have brought a wealth of female experience which enabled the workshop leaders to deepen their understanding of those issues, and of what it means to grow up a woman in society. In this book some of those workshop leaders describe what they have learned from running those groups.

They do not write as faceless experts, and do not deny their own personal involvement with the topic of the workshop. Often they face or have faced the same problems themselves; they draw on their own lives and share what they have learnt to assist other women. They describe their thought processes and feelings as group leaders. Their detailed accounts of the sessions give a vivid impression of how it feels to run a group, the successes and pitfalls that can be encountered.

Since we wrote *In Our Own Hands*, self-help therapy has blossomed in a life of its own. Initially, women from the Red Therapy group, to which we belonged, made a major contribution to the Women's Therapy Centre workshop programme, teaching different therapy techniques and skills for tackling specific topics and running self-help groups. Over the years the Centre has consistently provided support for the spread of self-help therapy, helping to initiate and sustain a network of groups. We are happy to feel part of a movement in which the work initiated by Red Therapy women has, under the Centre's auspices, been inherited and developed by others.

When we wrote *In Our Own Hands*, we were concerned to show that self-help groups were possible, and to provide people with an accessible way of learning some techniques and structures for those groups. This book takes that process a step further and elaborates the understandings that the intervening years have thrown up. While we were struggling to describe how we had started to grapple with the group process, here the writers of the last chapter have been able to work out a theory for understanding the development of self-help groups. Not understanding the process your group is going through can be very confusing and ultimately destructive for the group; we think that having a theoretical model will be sustaining and enabling.

In other ways too, *In Our Experience* has enriched what we wrote. The range of women whose needs are addressed has broadened, for example with the workshops for lesbians, black and working-class women. Another important development lies in the theme-centred groups on agoraphobia, depression and creativity. We hope that the programmes for disabled women which the Centre has more recently been pioneering will also find their way into print in the future.

*In Our Own Hands* was written from our experience of seven years in self-help therapy, for people starting out. We tried to sketch what it is like for women to work in groups which are not based on adherence to any one 'brand' of therapy but on commitment to a feminist and socialist perspective. Seven years on, this book fills out that picture, drawing on the further development of self-help, the workshop practice and on the long-term therapy work at the Centre, which has combined a feminist perspective with some of the understandings of the psychoanalytic tradition. In this way the book has moved into another area, addressing a different audience. With its focus on the process of group leading, it demystifies that process. We hope that those in the caring professions who are involved in setting up groups gain valuable ideas about running workshops for themselves and others. But while the professional element is more emphasised, we hope that women in self-help groups also find in it concrete exercises and structures they can use, and that they will benefit from the surrounding wealth of insights about what those exercises may stir up. We can picture the book in many living rooms, with the practical bits highlighted in fluorescent pen – and we can imagine lively discussions about the ideas it raises. *In Our Experience* offers new ways to understand ourselves and help each other which can empower women.

Sheila Ernst and Lucy Goodison, February 1988

# Introduction

All the contributors to this book have drawn on several years of experience of running workshops at the Women's Therapy Centre in London and, occasionally, in other parts of the country and abroad.

The contributors come from different countries and different trainings and different class backgrounds, have different sexual orientations and are of different ages, but all share a commitment to understanding women's lives and women's psychology in a social and political context.

Each of the contributors has drawn on her own experience of running workshops for women at the Women's Therapy Centre, her experience of meeting regularly with dozens of other workshop leaders and the written feedback and evaluation she has received from women after they have attended her workshops. We are greatly indebted to the women who have attended the groups and shared with us their hopes and fears. We hope that they will recognise in this book their own contributions, though names and details have been altered to preserve confidentiality.

The book is for a wide range of readers. For women who may be feeling isolated within their difficulties and thinking about whether to seek help, we hope it will demystify therapy and help dispel some of the misinformation that has grown up around it. For women who want to learn to lead workshops, we hope it will encourage them to start workshops in different parts of the country, as they are greatly needed and as yet largely available only in London and a few major cities. For women who are thinking of setting up or joining a self-help group as a way of dealing with problems they cannot manage alone, we hope this book will provide a good base to work from. Lastly, we are glad of the opportunity to share our experience with any women or men who are simply interested and may identify with the feelings and experiences described in the following chapters. We have organised the book with this diversity of readers in mind. Each part contains chapters around a general theme.

As it is in our families that we first experience ourselves, so it is in our later relationships that many of us first notice intractable difficulties, and the workshops focusing on three of the most important areas of relationships come first in the book.

Alongside our personal relationships we are also likely to discover something about the outside world, and how assumptions about women taken for granted socially affect our inner feelings and attitudes as well as our real life opportunities. So Part 2 contains descriptions of workshops on specific social oppressions and how they affect the inner world, and on one apparently personal problem, agoraphobia, that predominantly affects women and is intimately linked with women's position in the social world.

Once we realise that recognising external oppression is not a magic solution to our problematic feelings, we may turn more to trying to understand our internal world, and Part 3 contains chapters on the confusing relationships we may have within ourselves.

Many women may have specific problems in relating to their own bodies; moreover, it is through our bodies that we both express and sometimes discover our deepest feelings. Part 4 is written by three leaders of workshops connected with understanding and using the body.

Each of the chapters can be read for what it has to say about women's experiences; it is also intended as a source of information on how to lead workshops, and what it feels like to do so. This focus is specific in the last part of the book, which contains a practical guide to setting up and running a theme-centred workshop, and a chapter on the complicated issues raised by leaderless self-help groups.

Although these chapters come last in the book, before the reference section, they can be read first as a general introduction to how workshops function.

## The Women's Therapy Centre

Susie Orbach and Luise Eichenbaum opened the Women's Therapy Centre in Islington on 8 April 1976. They had previously been involved in the mental health field in New York, where they had participated in the struggle to establish a feminist-orientated therapeutic practice. On coming to London and realising that it was even more difficult to obtain psychotherapeutic services that addressed the needs of women and took account of the social realities of women's lives here, they took up the struggle again and founded a Centre where women could be treated by women who had a feminist awareness and where women therapists, counsellors, social workers and other mental health practitioners could share their thinking on women's psychology from a feminist perspective.

The first home of the Women's Therapy Centre was a basement flat in Hartham Road and consisted of two large consulting-rooms and an office–kitchen. It rapidly attracted women from all over London, and further afield, both women who wanted psychotherapy and women workers who recognised in the project their own concerns. Charitable status was applied for, but funding was non-existent then. Susie and Luise had sunk their savings into setting up the Centre and it now had to be self-financing. Before there was any funding, fees were charged on a sliding scale according to income so that women who had no money or were on subsistence level could receive free treatment, subsidised by their better-off sisters. The therapists worked for very low fees, as often happens in the voluntary sector. Most of the workers were fired by their commitment to the principles of the project and the sheer excitement and exhilaration of initiating change in a field where it was, and still is, so badly needed.

The staff group consisted of full-time and part-time therapists who collectively ran the Centre, decided policy and offered psycho-analytically-orientated individual and group psychotherapy. The Centre was soon overwhelmed by the demand for individual therapy and ended up with a two-year waiting-list (which no one was very happy about). It was partly in response to the enormous demand and precious few resources that the workshop programme was initiated.

## Development of the Workshop Programme

Discussions among the therapists at the Centre revealed that certain themes came up in individual sessions again and again, themes that seemed part of the very fabric of being a woman in this society: pain and anger between mothers and daughters, tensions about dependency and independence, huge problems over separation, anxieties about sexuality, feelings about being stuck in a caring role and not being allowed to have needs. Though not exclusive to women, they seemed endemic among us.

It was decided to set up short, time-limited groups that would focus specifically on certain of these issues as a way of raising awareness, giving specific help, and enabling women to decide what further steps they might take to help themselves. It was hoped that workshops would also teach skills for the self-help groups that many women wanted to set up.

The women's movement had developed the consciousness-raising group, in which women came together with no designated leader to explore the links between their personal experiences and their collective social oppression. It was often a startling experience to identify for the first time a personal shame or anxiety as part of a social reality, and it made changes in many women's lives. Wives challenged husbands over stereotyped expectations; women workers made demands for better treatment by employers; women discovered women as friends and allies. Collective action sometimes resulted in childcare campaigns, demands for abortion rights and access to contraceptive facilities, strikes by women who had never thought of industrial action before.

The internal realities were harder to deal with. Women often found a discrepancy between the independent attitude they adopted in the world and the feelings they carried around of dependency and insecurity. Some felt ashamed to speak about their unregenerate feelings to other women who seemed wholehearted in their feminism.

The picture seemed something like this: patriarchal culture has given the task of nurture – of the young and old, and of men, who can thus get on with the external work of the world unhindered – to women. Women learn early to care, and to deserve, not to be overtly demanding. We grow up with an expectation that our future lies in success at relationships and that we will be defined by them, our success judged by whom we marry, how our children turn out. When things go wrong, we have a tendency to feel not only pain but also the self-hatred of failure.

Both sexes lose something by the implicit and pervasive demand that women do all the 'emotional work', but it is women who experience the guilt when there are difficulties.

Out of the blunting of little girls' autonomy, so that they may be accepted and loved, spring the characteristic deformations of the 'feminine' psychic structure: the problems over separation/individuation, unresolved dependency, the fear of insatiability, the immense guilt, the manipulativeness that results from needs and demands that are not admitted to conscious awareness, the insecurity and feelings of rejection. Obviously, there are major individual variations. People are born with different capacities and characteristics, and personal history within families is infinitely variable. Yet this outline sketch is recognisable to a great number of women of different class backgrounds and from different countries within Western industrial culture. We should point out that so far most of these women have been white. There are differences both in the history and in the current experience of black women and women of colour, even within Western industrial culture, that may alter materially the internal picture of what it means to be a woman.

Some women, including those at the Women's Therapy Centre, had begun to try to understand the impact of internalised social attitudes on psychic development and structure, as a way of understanding these emotional difficulties. There were, in fact, several mixed groups in the early 1970s that were grappling with similar issues in terms of class. Red Therapy was a radical self-help therapy group in which the women had formed a separate group to explore particular issues of womanhood. Against a background of psychoanalytic theory they were experimenting with self-help and mutual support, with the aim of demystifying mental health, and had begun developing exercises and group games, derived from 'humanistic' psychology, as a way of getting in touch with people's inner experience.

When the simple but new idea of running groups for women focused on a theme came up at the Women's Therapy Centre, several women from Red Therapy were invited to join the workshop programme. Thus several strands of experience and theory were brought together.

Consciousness-raising groups did not occur in isolation but contributed to, and drew upon, an increasing body of sociological writing by feminists who had at some time participated in such groups. The structural position seemed fairly clear, at least for Western industrialised societies: that in any class or racial group, the power-holders in the outer world are men; that women, whether working at home or in that outer world, are economically disadvantaged by comparison; and that the socialisation processes that maintain this position result in women taking practical and emotional responsibility for things designated domestic, which are defined as inferior in importance.

Equally, just as the human responsibilities delegated to women are defined as inferior, women are seen as inferior beings, hence capable of performing only low-status functions.

The feminist challenge to the assumption of women's inferiority extended, as we have seen, to the realm of psychiatry, and became part of a more general questioning of established authority on the issue of mental health and illness. The 'anti-psychiatry' movement led in one direction to a romanticisation and idealisation of madness as a special sort of insight, in another to a denial that insanity exists, except as an extreme response to social conditions, in a third, to the forming of self-help groups of various kinds, in attempts both to examine how social reality imposes itself within individuals and to change the individuals' relationship to the power structure within themselves.

Such groups were not composed exclusively, if at all, of ex-patients. Many participants were politically concerned, and a large number of professionals in the psychiatric services and social work were involved.

The ground had been prepared by the therapeutic community movement, with its emphasis on mutual challenge and support in a safe environment, and by the increasing use of groups in various settings as a means of healing.

There are many ways of looking at group processes and of running therapy groups. The workshops, on the whole, though they may draw on the large body of available knowledge about the details of group processes, tend to focus more on what women bring from the outside world to share than on what being in the group does to them. Hence some group analysts might consider that the workshops consist of 'individual psychotherapy in the group'.

This is not entirely the case, however. Membership in the group, entailing an open acknowledgment of difficulties in common, sets up currents among the women that enable interpretations at times to be addressed to the group as a whole. Often, unlike a group therapist, the workshop leader may link her interpretations not only to feelings in the room but also to realities in the outside world. This is particularly common in those groups that have met because of an 'outside/inside' problem, such as class, race or age.

At times, the leader may address an interpretation to the whole group about processes she has become aware of – collective demands she may feel pressured by, for example – and, in effect, offer at that moment the classical 'psychotherapy of the group' approach. A good example of such a moment happened in a workshop Sue once ran. Her group of incest survivors were stuck in what seemed like angry silence, and when Sue recognised that to their unconscious selves she had become 'the mother they could not tell' and said so, the repressed feelings began to emerge and the group could move on again.

Because of the currents of sympathy that start to flow as women relate their personal stories to the theme of the workshop, it is often possible to see a form of 'psychotherapy in the group' beginning to happen. Not only do other members offer direct interventions, such as pointing out repeating patterns, but the fact of group membership itself offers much-needed support to many women and enables them to think what was unthinkable before.

## A Range of Theoretical Backgrounds

The attempts, to which we have alluded, to use psychoanalytic theory as a way of understanding the perpetuation of unwanted behaviour and attitudes are founded on the recognition that it is very hard to change. We may know about injustice, we may be good at recognising sexist or racist attitudes in other people, but when it comes to how we feel about ourselves and, crucially, how we behave in relationships, we often find ourselves bafflingly inconsistent and out of line with our principles.

Something is obviously going on that we do not know about, and psychoanalysis, in theory and in practice, is founded on the notion that a large part of human experience is unconscious. Conscious awareness may be just the tip of our iceberg.

Sigmund Freud, who developed psychoanalysis in the last part of the nineteenth century and the first four decades of this one, suggested that impulses and wishes become part of the unconscious because they are repressed, pushed out of conscious awareness as unacceptable or unmanageable. Some later theorists have postulated that it is not wishes but very early relationships that are unavailable to our awareness. What is unanimous is the recognition that we repress, not by conscious effort but by being unable to bear the reality, what is unacceptable to our conscious selves. The colloquial phrase 'They just don't want to know' sums that process up rather neatly, although the act of repression itself is not allowed into consciousness.

Although he analysed many women, Freud was not satisfied with his own formulations on the subject of women's psychology. (Susie Orbach and Luise Eichenbaum took the title of their well-known theoretical book *What Do Women Want?* from the title of one of his late essays.) He based most of his theory on what he understood of men, partly as a result of his lifelong adventure of self-analysis, and left a suggestion that later analysts, perhaps especially women, would make more sense of feminine psychic development.

Some of his early followers took up this suggestion within the taken-for-granted framework of women's social and economic inferiority. Helene Deutsch is notorious among feminists for her classically 'sexist' pronouncements about female sexuality.

Others, notably Karen Horney, began to look more closely at the social framework within which people lived and moved, and to relate the social world to the inner world. Though she did not make a specific link with gender issues, her ways of looking at socialisation are useful to feminists.

Wilhelm Reich, working in Germany in the 1920s and 1930s, made explicit the now familiar link between the personal and the political, and examined the dialectical process whereby each influences the other. He believed that political oppression, mediated through the family, results in rigid personal repression, which is expressed most acutely in the systematic denial and frustration of the needs of the body. In his view, the liberation of the body-self would create hopes and demands that would ultimately crack oppressive systems from within, as free people refused psychic and political servitude. He created the form of therapy known as bioenergetics.

Part 4 of this book owes much to his work. In it you will find a description of a bioenergetics workshop, as well as of other ways of working with the body.

The development in psychoanalytic thought that has been particularly fruitful in the attempts by women to understand themselves is that of so-called object relations. Freud saw human psychology as derived from instinctual drives and their encounter with reality. Towards the end of his life, he became more and more interested in the detail of the relationships that constitute reality for each individual, but he never reformulated the theory in relationship terms.

Melanie Klein, who came to Britain from Berlin in the 1930s, was an analyst of young children as well as of adults, and she became convinced that the human infant is not just a bundle of instincts but is from birth a being-in-relationship.

Dr W. R. D. Fairbairn, working on his own in Edinburgh, made an impressive restatement of analytic theory in those terms. His writings are fewer than Melanie Klein's and his theory differs in several respects from hers, but it is interesting that they were working on the same project at the same time in psychoanalytic history. Perhaps it was 'an idea whose time has come'.

The reason for using the clumsy term 'object relations' is that initially the baby has not the sensory or emotional experience to recognise a separate whole person. The objects of her emotions are what she can perceive: the blissful experience of warmth, comfort, being held and fed, and the potentially overwhelming terror of hunger, wetness, cold, not being held. Ambivalence is just too much for the very new baby. She keeps the experiences separate in her mental world, 'splits' them into a good and a bad object. She then responds to experience in a split way, as though everything is either wonderful or terrible, which can be upsetting for her objects, especially her parents, and may indeed affect the way they respond to the baby. In good enough circumstances, the infant gradually recognises that the provider and the persecutor are in fact a person, and the same person, hence that mother is neither all good nor all bad. The child can be said to have a whole object in her mind, about whom she must learn to tolerate the pain of ambivalent feelings.

Some people never do quite reach the point of being able to bear mixed feelings, and most of us resort to splitting and blaming at times. It is important to face the anger and fear that are at the roots of blaming.

To many women, the project of trying to understand present relationships by reference to buried earlier ones makes sense in an immediate way that is not our experience when we try to think about instincts as separate from their objectives.

Although it forms a useful theoretical background for many workshop leaders, psychoanalysis is, in practice, a long and difficult process, mainly because patients unconsciously resist knowing what they don't want to know. Hence, though some workshop leaders find that an understanding of unconscious processes helps them work out what is going on in the group, no workshop at the Women's Therapy Centre is, strictly speaking, an analytic therapy group.

To clarify the ways in which an awareness of unconscious processes may be used, it may be helpful to examine the phenomenon called transference. We all carry with us from our early lives unconscious memories and feelings that we transfer on to situations or people in the present. It is quite common, for instance, in quarrels, to discover that the feelings aroused and the abuse hurled have a familiar ring, one that resonates from childhood.

Transference is likely to be particularly strong in a situation like a workshop, where someone is looked to for help or 'rescue' (and hence can be said to have a parental function). Primitive hopes and expectations, and early experiences of disappointed rage, may all be transferred on to the workshop leader. There are ways of addressing this issue in therapy that are too intense in their effect to be appropriate in a workshop setting. The workshops are all very different, having in common only that they each have a time-limit and a specific focus of work. Within this boundary there are wide variations in the ways in which issues such as transference may be taken up. Indeed, in some styles of work the question would not arise.

Vin Gomez, in her chapter on depression, gives a good example of the direct use of transference by an experienced workshop leader. In the second session of her group, rather than let resentment and blame be continually directed outside the room, she draws it to her herself. Her perceived strength then makes it safer for the group to be open about anger.

Mira Dana and Pat Land used the 'transference to the group' to point out how members were, as must inevitably happen, bringing their problems into the room with them and communicating them by their behaviour in the group.

Tricia Bickerton's description of the Mothers and Daughers workshop gives a sustained example of the use of transference information without touching directly upon it unless it hits you in the eye.

Another good example of the indirect use of transference information comes in the unexpected context of the self-help chapter, where Jocelyn Chaplin and Amelie Noack describe how their experience of leading the training group, that is, their countertransference (how the transference issues felt to them as leaders) helped them develop a better structure for their model of group processes.

By no means do all therapists subscribe to a belief in the usefulness of the unconscious, either as concept or as tool. Some would argue that there are many levels of awareness that are potentially available to consciousness without being obvious on the surface, and that therapies can most usefully address these pre-conscious phenomena. The group of therapies that come under the broad heading humanistic stick to opening up areas that their patients are willing to explore.

Many of the exercises and games described in these pages derive from one or other of the humanistic therapies:

Rogerian counselling, in which the patient is encouraged to explore her thoughts and feelings and the counsellor 'reflects' them back, enabling her to face them and take them further.

Gestalt, derived from Gestalt psychology, a theory that we learn by recognising patterns. In Gestalt therapy, everything the patient talks about is treated as part of herself and she is encouraged to talk to, or on behalf of, each of these parts and thus to integrate them. In dream work, the patient speaks from the role of each object in the dream and the therapist takes up what they seem to be telling her. In discussing relationships, the patient may be encouraged to 'place' the absent party on a cushion and talk to him or her.

Psychodrama, a form of group therapy in which members of the group enact parts of one another's personal dramas and learn from the interactions thus created.

Transactional analysis, which identifies feeling/thinking states as pertaining to the child, parent or adult level of the personality, and examines the transactions thus set up within relationships as well as within the self.

Co-counselling, which is not a therapy in the same sense as these others, because there is no therapist. Two people take turns giving attention to or counselling each other, and use techniques, usually taught in a group, for helping each other go further and deeper. A well-known network is re-evaluation co-counselling. Most workshops do not utilise the full range of co-counselling techniques, but many leaders suggest paired exercises on a theme relevant to the workshop title, and these are part of the early stages of learning co-counselling.

In summary, the theme-centred workshops developed by the Women's Therapy Centre seemed a means of combining insights from all these ways of working and thinking to help women focus on specific difficulties in their emotional lives. The sharing of awareness is in itself useful to the participants, and is also a good way to enhance understanding of a woman-centred therapy.

## What a Workshop Can Achieve at the Women's Therapy Centre

Women come to the workshops at the Centre by their own choice. Hence they will have identified the theme as one that is relevant to their own lives and something they want to work on. This gives them more control over the process than they can expect in most individual or group therapies, and this may attract both women whose lives are going reasonably well and who want to focus intently on a particular issue, to 'get it moving' within them, and women who are too scared of the extent of their unconscious internal damage to face ongoing therapy, and a whole spectrum of need in between.

A workshop can paradoxically be effective at both extremes as well as in the middle range. The sharing of experience in a safe environment, where everyone gets time and attention, may enable a woman who is already strong to move a long way towards recognising and changing specific patterns that bother her in herself. Others may use the workshop as a stage on the road to self-discovery. It may eventually lead to therapy, or a commitment to changing careers or joining a self-help group, or the journey may simply be enjoyable in itself.

A deeply needy woman may not be ready for change as yet, but may receive some solace from the sharing and care, and may be helped by finding she is not as isolated and different as she thought, may go to many more workshops, in fact, and perhaps seek long-term help. In most of the work we share conscious experience and also tap the rich vein of pre-conscious knowledge that women bring to a workshop, things they had almost faced, almost realised, 'didn't know they knew'.

## Who Comes?

Thousands of women have participated in the workshop programme since its inception eleven years ago, during which time the programme itself has developed and expanded enormously. The staff collective now employs over forty women on a sessional freelance basis to run workshops in the evenings and at weekends in the Manor Gardens Centre, which the Women's Therapy Centre made its new home in 1979. The Centre has also been successful in obtaining funding for its many expanding areas of work. Whereas initially the fees charged to women attending workshops subsidised the running of the Centre, the workshops themselves are now subsidised by Centre funding.

In the beginning, the great majority of women who attended were white and mostly middle class, often, in fact, in the caring professions themselves, though frequently 'first generation' educated, uprooted from working-class backgrounds. Gradually more black women and women of colour have started attending.

The Centre has received some funding to put into practice an equal opportunities policy. This funding has been used both to train the workshop leaders in disability and racism awareness, to appoint more black women, women of colour and disabled women as workshop leaders and to make the workshop programme more accessible to women with disabilities, black women, women of colour and lesbians. Unfortunately, the Centre has not been able to fund workshop spaces for women on low incomes, although it has an unwaged rate, which is kept as low as the budget allows.

The fact that fewer black women and women of colour used the workshop programme from the start points up a more general issue about the accessibility of therapy of all kinds. However earnestly therapists in general may feel that what they offer is useful to anyone who is willing to investigate her inner world, in practice, black, working-class, lesbian or disabled women may feel excluded by what is seen as an elitist and, on the whole, patriarchal provision. Of course, stereotyping by professionals is not extinct and may work to exclude such women from access to therapy by preventing referral. Moreover, as Pam Trevithick points out in her chapter on working-class women, such women may feel defensively scornful of the very idea of an 'inner world', as though only the effete middle class could afford such a thing.

Women in this category and others who have had bad experiences of therapy or psychiatry in the past can now attend a short introductory workshop to test the water, air some of their fears and conflicts about therapy, and dispel some of the prevailing myths before plunging into a longer group.

The workshop programme, able to change rapidly to fit needs because of the short-term nature of the work involved, may serve as a gentle introduction to the world of therapeutic possibilities for women who might otherwise never have had the chance to think about whether some sort of therapy is what they need.

# Part One
# Relationships

# 1
# Mothers and Daughters
## Tricia Bickerton

The Mothers and Daughters workshop has been led by Stef Pixner and myself for the last three years. It is a short-term workshop lasting between five and six weeks, with three or four evening sessions and a whole day near the beginning. Although we usually run the group together, this part of the chapter is based on my own experience and is written from my own viewpoint. I would like to thank all the women who have come to the workshop over the years and who have participated in what was often a new and risky experience.

Mothers and Daughters is probably one of the longest-running workshops at the Women's Therapy Centre. It has always been fully booked and continues to be popular. This is not surprising given that for most women the relationship with mother is the first and most formative. It is she who usually takes care of us, feeds us and teaches us the skills of growing up. It is from our mother that we learn in a fundamental way to be women. The focus of the workshop is on the daughter's experience of her mother, even though many of the women may be mothers themselves. I do not intend to explore in detail the theoretical complexity of this relationship; it has been written about extensively elsewhere. What I will try to do is to give a description of the format of the workshop and illustrate with various individual accounts some of the general issues that are raised. Because it is a short-term workshop, there isn't time for a gradual exploration of thoughts and feelings. From the start we use a number of exercises, including fantasies, drawings and role-play, to encourage and stimulate the group.

We are all women; we are all daughters. The first evening is an introduction to each of our mothers and to ourselves as daughters. I have two exercises. One involves each woman in the group choosing a partner and spending five minutes describing her mother. When both have had their turn they come back to the group. Then each woman introduces herself out loud as her partner's mother, using whatever details she has been given. I sometimes ask questions to which she tries to respond in character. It doesn't matter whether the portrayal is strictly accurate, since the distortions may in themselves evoke a response in the daughter. At the end of the process every daughter's mother is in the room.

I then ask each woman to draw a picture of her own mother and herself as the daughter, using crayons and paper. I invite them to share the pictures with the group. This usually takes up the rest of the evening. A picture can be very revealing. The images provide access to unconscious feelings and attitudes. When each woman draws, she does not necessarily know what she is drawing. But in the picture she often discovers, perhaps with the help of other members of the group, something new about the meaning of her relationship with her mother.

There are various things to look for. Is the mother smaller than the daughter or larger? What does this mean? Is it that the daughter sees her mother as a child, as fragile and weak, and herself as more powerful? Are her own needs therefore felt to be huge and demanding? Does she have to protect her mother from her anger? Or perhaps she is small and helpless in the face of a large and looming mother. Does she feel intimidated and unable to grow up? Do mother and daughter look alike? Are they wearing the same clothes and standing in similar postures? Does this indicate a similarity that is desired, or is it an inability to construct an identity separate from mother? Do mother and daughter link or connect? Are they holding hands or facing each other? What is the distance between them on the page? And is anything missing in terms of their bodies? For instance, do they both have hands, feet and, if they are naked, breasts and genitals? What is lacking is often very telling. If the daughter doesn't have any feet, how can she stand up? If the mother has no hands, how does she reach or hold? Are they both allowed to be sexual?

Maureen held her picture in front of her. She pointed to the child who was kneeling with her arms outstretched towards her mother, pleading for help. 'This was me as a child,' she said. 'My father was very abusive and violent, but my mother did nothing to protect me. Look how she's standing here, very stiff and cold. The message was always not to feel anything.' As Maureen was talking I felt very sad and wanted to reach out and care for her, but I too experienced myself as helpless and frozen. I asked her if it was difficult to trust us and I was amazed to find that although she was in her early thirties she had rarely talked about her childhood before. She admitted to being very frightened, perhaps of the extent of her pain, perhaps of how we as the group might respond. I guessed it would take a long time before she could really allow the desperately needy child to emerge. It had taken a lot of courage to come to a Mothers and Daughters workshop and begin to talk.

In the centre of Lisa's picture there was a mother slumped in front of the television and, in the corner, a tiny but quite colourful butterfly. She told us how much she hated her mother's depression. Someone asked her if she wanted to escape, to flit away like a butterfly. This desire would have been quite understandable, since she lived in a flat very close to her mother, visited her every week and felt obliged to fetch and carry, even though her father was healthy and capable. Her friends advised her to make more of an independent life, but for some reason she couldn't act on their advice. As Lisa talked she became increasingly agitated. 'I don't really want to talk about my mother,' she said, and laughed. 'I don't really like listening to all this pain. I just think it's time we all got away.' The phrase 'fight or flight' came to my mind, and it seemed as if Lisa wanted to escape the group rather than confront the mother in her own mind. She agreed.

It is important that everyone has a chance to share their picture and to leave with the feeling that they have made contact with the group. It is the first meeting and trust is still tenuous. I try to make sure that each woman is given some attention, but I rarely work with any particular woman in depth. Hopefully, enough of a bridge has been formed to carry us all through to the next session.

The full day, which is always the second meeting, begins with feedback from the last session: any anxieties, thoughts or insights that the women want to share. Sometimes I do some relaxation exercises before exploring their relationship with their mothers further. With a group of women who lack much experience of therapy I use an exercise which allows them either to go back into the past or to remain in the present if it feels safer. I ask them to recall a significant event involving themselves and their mothers. Some women may have little emotional support outside the workshop and it is not always wise to dismantle too many defences. There is always a likelihood that if a woman feels too exposed she will be frightened and construct even stronger armour to cope with everyday life.

However, when it is possible, I prefer to use a more powerful regression exercise. I ask the group to find a comfortable position and to close their eyes. First I go back ten years and I ask each woman to reflect in her imagination on where she is, what she is doing and with whom, and how she is feeling. I then ask her to say goodbye to this time in her life and to go back another five years, and then another five, and at each stage to reflect on herself and her situation. Finally, I ask her to go back to an age somewhere between two and ten. The exact choice of age is left open so that each woman can go back as far in time as she desires. Then, on my suggestion, she enters her own room and looks in a mirror. I ask various questions: 'What do you look like?', 'What are you wearing?', 'What are you feeling?' As she regards herself in the mirror, I ask her to become aware of another reflection – that of her mother. 'Look at your mother. What does she look like? What is she feeling? What does she feel about you? What are you feeling towards her? Is your mother saying anything? Are you saying anything in response? Is there anything you'd like to say?' When the group has reflected on their thoughts and feelings for a few minutes I suggest that they remain in touch but come back to the room and open their eyes.

My intention is for each woman to bring her child-self into the present. Naturally this may feel painful and it is not unusual for one or two of the group to be crying. If this happens I try to work with those women immediately, while the feeling is close to the surface. Sometimes it is enough simply to talk about what happened and to have the group listen. But often there is a complexity of feeling that requires more intensive work.

Claire as a seven-year-old saw her mother in the mirror, looking away, scarcely noticing her. She felt her mother expected her to be grown-up. She tells us how she was sent away to boarding-school in another country because her mother was too preoccupied with her career to look after her. Once, when she was 11, her mother met her at the airport but didn't recognise her. Claire, as she talks about the incident, clearly feels in touch with the little girl who desperately wants to be close to her mother but daren't reveal her need. She is torn in herself as to what to do in the group. Should she allow herself to cry? Or should she keep her feelings to herself, which is more familiar? It is important that I stress my continuing attention and interest and encourage her to share the little girl's feelings. With reassurance, she begins to cry for the lost mother, and when the crying subsides she emerges feeling somewhat relieved that the group have responded with sympathy and understanding. It surprises her into thinking that perhaps it isn't always necessary to maintain a coping façade.

Hilary's picture is different. In the mirror is a mother standing in judgment. She is Victorian in attitude, straitlaced with high moral standards. Hilary is not good enough. She is lazy, sluttish; her hair is a mess; her room needs cleaning. The mother seems all-powerful and

Hilary shrinks. She can neither please her mother nor stand up to her. She feels helpless and intimidated. I try to encourage Hilary to feel that she does have resources, that in reality she is no longer a little girl dependent on her mother. Now she can fight back and adopt her own standards. But she is not impressed. I suggest that she imagine her mother is sitting on a cushion in the room and that Hilary has been given permission to say exactly what she likes. At first she is quite enthusiastic about the opportunity, but when she is confronted by her imaginary mother she is unable to utter any word of dissent. It is almost as if she is attached to her subservience.

The other women in the group clearly feel agitated and I invite them to share what's happening to them. Almost everyone mentions their irritation with Hilary that she won't stand up and fight. I wonder in myself if she is afraid of the extent of her anger. After all, as a child it could have felt dangerous to invite further disapproval and punishment. Perhaps her own aggression had to be buried, to the extent that it is no longer conscious. It is possible that as a group we sense her unconscious feelings and we're expressing them on her behalf. As yet she is unable to take responsibility for this part of herself. She prefers to perceive her mother as powerful and herself as very weak. To discover that she is critical, hostile, aggressive, not unlike her mother, might be rather upsetting. However, there is a glimmer of hope in that she is able to acknowledge intellectually that there might be truth in what we are saying, and this could lead eventually to a greater emotional acceptance of her own power.

Both examples illustrate how the child, because of her dependence on her mother, may have been unable to express certain aspects of herself. When a little girl has feelings that she cannot acknowledge, the feelings become unconscious to her but they still continue to determine her experience of reality. Hilary painted a picture of a very persecuting mother, but it is quite possible that her unconscious anger distorted her perception. Her mother, like most people, probably had good qualities as well as the bad. When I am exploring with daughters their experience of their mothers, I never assume that what I hear is the truth. Rather, I search for what is concealed. It is only when the unconscious feelings are made available that the daughter can perceive reality more clearly. Sometimes the very process of going backwards reveals parts of the psyche that have been buried.

Christine was rather detached and intellectual during the first session. She had an ironic way of talking that made people laugh. But in the regression exercise she saw a little girl in a pink dress, her hair in pigtails, staring back at her from the mirror – a little girl, she said, who was shy and awkward and wanted to please her mummy. The image of herself as a child was in direct contrast to the image she presented in the group, where she wore jeans and a long jumper and gave the impression of not caring too much about her appearance. When she saw her mummy in the mirror, she asked her whether she was loved. She thought her mother replied in the negative and she looked as though she wanted to cry. I referred to the sad little girl who wasn't certain of her mother's love and she began to laugh mockingly about well-trained little girls. This was very disconcerting. For a brief moment she allowed us to be aware of a vulnerable child; then, having regained her composure, she flipped back into a cynical stance. Later in the day, in response to Hilary's inability to acknowledge her anger, Christine suddenly threw her shoes across the room, as if at her mother. I encouraged her to let rip by hitting a cushion, and she threw herself into this with passion. But when the passion was spent she just as speedily returned to her rather off-hand adult manner.

I do not usually encourage such explosions, since the problem is one of how to acknowledge and contain rage and understand its source. However, with Christine I felt there was so much locked-in feeling that she needed to release it in a way that felt unthreatening. What was difficult was that Christine's child-self was very disconnected from her adult-self, so that the feelings arose only in fragmentary moments and couldn't be easily accepted or integrated into her everyday self. Because there is much identification between the members of the group, it is quite common for one woman to trigger a childhood memory or an outburst of feeling in another. But in a short-term workshop there is neither the time nor the continuity of relationship to help each woman to achieve an integration of all the unconscious and conflicting aspects of herself. It is, however, helpful to give every woman as much time as possible to reflect on her emotional experiences, to talk about them and try to understand their meaning. This may do little more than point to the problems, but it will have a containing effect. As I give everyone the chance to explore their response to the exercise, it tends to take the whole day. We will meet again in a few days' time.

At the next session we discuss the idea of perfect mothering. We talk about the fantasy of the mother we would have liked, the mother who would have been always available, who would have fulfilled all our wishes and desires. The group are asked to write a fairy-tale about their ideal mother, beginning with the words 'Once upon a time . . .' More often than not it is a story of abundance, of nature, flowers and fields and the sun shining; a happy picture of mother and daughter entranced in each other, in love. There is no domestic routine and rarely an intervening father or other children with whom to compete.

Almost every woman in the group can produce an ideal mother in comparison to whom her actual mother seems enormously inadequate. How does this wish for a perfect mother come about? One way of understanding it might be to look at the very earliest experiences of the infant. This is a time when she is utterly dependent and so it is necessary for her to feel that her mother exists more or less totally for her. When the mother is in tune and responsive to the little girl's needs, it seems to the daughter as though they are one person. She is as yet unable to appreciate that her mother exists as a separate person with her own, sometimes conflicting, needs and desires. But however good a bond is established between mother and daughter, the infant inevitably experiences a certain amount of frustration. She copes with the intensity of these feelings by dissociating them from the pleasurable feelings attached to the good, feeding mother. In other words, in her imagination she creates two entirely separate mothers, one who is wonderful, generous and giving, and the other who is a terrible mummy, a witch. As the infant's capacity to tolerate frustration develops, so does her ability to perceive the mother as one person. But the split is not always healed. The degree to which it occurs varies a great deal from one person to another, depending on their predisposition and on the balance of good and bad experiences they have had. The more bleak and empty the world is in reality for the tiny infant, the more crucial it is to her survival to construct in her mind an image of a perfectly satisfying mother. And this psychological device may continue to be used by the daughter as a way of coping with any frustration or distress.

Barbara wrote a story about herself and her mother sunbathing naked in the garden. She imagined the two of them together, admiring and touching each other's bodies as they basked peacefully and uninterruptedly in the warm sun. Her mother, she said, was beautiful and sensuous. When she talked about it afterwards she revealed that as a child she hadn't spent much time with her mother, who had been depressed and withdrawn. Her father had taken care of her instead. She couldn't remember being held or caressed as a baby. In her life now she found it hard to enjoy an adult, sexual relationship with her husband, but she drew much comfort and warmth from her small daughter. She delighted in the little girl's sensuality and her spontaneous enjoyment of cuddling. It seemed as though she identified the child part of herself in her small daughter and was able to give her the physical love that she hadn't received herself. But this did not provide a resolution for her own feelings of neediness. She yearned to be touched and held. I suggested that she be cuddled by the group and with our encouragement she allowed herself to lie down and be caressed. This was a powerful moment for every woman in the room. For some it was experienced as a healing and reassuring process; for others it was less comfortable.

Jane, who looked particularly tense, was irritated with Barbara. She thought that she was expecting her little girl to mother her. She said this was unfair. I asked her what it meant in her own life and she angrily retorted that her mother had been just like Barbara. She told us that her parents were unhappy together and that her mother was often left alone. She looked to her daughter for comfort. Jane's fantasy revealed a wish for a strong and independent mother who pursued her own interests with enthusiasm, a mother, she said, who could encourage her to grow up.

Ann held herself at a distance. 'I know it's unfair,' she said. 'I know you've suffered, but I can't help feeling, "Well, at least you've had a mother".' Her own mother had died when she was six. She now couldn't remember her. She envied the attention that Barbara was receiving, but when I suggested that she come closer she was resistant. 'I've always been grown up. I've always had to cope.' She was too angry to allow herself to receive anything. Yet another woman had recently had an abortion and cried for the lost child.

Witnessing a group member being mothered arouses many contradictory feelings. On the one hand, it arouses the desire to give and receive; on the other, it inflames resentment and envy. It touches poignant memories, reveals what is lost.

For Barbara, it was a brief moment in which she experienced herself as the star of the group, not unlike a small infant who is loved and admired by everyone. I pointed out to her that perhaps she was reluctant to have a sexual relationship with her husband. 'It's risky to love another human being who is recognisably separate,' I said. 'Then you are forced to confront differences, conflicts, frustration and disappointment. Sometimes it's easier to love a child who cannot leave you.' I thought that Barbara imagined that she and her daughter were the same and that their needs and desires coincided in such a way that they couldn't possibly hurt or annoy each other.

What I aim to bring to light in the session is the discrepancy between the ideal and the reality, the difference between the desire for the perfect mother and the daughter's inevitably mixed experience. Each woman has the chance to share her fantasy by reading it to the group. Sometimes I also use a co-counselling exercise which begins 'My mother wasn't perfect because . . .' The group divides into pairs and each woman has 10 minutes to talk, while the other simply listens. When they come back to the group I work with whatever arises.

Sheila told us how angry she was with her mother, who had always been working and preferred her brother. She was a mother herself and felt she was disappointing her own daughter. We continued to talk about it and she revealed that she'd written a letter to her mother recently about a traumatic incident that had happened in her childhood. Her mother had responded with sympathy and understanding. 'I think I do love her,' she said cautiously, and clearly couldn't square the feeling with her miserable childhood. 'Your mother wasn't perfect,' I said, 'but then neither are you.' 'I'm more perfect than my mother,' she replied, and laughed. Her joke was a kind of admission that perhaps her mother had given her things that were important to her, but because of her own hostility she'd pushed her away. This seemed to ring bells for lots of women in the group, who felt that as daughters they'd been over-critical.

The problem with the idea of a perfect mother is that it is used to devalue the ordinary mother who is perhaps good enough but inevitably makes mistakes. Of course, it can be very disillusioning for each woman to come to terms with the reality of her childhood and her relationship with her mother compared to the fairy-tale version. And how much easier it is for the daughter to imagine that she is innocent and her mother is totally to blame! Sometimes it is very hard to shift her viewpoint, because then she is faced with her own imperfections, which may seem at first to imply that she is all-bad. However, it is important to keep on stressing in this session that there is no such thing as a perfect mother – nor, indeed, such a thing as a perfect daughter.

At the next session I concentrate on the issues of individuation, of separation and identity. In what way are we the same as our mothers, and how might we be different? Sometimes as a daughter we are afraid to disentangle ourselves from our mother for fear of hurting her and losing her altogether. One of the exercises I use is to ask each woman to write a list of her mother's positive and negative qualities. She might write, for instance: 'Controlling, weak, friendly,' etc. I ask them to read out the list of qualities to a partner, prefacing each of them with 'My mother is . . .' Then I suggest they read out the same list with 'I am . . .', so it would read: 'I am controlling, I am weak, I am friendly.' I don't reveal this part of the exercise at the beginning as it might have an inhibiting effect.

Surprisingly many women discover a similarity between themselves and their mother, but it can be disquieting, particularly if they have tried to distance themselves from her. A common example is for women to describe their mothers as possessive and demanding and unable to let go of their daughters. What they cannot always acknowledge is their own demanding self and their wish to remain close to their mother. I sometimes do some Gestalt work with anyone who is confused. I ask the daughter to imagine her mother sitting on a cushion in front of her and to talk to her, and then to reverse positions, to sit on the mother's cushion and become the mother talking back to the daughter.

Jenny described her mother as jealous and controlling. She told us how her mother rang her every evening and persistently asked her to come back home for holidays and weekends. She imagined her mother relished the fact that she didn't have a lasting sexual relationship. When Jenny became pregnant her mother, far from being dismayed, seemed to like the idea of a grandchild who would belong exclusively within the family. Jenny felt incapable of standing up to her mother and asserting her own independent life. She was afraid of giving her mother any reason to feel rejected. When she talked to her mother on the cushion she was cautious, tentative and timid. When she sat on the mother's cushion there was an immediate difference. Jenny as her mother became powerful and demanding. But in the process of moving backwards and forwards her own voice and arguments became stronger and herself as her mother seemed to be disarmed. As a result she felt more powerful and felt she could possibly tackle her mother in real life.

Although this exercise may be perceived as an actual dialogue between mother and daughter, it is more an expression of the relationship between these figures in the daughter's inner world. It is helpful to separate out the different parts of this world and explore them in turn in order to discover the substance of the conflicts. Identity is created not by merging and blurring the differences but by distinguishing them. It may feel dangerous for the daughter to see in herself the qualities she has attributed to her mother. But it is easier when she realises that they are only a part of her, not necessarily the whole, and thus not as consuming as she might believe. The daughter's sense of herself as a whole and separate person grows as she learns to integrate within herself the parts that she usually projects on to her mother. Sometimes it is then possible for the daughter to establish a more realistic relationship with her mother, one that is less distorted by her projections.

Towards the end of the session Jenny suddenly blurted out that she was angry with two women in the group for taking up so much space. When she had given vent to her feelings I suggested that perhaps this was the anger that she felt towards her mother, who had taken up so much space in her head. I wondered in myself if the previous exercise had stimulated the outburst. Jenny was clearly still irritated, but she began to apologise, then withdrew the apology. She held the attention of the group for some time and I suggested that perhaps she was in conflict with herself. She wanted to be angry but she was worried that if she was loud and powerful like her mother she would wipe people out, as her mother had seemed to wipe her out. She said she was afraid that the two women would leave the group and wouldn't return, and she only felt reassured when they acknowledged her anger without seeming to be too upset. Sheila said: 'Well, I got very angry with my mother and she survived.'

The session ended on a rather uncertain note, which is often the case if conflict occurs between the women in the group and there isn't enough time for its resolution.

The last session is mostly about tying up the loose ends in preparation for leaving the workshop. I make a point of asking whether there is any unresolved issue that anyone wants to explore in the group. Sometimes, if there is nothing pressing, I suggest that each woman, with a partner, talks for 15 minutes about how her relationship with her mother might be influencing her work, her friendships, her children and her sexuality in her present life.

Pat described how she took responsibility for her husband's feelings, very much as she had for her mother's. Her father had died when she was only seven and she had felt obliged to sleep in her mother's bed. She told us how difficult it was to obtain any space for herself. Either she obliged her mother and relinquished her autonomy or else she fought ruthlessly for her independence, hurting her mother in the process. Her marriage, she said, was on the rocks. She very much wanted a room of her own in the house she shared with her husband but he was antagonistic to the idea. Later, she thought that he had probably understood this desire as signalling the end of their sexual relationship. Having understood the background to her present conflicts, it occurred to her that perhaps she could be more independent within the marriage. Her husband might be rather insecure but it wouldn't necessarily be disastrous. Perhaps if she explained the meaning of the change to her husband there might be more room for negotiation. It didn't have to be so all-or-nothing.

Carol felt worried about her relationship with her five-year-old daughter. She told us that almost every day she felt driven to smack her. It shocked her to think of how enraged she became at her daughter's defiance and how hard she hit her. Her son, who was equally strong-willed, was not a problem, and she wondered if her relationship with her own mother had some bearing on her difficulties. In all the previous sessions she had drawn a blank when trying to remember her own childhood before the age of 11. Yet as she talked to the group about her daughter, memories came flooding back. She recalled how she once dressed up in stiletto heels and deliberately spiked holes in the back lawn. Then it occurred to her that her mother often flew off the handle, shouting and screaming and hitting her. When I suggested that it was the little girl inside her that really gave her a problem, not her daughter, she began to cry for the first time. She identified with her daughter's rebelliousness but, like her mother, she hated the little girl's will and wanted to beat her into submission. Carol was re-enacting her battle with her mother in the past with her daughter in the present. She was relieved to discover that her behaviour could be understood in terms of her own history, and that perhaps she had a chance to do things differently with her daughter.

At the end of five or six weeks most women are very loath to leave the workshop and feel that much work has been left undone. There is often talk of trying to continue the group afterwards. As a leader I very much resemble the mother who promises much but is inevitably disappointing. Anxiety is increased by the thought of the approaching end. Sometimes this is expressed in the need for immediate answers. I find myself being asked abstract questions, such as 'Do you think my relationship with my mother will ever change?' I cannot know the answer but I can suggest that leaving the group may be a reminder of being left by mother to rely on one's own resources. The question expresses a wish for reassurance about the future. One or two members of the group may find it difficult to appreciate what has been gained. The ending presents a limit and as such seems to spoil the pleasure of the past few weeks. I always give time for any negative criticisms of myself, but I also look at them in the context of it being the final session. Perhaps it is easier to leave the workshop with the belief that nothing has been received. That way there is no sense of loss. However, there is often a feeling of appreciation, not just of me but of all the women in the group, especially when they have been supportive. For many it has been a relatively new experience to talk intimately about their childhood and their relationship with their mother, and perhaps it is the first time that the inner child has been felt to be worthy of respect and understanding. Of course, a six-week group is only a beginning, and it is quite right that everyone should want to go on developing in whatever way they can.

A last exercise that is useful is to ask each woman to find a partner and discuss with her how she might move forward. I ask her to be practical and to think of realistic possibilities, however small. This could mean anything from making a decision to go into individual therapy, to saying no to visiting mother twice a week, to simply ringing friends when lonely. This decision will be a reminder of the emotional work that has been done, and it may also be a practical step towards further change.

# 2
# Fathers and Daughters
Stef Pixner

My own father left England when I was a baby and I didn't meet him again until I was 18. I wasn't aware of a lack, though I was aware of my mother's difficulties as a single parent. However, the picture I built up of him from my mother's stories (she told only of his admirable qualities), her worries and warnings (in which she communicated the negatives) has significantly affected my identity and my major choices in life.

Looking back, thinking about my own investment in running Fathers and Daughters workshops (three times a year for seven years), I think I have perhaps been searching for a sense of what fathers are, what they do, of what it was I didn't have. The search is illusory ('I had a father and I still don't know what they're for,' remarked a therapist friend.) However, I do have something I didn't have before. A series of pictures; a sense of a range and variety of relationships; a gap between this material and the theories (feminist and non-feminist) bearing on it; a growing awareness in me of gaps and of the meaning, for me, of absence.

A workshop is about to begin and I check out how I'm feeling. (I may need to know later whether I was tired/anxious/irritable at the outset, or was it just when Sue or Fiona or Dierdre started talking?) I check out what issues are around for me in relation to my father and other men in my life. My feelings are an important resource; I aim to be aware as far as I can in order to be usefully separate from the women in the group. Also, the more in touch I am with myself, the more likely I am to enjoy the workshop and to feel energetic rather than drained at the end of it. Compared to Mothers and Daughters or Sisters, both of which I would rather run with a co-leader, I find Fathers and Daughters an easy group to run on my own. The men are 'out there', and transference and counter-transference issues tend to be less strong. However men *are* 'in here' too, inside each one of us.

We learn each other's names. Everyone says a little about why they've come and whether they have any experience of therapy. This helps me pitch the level of work I may undertake with the group, or with any particular woman. I make a few introductory remarks, starting at the most general social level: 'As between the sexes, men have the greatest economic, political and cultural power. For most of us, our first and most formative relationship with a man has been that with our father. Your father may or may not have been an especially powerful man; we will be exploring the particular significance he has for you. There will be time for work in pairs and for individual work in the group. Everyone won't get exactly equal time – be aware of how you feel about time and attention (we won't be going round in a circle) – and about other women taking it. It may relate to feelings you have about your father's time and attention.'

Having acknowledged the social context, I rarely mention it again, although it is a backdrop in my mind as I work, at several different levels. For example, the organisation of work in society, housework and childcare (in particular, mothers are much more likely to have been present in the early years than fathers); the representation of women in the media and common social attitudes about gender; father's absences through war, death, divorce, long working hours and/or an inability to make emotional contact; male domestic violence; father–daughter sexual abuse. But all this is only a backdrop. I try to put it on one side and listen to each woman's story, and the story behind the story – her hidden as well as her official agenda with her father.

Another backdrop somewhere in my mind as I work is my knowledge of different understandings of the psyche (drawn mostly from object-relations theories, and neo-Reichian notions of character structure) and its embodiment, as well as attempts to understand psychic differences between women and men. I started running groups without much knowledge of theory, and although I find it very useful, the best theory in the world won't run you a good group. Putting all this to one side again, I try to get a sense of:

1   the 'outer' reality of each woman's life, with particular regard to her father (I work hard to memorise every piece of information given);

2   her own response and choices, conscious and unconscious feelings and 'patterns' in relation to him – her inner reality;

3   my own responses to her, emotional and physical – particularly if what she's saying and how she's saying it do not quite fit.

I usually start the group with a brief exercise in pairs: 'What's on my mind at the moment about my father.' I follow with a drawing of 'My father and myself'. Drawings are a good opener, allowing the women in the group to consciously choose what they want to present (if they so wish; some are able and willing to 'just draw' and see what comes), while expressing unconscious aspects which may startle or clarify. Women talk about the meaning of their pictures for themselves, and listen to comments from me and from others: 'He looks like a shadow over you', 'Is he giving you a present?', 'He has feet, but you haven't', 'Why are you green?'

Mothers may appear in the drawing: between father and daughter, closer to daughter, closer to father (in bed together, for example), or cordoned-off in a boxing-ring. Stepfathers may also appear, as may siblings.

Occasionally women find it too threatening or they are too angry to draw themselves on the same piece of paper as their father. In this situation they usually leave themselves out of the picture altogether, and it's the father who takes up all the space.

Sometimes fathers appear in boxes or behind glass, walls, fences or bars. These barriers may be seen as the father's creation: he's made himself remote and unavailable. Or they may be the daughter's, to protect herself from invasion – violent, sexual or emotional. Occasionally father and daughter are represented as two incomplete shapes which together make a whole, for example sun and moon shapes, or curved phallus and egg shapes.

It's interesting to compare these drawings with those that come up in the Mothers and Daughters workshops. My impression is that barriers are more frequent in the drawings of fathers and daughters; 'merging', 'one-inside-the-other' or 'same as' drawings are more common in the drawings women do of themselves and their mothers. In both, however, the parent is usually drawn larger than the child.

I often work further with one or two women, using the drawing as a starting-point.

'Mary, if your father had hands, what do you imagine they would be doing?'

'Smacking my bottom.'

I might then use cushion work, fantasy work or simply give Mary a chance to tell us what she remembers, what it was like for her, and explore how it connects with her life now.

Vicky has drawn herself as a tiny, pink little girl in the corner of a prison-like room. Her father, a huge grey-brown hulk, advances towards her. The picture has a nightmarish quality, and Vicky's fear is very apparent as she speaks. I suggest that she draw a second picture in which she is bigger than her father. She refuses. 'It's impossible.' However, after further discussion and some encouragement, she has a go. To her surprise, her father turns out to look like a two-year-old (with moustache and glasses): 'A big baby!' She laughs, getting a glimmer, perhaps, of changing – not the reality of past events, which can never be changed, but their hold over her, the powerful and fixed position her father takes up in her head.

Most, but not all, of the work the women do in the group is with this 'father-in-the-head' who they are raging or rebelling against, longing for, frightened of or seeking approval from (often all these at once), usually unaware that he is now a part of them. A woman's father may be dead or live across several oceans, yet she responds as though he is still telling her what to do, withholding his love or his presence, needing her, punishing her, invading her, etc. I suggest that to own, voice and integrate that inner tyrant may mean he will control her less. (I am not suggesting that the woman's real father was necessarily a tyrant – although he may have been – but that the father she has internalised often has a tyrannical hold over her, not open to reason or negotiation. The more she owns it, consciously, as part of her, the more open to other influences inside herself, the less absolute and the more negotiable it becomes.) A woman's real father may never change, and even if he does, the inner father of her earlier years is unlikely to change apace. However, her internal father is a part of her that she has greater power to affect.

Rosemary draws herself with her arms reaching out towards her father, and her body slightly turned away.

'What do you imagine you are "saying" to your father in the drawing?'

'Come home!'

'And what is he "saying" to you?'

' "I can't. I'm working. You see, if I came home I'm not sure who I'd want – you or your mother." '

These words come as a surprise, and we work further with the issue of sexual feelings between Rosemary and her father.

Sometimes very strong feelings erupt from the past. Helen has drawn two thumb-sized blue figures with red tears and the words 'sad, sad, sad'. What strikes me is how little space the figures take up on the page, how similar they are and what a lost, isolated quality there is about them. I have a sense of Helen as quietly responsible and undramatic, concerned for others while at the same time in touch with herself. I notice that I feel protective towards her. She explains how her father left the household after her mother stabbed him in an outbreak of psychotic violence. She talks of the ensuing tug of loyalties, of wanting her father's protection, of the loneliness of taking on adult responsibilities while still a child.

When first asked to draw, Helen felt an impulse to make slashing marks on the paper. She reports pains in her left arm. I suggest that she try drawing slashing marks now. She doesn't want to hurt the blue figures and asks for more paper. Suddenly she slashes and stabs at it, tears at it, screams and screams. I suggest that she keeps her eyes open, to keep in touch with reality, but she indicates that she knows what she is doing and is not out of control. Eventually the screaming subsides and she curls up quietly on her own. At the end of the evening she's feeling calm, grateful, relieved.

Over the next week, however, she feels great fear of men breaking into her home with axes. Women in the group comment on her strength and say that they feel protective towards her. She doesn't like to hear the second piece of feedback; the piece that seems to me to relate most directly to her issues with her father. I suggest that in addition to stirred-up memories of uncontained violence, the fear has to do with her own destructive feelings from that violent time demanding recognition and outlet, and that if she can acknowledge these, she will probably feel less frightened. At the final session Helen isn't feeling too good, but she has felt safe working with me. I offer my phone number in case she needs individual sessions to come to terms with the feelings which have begun to surface.

'I'm Donal, Orla's father. I have 11 children and work on a farm in the West of Ireland . . .'

Instead of a drawing, I may start the workshop with an exercise in which each woman tells a partner briefly about her father. The partner then introduces herself to the group as though she were the woman's father, and the group asks 'him' questions: 'How do you get on with your wife?', 'Are you happy in your work?', 'How do you feel about Orla?' If the partner doesn't know the answers, she invents them. The discrepancy between the woman's memories and her partner's account can turn out to be very useful. Orla, listening, sees her father from a new angle. Suddenly he has shrunk in stature in her eyes. At the same time she appreciates his worth and the struggle of his life for the first time. She feels angry with her partner, Gill, for suggesting that Donal's life is a pleasant one, slow-paced and organic, surrounded by the beautiful Kerry countryside. But then it makes her think, especially after having heard Arthur (a well-off urban academic with only two children to support) introduce himself as a failure with a history of depression and breakdown, that maybe Donal's circumstances and his unhappiness aren't as automatically connected as he (and she) has always believed. For a moment, Orla feels less burdened by the weight of his life, and imagines feeling less burdened by her own. She is intrigued by another reply of Gill's as her 'father': 'I want Orla to be attractive to men, but not to get involved with one.' We explore this in another session.

It is the second session of the group and the focus is on the past. I have developed a memory-scanning exercise, which I improvise and change but which goes roughly like this:

Shut your eyes and get comfortable. Be aware of your breathing. Be aware of what you're feeling at this moment.

Picture your father (or father-substitute). Picture him eating, drinking, driving, going to work, coming back, talking about money, about politics, doing the housework . . .

Be aware of how you're feeling now.

Think of times when your father played with you. What kind of games did you play? Can you remember playing games with your father?

The exercise continues, ranging over anger (Can you remember times when you were angry with your father? Can you remember times when he was angry with you? How was anger expressed between you?), fear, cruelty, humiliation, affection, nurturance, longing, approval, recognition, advice, admiration . . . I vary the list and the accompanying suggestions, but always stress: How did you feel?, How did you/he express/not express, respond/not respond?

Think yourself back to puberty, to your first period(s), to the time when your breasts were beginning to grow. How did you feel about your father at this time? How did he respond to your growing womanhood? How did he react to your first boyfriend or your first girlfriend; your first sexual relationship(s)?

Picture your father's body. How do you, or how did you, feel about it? Is he, or was he, an attractive man? Did he give off sexual 'vibes'?

Now I want you to imagine touching your father. What is your impulse? It's your fantasy, you can do it in any way you want, positive or negative.

As a child, what was it you wanted and needed from your father? How did you try to get it? Did you get it? What is it that you want and need from him now? What do you receive now?

Think about men who are significant in your life at the moment (husband, lover, son, boss, colleague, etc.). What is it you want or need from them? How do you go about getting it? What do you get?

How are you feeling right now? Scan over the range of what you've been feeling in the last half-hour.

Now think of a word that sums up your father for you at the moment – the first word that comes into your head. It doesn't have to be accurate or just.

In your own time come back into the room. Look around you. Make eye contact. How are you feeling? Turn to the woman next to you and tell her the word.

Some women find this exercise difficult: their memories of their father are not available to them. Others are overwhelmed by the number of memories and the painful or pleasant feelings which accompany them. Memory and feeling are often disconnected, one emerging in the absence of the other, which is cut off from conscious awareness. Sometimes a 'new' memory emerges from the depths, or an old memory takes on a different meaning – small changes that can become part of shifting a pattern.

'I can't remember him ever playing with me.'
'I've just realised that Mum was always in between us. I couldn't remember him without her being there.'
'For the first time, I wish he was here.'
'He's always been a blank, a complete stranger.'
'I could see him as he was before his illness.'
'I could only see bits of him at a time: he's too big to see whole.'
'I was angry with you, Stef, for drawing it all out of me.'

It's common for good memories to bubble up for the first time with feelings of surprise. Sometimes it's first negative memories and feelings. (Not surprisingly, fewer women who idealise their fathers or who have had genuinely good relationships with them come than those who are aware of difficulties.) Often it's familiar feelings very much intensified.

*

Georgie's words for her father were 'pure goodness'. She came to the workshop because, although he died many years ago, she still hasn't got over his death. Her face lights up as she talks about him: 'He was a wonderful man!' Georgie was an only child who had always longed for a large family of brothers and sisters. She was a 'good daughter' who tried hard to please her father, but 'He never saw me'.

Georgie has been 'good' in the group too. There's something clingy in her voice and eyes, and my impulse is to draw away from her at those moments. This reaction gives me a clue as to how best to work with her. On my suggestion Georgie chooses a cushion to represent her father. The memories that have surfaced most strongly are from her adolescence rather than the time of his death, and she talks to him as though she is a teenager.

'You're hiding. You're not there for me.' Her voice has a sad, pleading quality, and I have an image of her oozing like treacle from her cushion to his. I suggest she reverses roles and acts her father. 'You overwhelm me. I can't handle you,' her father says to Georgie. She goes back to her cushion and I take the father role.

'Why do you hide from me?' she asks. Her face melts and she reaches out her hand, expecting an enactment of the close union she has longed for over so many years. But I replace it, repeating back to her the words she spoke as her father. 'You overwhelm me. I can't handle you.' Expressions of sadness and anger come and go across Georgie's face. 'I'm not what you think I am,' I continue, ad-libbing. 'I can see you're hurt, I can see you feel badly, but I can't give you what you want. Nobody can.'

'Then who can make it better? It's so lonely . . .'

We end the role-play at this point, and the group gives her feedback. I suggest that for the last 10 years, her fantasy of her father as perfect has served both to keep him alive inside her and to keep alive the hope she had as a child that one day he would give her the loving recognition and closeness she wanted from him: 'One day my prince will come . . .' To get over him she needs to give up this fantasy, but to let go of it is also to let go of her lifelong hope, and that is painful. If she can accept that she will never get what she didn't get *as a child*, she will be able to receive more in the here and now. During the break, Georgie lies down by herself; she doesn't run from her empty, lonely feelings but wants and is able to stay with them.

She comes to the next session feeling lighter. Her father wasn't a saint; he was an *ordinary* man. It is a relief. He was ordinary, but she loved him. For several days after the exercise she had felt a sense of loss. She realised that her relationships with men have often followed a similar pattern to that with her father. Now she feels more able to get over his death. I feel very moved by her work. 'It's as if you've laid a ghost,' remarks one of the women in the group. The change in Georgie is certainly striking. She seems more centred in herself, less blurred and uncertain, her eyes less clingy.

In playing her father I was trying, in the words of my training supervisor, to 'put a bottom to the bucket'. You can't fill a bucket with a hole in it, no matter how much you go on putting in; you need to stand it on the ground. My way of 'grounding' Georgie was to help her face what *is* (his death) and what *was* (what he didn't give her); to face the lack, both of him and what she had never received from him. Without value judgments as to whether or not he should have given it, and without any way of knowing what he actually did give, the fact remains that Georgie hasn't got it, inside her. But the role-play between us wasn't a simple repetition of the past, i.e. of not getting. My aim was to give her something she hadn't had: an honest, firm 'No', a boundary within which I didn't withdraw, punish or comply with her (unconscious) manipulation – 'If you don't give me what I need I will be terribly hurt' – but showed that I saw her, was concerned for her and would stay engaged with her.

This wouldn't be an appropriate way to work with everyone; I drew on my knowledge of different cross-gender character structures and styles of defence. When I first started running workshops I would not have had the confidence, experience or theoretical backing to work in this way. I wanted to be able (a common misconception of 'feminist therapy', an unconscious hope of my own, shared by many?) to give women coming to the groups what they felt they needed so they could go away feeling comforted and nurtured. That can be appropriate in some situations. For example, Annie was sexually abused by her father from early infancy until late childhood. She told no one for years, fearing that it might break up her parents' marriage, that it might hurt him, that she might be blamed, that her mother knew anyway and it was normal paternal behaviour. Telling the group is frightening and new, and the fear shows on her face. Most of her family still don't know; her secret has cut her off from them and others all her life. Her most immediate need is for acceptance, reassurance and recognition, which I and other members of the group have no trouble in giving.

Sonia, however, arouses a different reaction in me. She too has been sexually abused by her father, in late childhood and early adolescence. She describes her dread of his feet on the stairs, the smell of alcohol on his breath, her decision to keep quiet about it for similar reasons to

Annie's; however, as she speaks I pick up no sign that she is feeling what she is saying. She has me spellbound, and yet I feel curiously pushed away. I have the feeling it is a story she has told many times before. What I am most strongly aware of is her need for reassurance, and for allies rather than insight. I do have an impulse to reassure her, but it feels pulled out of me, and I ask myself why. My guess is that it's because she needs the reassurance in order not to feel what happened or accept that it did. Rather than give her the reassurance she desires (which I can't genuinely give in any case), I ask Sonia what she is feeling as she talks. She doesn't know, seems hardly to understand the question. We talk a little about this and what might underlie it. I don't push her; it will probably take some time in a more secure ongoing situation before she can connect with what she feels. At the end of the evening she seems disappointed and unsatisfied. However, three sessions later, she tells us (sounding a little bewildered and surprised) that although she can talk openly about her father's sexual invasion, she realises she is cut off from it inside. Perhaps this discovery will turn out to be one step in a longer process of freeing herself from the effects of her father's abuse of his power and her trust.

Sometimes the enactment of what a woman hasn't had can be very creative: when, for example, any conscious longing, any possibility or hope of getting something good is faint or non-existent, or continually attacked by the woman herself internally. Margery can't remember her 'real' biological father, who died when she was three, although she is sure he was gentle, understanding and intellectual. Her mother's boyfriend, who had spent a lot of time in jail, she experienced as brutal and humiliating. Margery herself is at a low ebb; everything is wrong with her life. Although she is recognised as a gifted and original painter, she feels depressed by her work and unable to carry on with it. She has difficulty getting anything out of the group and her contributions tend to be carping and negative. She often refuses suggestions and 'spoils' positive comments. Intrigued by her certainty as to the qualities of her real father, I ask her to imagine what an ideal father would be like. He would be gentle, intelligent, interested in what she had to say; interested in her world, even if it is different from his own, and in that of her friends. I suggest that she choose a woman from the group to be herself and role-play her fantasy ideal father. She seems pleased at the idea and in a matter of minutes we see a very different side to Margery. As her fantasy father she is a quiet, anchored, content sort of person who introduces 'his' daughter to each member of the group proudly, listing her accomplishments, takes her out to listen to music and to the theatre, asks her about her life and tells in turn about 'his' own work as a musician. At the end of the evening, and for the remaining sessions of the group, Margery exudes a shy, bubbling pleasure and enthusiasm. Other women remark on how different she seems and say that her work has helped them too. I don't know what significance Margery's work here has or will have in her life, but I hope it gives a glimpse of what is possible when the self-attacker inside (perhaps the internalised voice of a real person in her childhood), makes room for a more accepting inner voice.

Role-playing an imaginary father is an unusual suggestion; I was working on intuition. A more usual exercise is to act from the inevitably imaginary but often uncannily accurate point of view of real, known fathers. Sometimes it's easy: 'I *am* my father,' says Carole, sprawled, legs wide, in an imaginary armchair – wife in the kitchen, snooker on TV, daughter trying to engage him in political argument. Sometimes it's difficult: he's a mystery, a stranger, a blank. Or he's too familiar: to act him in his company would be a betrayal. Or he's 'that which I despise/detest/hate/fear and never want to be . . .'

It's the third session. Karen is telling us about her father, who is a religious dignitary. Every week he stands before a large congregation. Though he is an impeccable moral figure in the public eye, at home she was frightened of his sexual feelings towards her, his outbursts of rage when she first went out with boyfriends. Karen herself speaks very quietly and dresses in a way which draws little attention to herself. I suggest she role-play her father with the eyes of the congregation upon him. Impossible. 'What if you try standing up?' Her voice is hardly a whisper. 'See how it feels to stand on your chair. If it feels right, try saying, "Look at me." See if you can enjoy the attention. Let your voice get a little louder.' Eventually Karen is standing on a chair, booming: 'Look at *me*! Listen to *me*!' She has discovered a part of her that has been locked away with the father-in-the-head she has been trying to deny; a part of her that needs to be seen and heard, that enjoys some dramatic, theatrical expression. For the rest of the evening she goes around with a mischievous look on her face. There's something more vivacious about her, something more confident and alive.

Sometimes it almost seems that someone has made a promise, conscious or unconscious, to themselves long ago in childhood or adolescence: '*I'll* never be like *that*. I'll never do to anyone what he has done to me/my mother/sister/brother.' A vow to stay on the side of the angels. But it's pretty difficult for any of us, female or male, not to be like a parent or other important person we have grown up with, although what the 'like' means can vary enormously in quality, extent and depth, as we vary too in our awareness and acceptance of it. Often, the more we hate and deny, the more like we become. Inside us, there's a lock or jam of opposing forces which keeps the problem going and doesn't allow for change. Then rather than learning to integrate and handle the most difficult parts of ourselves, with the risks and moral choices that this involves, we avoid 'doing' in those areas and remain 'done to'. We may well have been victimised but then maintain a pattern of being the victim, even when taking more control of our own lives is a real option. There is usually a pay-off in maintaining this position; it entails not having to take risks and responsibility and assuming an air of moral superiority.

'When you were being your father, you spoke and seemed more convinced of what you were saying...' It is common for the 'father's' voice ('mother's' voice too!) to come across more strongly than the woman's own, dominating her moral and emotional centre-ground. When this happens I might encourage a woman to back herself up so her own voice begins to sound as definite, her feelings and moral world as legitimate, as her father's. (A common fear is that if he is no longer able to wipe her out, she will wipe him out. It's him or her; there can't be room for the two of them to have separate feelings and ideas, to meet in conflict and both survive.) Or I might, as I did with Karen, encourage her to own the qualities of the father-in-the-head she dislikes or is trying to deny.

Sometimes, through role-playing, women discover aspects of their fathers which come as a surprise to them. Liz doesn't like her father. She has hardly spoken to him for years, feels no love for him, no longing. 'Fathers are irrelevant.' When she goes home, which she often does, it's her mother she talks to. Her father interrupts with provocative remarks: 'He has to be cleverer, wind me up and put me down.' She sees the two of them as competing for her mother's attention. Suspecting that this account isn't the whole story, I'm reminded of the drawing she did on the first night of the group and a remark made by one of the women about it: 'You look like teenage lovers.'

Putting this aside for the moment, I suggest she act her father. In this role, Liz says to the cushion representing herself: 'I don't feel much for you.' Liz holds back the tears which might cast doubt on her apparent indifference. I suggest she choose a woman in the group to be her mother and I play the role of Liz. Liz, as her father, trying unsuccessfully to break into our female *tête-à-tête*, feels desperate. 'He' also feels the need for 'his' *daughter's* attention and approval. This is a new idea for Liz.

Recalling the drawing, I ask her how she and her father got on during her adolescence. 'He criticised me all the time.' I suggest she scan over those years as though she were there now. 'He wanted me to be feminine, but not sexual or sexy. Come to think of it, it was Mum who told me that's what he wanted.'

What strikes me is how sexual and sexy she comes across now, in a way that appears very natural, with a masculine style about her. I suggest that Liz talk to her father as though she were the adolescent she once was, and then talk to herself as though she is her father at that time. The adolescent Liz tries haltingly to assert: 'I am a sexual person.' Liz as her father, confronted by a newly sexual daughter with boyfriends calling her on the phone, doesn't feel jealous of the boyfriends; it's Liz he's envious of, for having them. He would like a boyfriend too.

From the role-play alone it's not possible to tell whether Liz's insights are accurate intuitions of her father's inner world or creations of her own unconscious. But over the span of the workshop they lead to changes in her real relationship with him, to some small, new, hopeful contacts between them.

Role-playing a cruel, tyrannical father, though the idea of it is frightening, can be particularly helpful. It gives a women permission to express 'dangerous' parts of herself in an environment in which no one stands to be hurt by them. And in her role of tyrannical father she is likely to experience herself the panic, loneliness, sense of inadequacy, financial worries, exaggerated sense of family responsibility and obligation, self-centredness, doubts about masculinity, fear and envy of women, etc. which underlie his sadistic domination. This often reduces her sense of his power and unassailability.

Many women, however, are already painfully aware of their fathers' feet of clay. Barbara, acting her father (a successful politician), strides purposefully round the room, frowning: 'I'm brilliant. I'm attractive to women. I have no problems.'

I ask him about his daughter and how he feels towards her. 'Barbara's like me. She's brilliant. She has no problems.'

'But didn't she have a breakdown when she was at university?'

'Yes. I can't understand it. She really has no problems.'

Barbara believes his picture of himself. He has a way with women; he has no problems. She wants him to recognise that she does have problems. But she also wants to fit in with his picture of her and not have any. When faced with her father on a cushion, however, what she is most aware of are his needs and insecurities. She remembers the awkward way he comes up to give her a hug or a peck on the cheek, and how she flinches, putting up with it because she doesn't want to hurt him. She looks after the vulnerability he denies. I suggest she tries what it feels like to turn round and sit facing the other way, turning her back on his problems.

'No. I couldn't do that.'

She feels responsible for the problems he insists he hasn't got. She tries turning round. It's lonely. It's also exciting. But if she stops carrying his problems, if she becomes a more separate person, aware of where she ends and he begins, perhaps she will lose what connection with him she does have, however unsatisfactory? If you're a part of someone else, you're never alone. But then you're never really together either. I suggest that becoming more one's own person does involve a kind of loss. However, it also creates the possibility of a more fulfilling, less desperate kind of connection.

Such issues of separation and boundaries come up in every area of therapy, particularly in relation to mothers, who usually do the primary physical and emotional nurturing of children, especially in the earliest years before a baby has a sense of separate identity. In theory, fathers are seen as key boundary makers, helping to separate the fused identity of mother and young child. Identification with fathers is assumed to be of a different kind to that with mothers, happening later on in children's lives and happening differently for girls and for boys. Leaving aside the how and the when and the why of it, what has struck me in running Fathers and Daughters workshops is the range and complexity of the ways in which we identify with, introject and model ourselves on our fathers (including our pictures of absent ones) despite having a fundamentally female identity; the complicated ways mothers figure in this process of identification; and its relative but certainly not complete autonomy from gender identity and sexual desire.

'I felt angry with my boyfriend after last week's session.'
'I rang my father in South America. It's the first time for years.'
'I felt depressed after last week. I kept waking up in the night and remembering things from my childhood I'd forgotten.'
'I felt comfortable after last time when you asked Chris why she couldn't challenge her father *and* want to hold his hand.'
'I felt better all week. I stood up for myself at work for the first time.'

It's the fourth session tonight and we're going to explore fantasies of the ideal, the perfect, the longed-for daddy that many of us harbour somewhere inside through an open-ended story beginning: 'Once upon a time there was a wonderful daddy. . .' I say to the group: 'Don't think about it. See what you write. Anything can happen.'

The idea for this exercise came out of discussions in a consciousness-raising group I belonged to in which we looked at our relationships with our fathers. Those of us who had grown up without them had ideas as to what we might have missed. One thought that as an adolescent girl a father would have given her a sense of her femininity and backed her up in that. Another thought that he would have supported and guided her ventures into the public world of school and work and politics. Although none of the women in the group who had lived with their fathers had experienced them in such ideal ways – indeed some disparaged them as weak, inadequate or impotent – they too harboured fantasies of an ideal father. We often based our ideas and ideals on friends' fathers or men who had been significant to us later in life – a man who was distinguished-looking and knew how to dance or call us 'Bella'; an artist or a revolutionary; a person who was mild, gentle and encouraging; a person who was strong, tempestuous, passionate, challenging . . . All this made us think about ideals of fatherhood and masculinity, motherhood and femininity, present in the dominant culture at large. We judge our parents in the light of available stereotypes as well as in relation to our needs and desires.

Some women sit in front of a blank sheet of paper, others can only manage a sentence or two. 'I haven't even got a fantasy.' This may arouse anger or despair. Some get a lot of pleasure from the stories, despite the gap between fantasy and reality. Others find the gap a painful one. Occasionally wonderful daddy and real daddy turn out to be one and the same. Sometimes the fantasies start out wonderful and go wrong: they can't be made to go right because there's always an unconscious expectation – daddy will leave, mummy/girlfriends/siblings will come between the daughter and her father.

Many of the fantasies involve being with daddy on his own in the world out there, living together in a lighthouse, crossing oceans and deserts, or just going down to the local park. Equally often, wonderful daddy is a Pied Piper figure, leading hordes of happy children off on adventures (a frequent complaint being that in real life childhood friends were discouraged and unwelcome). Or wonderful daddy is in the home, is nice to mummy (this comes up equally often in Mothers and Daughters workshops – mummy is nice to daddy), makes and mends things, doesn't drink, shout, criticise . . .

In the discussion and feedback afterwards I try to distinguish between, on the one hand, a tyrannical split-off longing for someone who will be everything we want and need all of the time, as opposed to the person we actually have who will never be any good: and, on the other, healthy hopes and desires that lead us to act and determine ourselves, that have a chance of being realised and are precious in themselves. But if there's a chance they may be realised, there is also a risk that they may not. We may be rejected, disapproved of, misunderstood. We may struggle and be defeated. Impossible longings protect us from caring too much about the present, which we devalue in comparison, depriving ourselves of it in the process. 'I never thought much of him when he was alive. But after he died, I went to pieces.' Valuing what we have is sometimes confused with resigned acceptance of bad conditions, of not struggling for better, more equal relationships, just as our struggles as feminists can get confused with our tyrannical longings for the impossible. All this being said, 'reality' and 'possibility' are always being redefined, and, as Mae West put it, 'Too much of a good thing can be wonderful.'

It's the last session. 'Shut your eyes. Focus on a memory of an event involving your father which was bad for you in some way. Imagine you're there now and it's happening at this moment. What's the setting? What are you and your father doing? How are you feeling about it? Now I want you to try and rerun the situation in your mind's eye, as if it's a film, and give it a different ending with an outcome that's more positive to you. You can use any methods you like; they don't have to be likely or realistic. Let your imagination go.'

Some women rerun the situation so that their fathers do something different: ask their daughters how they are, give them a hug rather than a cheque, say something appreciative rather than critical. Others rerun the situation giving themselves the active role: 'Stop the car at once!', 'Why do you read those porn magazines?' The changed response may bring up unexpected difficulties. Pauline's father gives her the longed-for hug and she feels the weight of his need or his sexual desire; or she realises she doesn't want him that close because in fact she is very angry with him and would rather stay angry. Maybe a cheque is easier after all! Maggie is assertive about her father's dangerous driving and then feels sorry for him. She doesn't want his self-esteem to be dented or for him to do as she tells him, because although she sees his fragility, if she stops believing he is a strong, daring man, she herself might have to change; she might have to become stronger and more daring herself. She fears losing the imaginary protector who in reality endangers her life.

The negative 'set' may be so strong that a woman finds it impossible to rerun it with a positive outcome. No force, whatever tools are open to the imagination, can counter his violence or disapproval; she is too ugly or unworthy for him to show a gesture of appreciation or love; if she succeeds in getting what she wants, she will be envied or attacked. Sometimes it seems most appropriate to help the woman to stay with her despair or to explore its significance in her life now. At other times I may work with her on a fantasy level. At this level she may be able to allow a glimmer of a new possibility. The rerun often reveals painful things a woman will need to face if her negative 'sets' or defences begin to change.

It's nearing the end of the last session. 'Find yourself a partner. You will each have 10 minutes on the theme: "How I'm going to get what I didn't get from my father in my life now." I want each of you to come up with something practical, something that's do-able in the next week, however small, within the constraints of your life *as it is now*, and that you can genuinely commit yourself to doing. No tall orders to change your personality! Your partner is there to help you focus on something concrete and to help you to fix a specific time for when you'll do it. You'll probably need the first five minutes to focus on the general issue of what you feel you didn't get.' The room buzzes with voices and laughter. After the 20 minutes is up, we go round everyone hearing what they have decided to do.

'I'm going to tell my father I'm a lesbian.'
'When?'
'Erm . . . Well, I could go home on Sunday night. I'll do it then.'

'I'm going to look for a new job.'
'When?'
'I'll buy all the papers tomorrow morning.'

'I'm going to buy a really sexy dress.'
'When?'
'Well, it'll have to be next week. But I will do it.'

'I'm going to write a memo to my boss objecting to certain copy I have to sub-edit.'
'When?'
'I haven't got much time this week. I'll write it when I get home tonight.'

*

On my way home I mull over the workshop in my mind: the mistakes I made, the laughs as well as the rages and the tears; images of women acting their fathers behind newspapers, desks, steering wheels, chequebooks, cameras, bottles of beer; the picture Sheila gave us of how her father celebrated the news of her first period – with red drinks, wine for the parents, cherryade for his newly menstruating daughter; Lorraine's story of how as a small girl she told her father she had been bitten by a dog when she had only scratched her finger on a wall, and of how he had examined the scratch with great care before winding an enormous bandage round it, of her pride and joy for days – it only occurred to her recently that he must have known the truth of it all along.

The good feeling of the group, which ended warmly, is still with me:

'Things with my husband have been a lot better since I talked about my Dad.'

'I don't feel I put very much into the group. I wish I'd had a go with a cushion.'

'I see my father very differently now. I hope I can keep it up.'

'I'm sad the group has to end. Does anyone feel like coming for a drink?'

# 3
# Sexuality and Intimacy
Pat Land

Many years ago I was in a relationship with a man to whom I felt deeply attached. He was not demonstrative, but he was around a lot and I was convinced that one day we would achieve real closeness. Indeed, at times, his barriers of privacy and refusal to get involved did seem to crumble and we seemed briefly to enjoy the oneness that I craved and thought he needed too. It took me some while to notice that these moments inevitably preceded a break in communication, and even longer to face that the intimacy that I thought suited me was what precipitated flight in him.

The more elusive he became the more dependent and anxious I felt, and the harder I tried, when he was around, to find out how he wanted me to be so that I could become an indispensable part of his life. Despite all the evidence I remained convinced for a long time that love was there for me, if only I could find the key, if only I could find out how to deserve it.

Eventually, even I had to recognise a pattern I knew of old, not only in my own life but in the experience of many women I knew. In fact, I was living out an embarrassing cliché, the stuff of wry jokes among women. How could I, an independent woman, a feminist, running my own life, making my own decisions, have fallen headlong into the same old trap?

As I struggled to cope with the end of the relationship, I had to do a lot of thinking. I began to have a strong sense that my feelings about this had something to do with my mother. There was something between us that caused continual disappointment, and at the same time made it impossible for us to let each other be. It seemed I had been longing all of my life for her unequivocal love, a love not conditional upon my being just that bit better than I was, and it was that frustration that kept me hooked. The analogy with the man I was involved with was obvious. I had chosen a man who could not love me, and had turned him in my fantasy into a kind of demanding mother whom I might one day learn to please.

Although I had been in women's groups where I had heard other women talk about their mothers, it was only when the notion of something not all right in my own relationship with my mother really 'clicked' that I became aware of the questioning going on all around me as women re-examined this central issue in their lives.

I knew from my working life as a social worker and as a group worker in psychiatric settings, as well as from listening to friends, that a great many women have problems in experiencing and understanding their sexuality. The two themes now intertwined in my awareness and I felt it was time to consider them together. When I put the idea to the workshop leaders' group, there was a sense of recognition and a general agreement that we should offer a workshop on the issue. The first workshops were held under the title Intimacy and Early Nurture. As we explored the connections between early childhood memories and worries over present relationships, we recognised that the liaisons at once the most intimate and the most threatening, the most desired and the most feared, are the sexual ones. So we changed the title to take account of this reality and the last one was offered as Sexuality and Intimacy.

Sexuality and intimacy: we wanted to explore 'what sexuality means for us, and in what ways sexuality and intimacy are the same; and in what ways they are different. What are the connections in our own lives? We would like to look at current attitudes and relationships in the light of early experiences in the family.' Over a span of about four years, I then ran several such groups, the first two with Sue Krzowski, then some on my own, and the most recent one in November 1983 with Mira Dana.

It is often not easy for women to talk openly about sex. As the workshop leader, you need to give some thought to what you will say at the beginning. (You may find some material in this chapter on women's upbringing and its relation to sexuality useful in preparing your introduction.) It is important that you feel comfortable talking about sex, and that takes practice. You will need to do some reading, and talking with friends; you should certainly try out any exercise you plan to use. I found that despite these preparations, it still took a while in each group for me to feel at ease. Perhaps, indeed, it is important for the workshop leader not to be able to distance herself too far from the initial discomfort that most of the group members will be experiencing.

I had also to do some work on thinking about lesbian sexuality. I had not at first made a distinction of approach between lesbianism and heterosexuality, because I believed that in exploring early childhood experiences, the connections each member made with adult attitudes would be equally valid and interesting. However, as I should have expected given the climate of compulsory heterosexuality in which we grow up, this meant that the one woman in the early groups who identified herself as a lesbian felt isolated and fearful of being judged against a standard of 'normal sexuality'. Having discussed the issue with other workshop leaders, and accepted some criticism, I agreed with Mira that in our joint group we would refer in our introductory remarks to lesbianism and heterosexuality, rather than to a more generalised sexuality that might be assumed to be straight.

It is interesting that in the subsequent group, although only one woman was a practising lesbian, several members proved to be struggling with this personal/political issue. We have no way of knowing what contribution was made by the outspokenness of the one lesbian, by the particular composition of the group, or by our joint mention of homosexuality, indicating that it was not a taboo area. It may also have been relevant that there were two of us: we could be seen in unconscious fantasy according to the need of the moment, as mummy and daddy, the sexual woman and the nurturing woman, the good and the bad, or as a lesbian couple; and not as the single, judging mother of that other woman's experience.

There is a sort of hierarchy of difficulty in each woman's assessment of her own problems. Most women who come to the Sexuality and Intimacy workshop have been in other workshops, facing what seemed to them easier issues first. It is not easy perhaps to admit to difficulty in what we have grown up believing should 'come naturally' to women, the area of love relationships. Hence the members are likely to have in common some anxieties, which may range from embarrassment to desperation and which will be hard at first to talk about.

Thus, though I often use relaxation exercises and movement as a way of focusing concentration at the start of a session, I find it more productive in the first meeting of an ongoing group to begin with a simple talking exercise. Either a paired exercise or a 'go-round', depending both on the size and on the feel of the group, on why members chose to come and what they hope for, can ease some of the shyness, as well as locating themes that will need to be worked on.

In later sessions I pay attention to the body. In one workshop, I used the combination of relaxation and stretching exercises, then adapted a meditation technique of imagining an energy source, a spring of life, that could move into different parts of the body. When I suggested locating it in the genitals I used the word cunt, and this had a strong impact on the work of the session. One woman was much emboldened by the idea of reclaiming 'that word' from its slang usage as a term of abuse; with much laughter at first, and then with anger, she told us how she felt men had treated her 'as a cunt', using her female sex as an excuse to bully and browbeat her for stupidity. She began to recognise how powerless she had allowed herself to feel, and how furious she was about it. Another woman was initially shocked and disgusted, but reached a point of real grief over the realisation that she too felt the disgust towards the female genitalia that she had perceived in men she thought intolerably sexist.

In another workshop, my use of a movement exercise – in this case, choosing different parts of the body to 'lead' you about the space, so that you move head first, left shoulder first, right hip first, pelvis first, bottom first, and so on – which made most women laugh and was intended to free some energy, made one woman furious. When we talked about it, it was clear that my behaving in what she saw as a sexual way had painfully emphasised her own feelings that she was not allowed to be openly sexual.

It is always important to allow time to talk about how exercises feel, so that points such as this do not get missed. If the feeling has to be buried again, unspoken, it merely exacerbates the woman's sense of isolation and frustration.

Paired exercises based on the simplest level of co-counselling practice are extremely useful and are an effective use of time, especially in a fairly large group or one with a short time-span. Many women find it easier to share sensitive material with one person first, the experience of relief and mutual closeness then helping them to open up in the whole group.

I have also found paired work helpful in getting a lot of material for discussion in a short space of time. You can have two or three brief co-counselling exercises, one after the other, before moving back into the whole group for feedback. Feedback, I should add, need not mean revealing your own or your partner's raw feelings; it can consist of thoughts that come up in relation to them, and in relation to areas of common or different experience.

A series of paired exercises on topics like what my mother felt about sex; what she wanted me to feel about it; and things that trouble me now in relationships can produce considerable emotional charge and some very useful material for the subsequent work of the group. I introduce the topics one at a time, so that the impact of the thoughts and memories is cumulative. By the end of the exercise, when the group meets for feedback, the connections between early childhood experience and teaching, and present relationships are very much alive in everyone's minds.

Jane cried all the way through this exercise, and she was willing to share part of her experience during the feedback session. She explained,

*I just felt so awful thinking about my mother and sex. I'm sure she hated it, in fact I know she did, because after I was safely married she told me so. And I knew it was true, thinking back. There was never any feeling of a happy secret between my parents; it was something shameful and upsetting.*

*In a way I still feel angry, because I'm sure those unspoken feelings had a deeper effect than anything she ever said while I was growing up. Yet she tried so hard not to inflict her shame and pain on me. She must have been so lonely, and Dad too, I guess. I think they really loved each other in their way, yet they made each other miserable.*

*I feel frightened when I think about how much all that confusion is a real part of me. There is a fear of never being understood and accepted, I suppose because I can't accept myself.*

Many women will recognise in such a context, perhaps for the first time, how deeply problematic is their attitude to sex and love, how confused they are and how angry and distressed.

A guided fantasy may be efficacious in opening up feelings and thoughts the group needs to explore further. It is not the same as exploring a particular woman's private fantasies, the point being to share similarities and differences around a common theme.

Sue Krzowski was good at inventing guided fantasies (see Chapter 12). The first we used was based on going back in imagination into early childhood, picturing the scene in some detail, finding your mother and asking her for something. This choice of theme was based on our preparatory discussions of the common experience among women that we learned when very young not to ask for too much. We have internalised a very strong message that we ought not to ask, and a feeling that if we do, we will not receive.

Sue and I said nothing of these ideas when we introduced the guided fantasy, as we did not wish to skew the memories and fantasies that each women would contact for herself. Yet neither in that first group nor in any subsequent group in which I have used it did any woman ever get what she asked for, whether a cuddle, an outing or even a biscuit. Mother was cross or busy or preoccupied; in several cases she wasn't even there. One cannot presuppose that it will be the case for everyone in all groups – and the dynamics would be fascinating if one or more members were able to fantasise having been satisfied – but so far it has been so.

Feeding this internal experience back into the group, first as each woman's painful recognition, which gradually becomes a shared pain and shock and often even amusement, has a dramatic effect on the group's sense of a common emotional reality. This is not to say that all the women had terrible mothers. I am talking about an inner experience, and will suggest later in this chapter some of the reasons for its apparent bleakness.

The other guided fantasy we used only once, for a particular group of women. Several members were part of a close social network and there seemed a strong taboo on examining competition among women, especially sexual rivalries. Sue suggested the fantasy of the 'sexual woman': you are in a mixed group of people, feeling good about yourself, quite attractive, when another woman comes in whom you see as very sexually attractive; what happens?

This exercise elicited much material about feelings of insecurity and readiness to be diminished, as though in the words of one woman, 'there can only be one goddess'. Most women in the group identified themselves as feminists and there was much anxiety over competitiveness and rivalry with other women, as well as a great fear of acknowledging fear in case, by admitting it to consciousness one were to admit it in another sense into a life whence it had been painstakingly banished. It is of course true that banishing feelings does not make them go away, and that it is ultimately safer to admit them into one's consciousness. But it does not feel safe and it is important to acknowledge and support the courage it takes to face the unacceptable side of ourselves.

It is a surprise to most women to recognise how closely bound up with their sexuality are their feelings towards their mothers. Most of us, in trying to make connections, think more readily of our fathers, who, present or absent, provide our first experience of 'the masculine'.

Naturally enough, in the course of a workshop on sexuality, much will be said about women's experience of their fathers. It is as though our experience of neediness and what it means is deeply connected with our feelings towards our mothers; our estimate of our capacity to get our needs met seems linked more with our father's attitudes. It was they who somehow decided what we deserved. Jane said of her father:

*I don't think he really liked women, which of course didn't help his relationship with my mother. He couldn't really cope with emotions at all, he tried not to have any, and if he felt any 'softie' ones, he'd turn them into loud angry ones. He could be very sarcastic.*

*When I think what he was like when I was a teenager, I feel really upset. I think now that he had a whole jumble of feelings that he couldn't cope with – maybe even some tenderness, worry about my safety, maybe feelings he couldn't face about finding me attractive, and so on. In practice what it meant was that he was constantly putting me down, doing his best to make me feel that I could never get a man, I wasn't pretty or popular enough.*

*I think it made me very insecure, really quite desperately so at the time. I was in fact quite pretty, and I married the first man who seemed to think so.*

In the most recent workshop, all the work consisted of talking in the whole group. Mira Dana and I had prepared a plan for our first evening's work but saw the various exercises as a way of facilitating talking. When, after our introduction, the women began one by one to share what had brought them to the group, there was such a swift and intense communication that we abandoned our plan of exercises. The only variation in the pattern of talking we introduced was at times to share out the available time equally among the women and at times just to let people claim their share, examining with the group what happened when someone took a lot, others less or none at all.

We did take responsibility for structuring the sessions to the extent that we paid close attention to the focal issues, and tried to help the women stick to the topic of sexuality and intimacy. We took up the implications of what they said and did in the group, as they related to the theme. For example, Caroline joined the group at the second session, thus missing the first powerful experience of sharing that had already formed a tentative unity in the room. She then enacted a pattern of talking herself only when invited by the equal sharing of time. When people were using the space freely, she never used any, and it was not until the last session that she told us how furious she was about this.

It was important to recognise with her how she was locating the deprivation in Mira and me as uncaring figures, but also how she was using the group to show us – and herself – the ways in which she was angrily holding herself back from getting what she needed, a pattern she had imported from her unhappy home-life.

Maura was talking about her resentment of John, the most recent of a series of lovers who had failed to discover what pleases her most in sexual play. Mira asked her whether she ever tells him what would be nice. She flushed deeply. She couldn't tell him. It would sound awful. Anyway, if he really cared about her, he would find out for himself; he could even ask her, then it would not be so hard for her to say. She paused and for a moment no one said anything. Then Janet, who had been simmering with unspoken distress since she came in, late, jumped into the silence to complain about a quarrel with her husband. Maura did not attempt to carry on with her thought; instead she sat and glowered. Janet noticed after a few moments and shut up, guiltily apologising. Maura then said she could not remember what she had been going to say. We pointed out to Maura that she had just reproduced in the group the difficulty she had been describing. She had not let Janet know that she had wanted to go on talking. Then she had succeeded in making Janet feel really bad, but not in getting her thought expressed. 'Oh,' she said in a strangled tone, 'I do make John feel guilty, that's true.'

A similar thing happened to Doreen. She stopped to think, in the middle of saying something about her disappointment in sex, and was interrupted. This time the offender did not notice and Doreen just glared, then started smiling nastily and making sarcastically friendly responses. Everyone got very edgy and uneasy, and we reminded Doreen of her description of the atmosphere at home when things have gone wrong in bed between herself and her husband. Perhaps some more direct communication might help? 'Right,' said Doreen, laughing suddenly. 'Shut up please, Anna, and let me talk, because I hadn't finished.' Everyone laughed, and someone made a bawdy analogy with the situation at home. Doreen got the point that she could try to be more open with her husband about her sexual needs and Anna fed back the information that she had felt awful when she was talking in the face of Doreen's bitter sarcasm and was more comfortable now that she knew what was wrong and could put it right.

The fact that in our workshop description we linked sexuality and intimacy gave our work from the start a particular slant. It signalled that we were intending to focus not only on the physical experience of sex – though this is an important aspect of such workshops – but also on the problematic nature of the feelings we experience in sexual relationships. Nearly all the women who came to the workshops, therefore, had already recognised that they had not got it 'all' worked out' in a way that suited them.

Sexuality is a complex concept, partly because we use it in different ways. I am using it both in its sense as feelings about oneself as a sexual being – with the assumption that we remain by our natural endowment sexual beings even when deprived or celibate by choice; and in the extended sense of self-expression within sexual relationships. Some women have managed a distinction between sex-in-relationship and sex-for-its-own-sake, and maintain that the latter is what they seek. Sexual pleasure is the goal, and the longing and pain associated with need is irrelevant. However, among women who have attended the workshops, this view is problematic. Pamela said sadly:

*I've had enough of men who can't relate to me as a human being, but I still desire men, not women. So I get my need for intimacy met by friendship with women and turn to one-night stands or old friends in town for the weekend, that sort of thing, no strings, for sex.*

*But sometimes I feel as though I'm doing with men what they've always done with me, and I wonder if it's really what I want. I like the idea of trying to get men to be more open emotionally, but that feels like a long-term project, and what am I supposed to do in the meantime?*

Many women, particularly those living without a long-term partner, will recognise the feelings Pam is describing, whether or not they opt for her solutions.

It is certainly the case that not all sexual relationships – whether heterosexual or homosexual – are intimate, just as not all intimacy is sexual. But what do we mean by intimacy? And what did the members of the workshop mean, and think I meant? What was it we were looking for? It did not seem to be precisely the closeness of friendship, though that seems related to the notion; there is something more that we seek through sexual relations, something of trust and loss of inhibition and freedom of bodily expression. There is a need to know and be known completely, which can feel like the dissolution of the boundaries between one person and another. Intimacy means that deep contact, 'the possibility of being real to one another' as one woman put it. And we may seek it sometimes with partners we would not choose as friends, which is a direct pathway to hurt and confusion.

Why is it that the closeness we believe we want is so difficult to achieve in practice? For one thing, our longings may be more ambivalent than we know. In the gradual separation of mother and infant, the child, as she becomes a conscious self, develops a sense of a boundary. She can let other people near or even inside at times; she can also choose to keep them out. Many women, in order to make a separate self from the mother who is too like them, have set up a boundary that is experienced as a barrier. Inflexible, fragile, it can be broken or overwhelmed but not stretched and opened up by conscious choice. So the need for closeness may be terrifying, the longed-for melting of the boundary seeming to entail total dependence, total merging, loss of self and the rights of selfhood; or there may be a fear that the need will not be met; indeed, the need itself may be too alarming to emerge into conscious awareness.

Also, if 'our bodies are ourselves', then the genital difference between the sexes must have an impact on our respective inner worlds. It seems probable that the heavily socialised gender differences that cause so much mutual misunderstanding and pain have an unconscious reinforcement in the physical fact that men have an organ that thrusts outwards from the body and women an inner space in which life may grow. Our bodies' forms, too, mean that men's orgasms happen physically in someone else's space, whereas women's pervade their own inner space. The sheer physical reality of intercourse is very different for men and women, which certainly adds to the possibilities for mutual misunderstanding.

And, of course, there is a huge difficulty in an exploitative society of having any relationships that are not tainted with the use of others in some way. It is not only in sexual life, though it seems particularly acute there, that we have to struggle for self-expression, mutual honesty, a reciprocal giving and taking.

A sexual relationship is directly reminiscent in our unconscious fantasy worlds of the experience of early infancy, when our physical and emotional needs were felt – and met, well enough or inadequately – as a unity. Desire and its fulfilment can arouse an unexpectedly intense vulnerability and neediness. Our infantile demands could inevitably never be entirely met in reality, and all of us have experienced rage, as babies, over the deprivation we felt.

Women, on the whole, are not at home with anger. Having been trained to placate, we fear its destructive power – often not having had the opportunity to learn that a relationship can survive it – and tend therefore not to know when we feel outraged. Thus our hope for intimacy may mean a wish for something much more infantile, the sort of symbiotic relationship that prevailed in our earliest weeks of life. We can regain it temporarily through happy sex, but often experience dismay and hurt that it does not seem to last. When the hurt turns to anger, unawares, we may find ourselves depressed or acting in subtly destructive ways in the relationship.

Most men have had a continuing experience of entitlement to nurture, however imperfect their actual circumstances. There is little expectation that they should earn this entitlement by looking after others' needs. Traditionally, men come home from working in the world to the ministrations of mother, wife or sister, which can be taken for granted. The pressure on them not to acknowledge need is the easier to comply with if men are not aware of needing.

It is important here to recognise that people in close relationships can act out for each other the disowned parts of the self. A common picture is that of the woman as emotional, tender and vulnerable, the man – apparently unencumbered by feelings – active, assertive and dominant. But each partner in such a role-segregated couple is relinquishing wholeness. We could now look again at that vexatious relationship and see that I was carrying for the man mentioned previously any need for tenderness he may have had (so that he could remain unaware and aloof); moreover, in choosing a man who could so obviously not bear closeness, I was really protecting myself against a level of intimacy that for various reasons I could not cope with at the time, while remaining the injured party.

It is not only in heterosexual couples that the emotional functions may become split. Many lesbians struggle with similar dynamics. Human beings find it hard to be whole, and very readily attempt unconsciously to get one another to carry the feared or despised attributes they are unable to face in themselves. This pattern is often evident in groups.

I can make this notion clearer with an example from the last workshop. Rebecca was telling a painful story about a relationship with a married man in the architect's office where she worked. She was in love with him, needed him, suffered for his suffering in a loveless marriage; from her description he was behaving in a casually exploitative way with both women. The other women in the group became indignant on her behalf. 'You shouldn't let him treat you like that. Tell him where he gets off.' But the more the group said, the more saint-like Rebecca became. Mira and I looked at each other. I tried saying to Rebecca that I thought she was quite angry with this man's behaviour. 'Oh no,' she said, 'how could I be angry? He has more than enough to cope with.' We looked at each other again. We were getting cross. Mira then used the experience of the split between Rebecca's conscious benevolence and everyone else's anger, and the increasing irritation we were feeling with the woman herself, to make a transference interpretation: 'I think you're using the group to express the anger and hostility you can't acknowledge.' Rebecca got very angry as she denied her anger, and insisted this made no sense to her; but everyone else relaxed, and there was some general talk about how much easier it is to be a martyr than to face anger in oneself.

If we are so afraid of our aggression that it is repressed and thus not accessible to consciousness, we will appear gentle and tolerant, even passive. Equally if we hate our timidity so much that we have pushed it out of consciousness, we will believe ourselves very tough. Feminism has helped us to recognise the dangers in the implicit demand of a patriarchal culture that men should be tough-minded, functional and unaware of emotional complexity. But there is a risk that in celebrating the neglected virtues of warmth, receptiveness, tenderness and openness to emotional need we may fail to recognise that women, including ourselves, can have 'nasty', angry feelings, can feel ruthless or envious, competitive or uncaring at times. We may also have our moments of feeling tough and functional, and cutting off our awareness of our own or others' emotional needs.

If we push all these hated attributes on to men, where we can then repudiate them, we keep ourselves as victims and maintain in a subtle way the socially sanctioned aggressiveness of men.

I wrote the first draft of this chapter fairly easily. I had been thinking and reading about the topic for years, and was quite experienced now in running workshops; the task seemed reasonably clear. Then I was beset by doubts. Every time I read it over or discussed it with other women, I conceived fresh objections to what I had written. It seemed to me that I knew nothing at all about sexuality, my own or anyone else's. How dare I write about it? Eventually it dawned on me that my hesitations and feelings of confusion and dismay reflect, much more accurately than my certainties, the doubts many women share about the meaning of our experience, doubts the workshops focused upon. Moreover, the women who came to the groups had each lived in fear that her difficulties were shamefully hers alone. And now I was feeling out there on my own with the task of writing about them. So, like them, I took courage in the end from what we had shared together.

Part Two
The Outer World

# 4
# Unconsciousness Raising with Working-class Women
Pam Trevithick

'Using co-counselling exercises, this workshop will focus on how we have experienced and internalised our oppression as working-class women and how "privileges" (e.g. education, high income, etc.) have been used to divide, isolate and confuse our sense of identity with our culture, family, friends and other individuals who share a commitment to end class injustices. We will spend some time reclaiming our heritage in all its diversity and richness and also look at how unresolved, hurtful oppressive past experiences have left us with feelings of powerlessness, despair and mistrust that hinder our progress and confidence to make changes in our lives. This workshop is for working-class women only, which for us means women who have a working-class parent. Since we don't accept that higher education should be the monopoly of the upper or middle classes, nor an excuse to dispossess us of our heritage, this workshop is open to women who have struggled through the classism of our education system to acquire a formal education.'

This chapter gives an account of workshops I have run at the Women's Therapy Centre since 1984 for women who recognise themselves in the above description. It is about the empowering and healing potential that is involved in reclaiming a sense of pride in and connection to our class. It begins with the influences in my own life that have drawn me to lead workshops for working-class women at the Centre and elsewhere. I then describe classism and look at its effects through describing some of the common feelings and experiences that have regularly come up during the workshops.

*

## Influences

The phrase 'unconsciousness raising' was coined by one of the women who attended the first workshop and it captures some of the major influences that have drawn me to lead workshops of this kind. The first was feminism, whose political insights and strategies for change have continued to excite me since I first sought out the women's liberation movement in 1972. The second was therapy, and particularly feminist perspectives within therapy and re-evaluation co-counselling, which I have been involved in since 1979.

Looking back on my life, I often wonder what would have become of me had I not stumbled across feminism. I had resisted its wisdoms for a long time, believing, like many, that I was a liberated woman and in no way restricted in what I could do or be. A long period of unemployment, a stream of low-paid jobs (as a barmaid, cleaner, usherette, typist, etc.) and work with homeless and 'vagrant' women in a London government reception-centre all played their part in shattering the myth of sexual equality. As a lesbian, I felt desperately lonely and trapped within a twilight life of secrecy, shame and closet relationships.

Feminism and my contact with the women's liberation movement exposed me to ideas and possibilities that I had never dreamt of. This was effectively my first journey into a predominantly middle-class culture and I thrived on it, not least because I felt accepted and respected by most of the women that I came into contact with. Joining a consciousness-raising group marked a new process of reflection, opening up a new way of seeing myself, women's oppression and the world.

I grew and changed enormously during this period, but my journey this far had focused almost totally on my oppression as a woman and lesbian. It wasn't until my mother's sudden death in 1976, followed by the deaths of my maternal aunt and grandmother, that I came face to face with issues of class, race and religion. These deaths left me locked in grief and outrage, not least because they left me bereft of a vital link with Ireland and even more estranged from the Catholic, mainly immigrant culture that I'd known as a child growing up in the north of England. My mother was buried in the bosom of that Irish culture that I'd become estranged from and ashamed of. Like many children of Irish immigrants I had been encouraged by my mother to think of myself as Irish – which was itself fraught with conflict and confusion, because I was born in England of an English father. My mother's death left me not knowing who I was or where I belonged: I didn't feel

Irish enough nor did I have any real sense of being English. Yet it became clear that my mother had passed on to me all that was important to her – a love of songs and stories, a passion for justice, particularly in relation to Ireland, and also a sense of grief for Ireland and its history of emigration, separation and loss.

During the years following my mother's death, I became quite lost, both personally and politically, and felt that I needed to look at my life again but from a different point of view. I wanted to open the door to the more emotional, secret parts of me but I didn't know how to do this. I began to read about feminism and therapy and to attend workshops at the Women's Therapy Centre, and eventually, after setting aside a host of fears and doubts, I decided to join a women-only re-evaluation co-counselling class. Initially this felt very similar to the many consciousness-raising groups that I'd been in, because of its emphasis on speaking from one's own personal experience. The difference lay in co-counselling's emphasis on 'discharge' and 're-evaluation', where a person is encouraged to revisit hurtful past experiences so that they can be released or discharged through crying, shaking, laughing, yawning, sweating, non-repetitive talking or a combination of any of these. Because discharge frees up the hurt, it allows us to re-evaluate the reality of the situation so that we can see the incident, ourselves and other people more clearly. Discharge then becomes a recovery process that frees us from our distress and from rigid patterns of behaviour that are the result of being hurt. The aim of this process is to reclaim our inherent abilities and integrity so that we can live life to the fullest, according to our own individual choices and not those imposed on by us by an irrational and oppressive society.

I felt excited by this thinking because it not only offered me a way of healing myself but also gave me a more hopeful political direction. It was through co-counselling that I began to reclaim my working-class and Irish heritage, and this marked the end of a long period of confusion and the beginning of a new understanding about the past and present. From these influences, I decided that I wanted to share with other women what I'd already learned about classism, to work through some of the pain and to revive some of the joy that's a part of being working class.

I had some doubts about doing a workshop at the Centre because for many working-class women the very mention of the word therapy can be off-putting, since it's seen as an indulgent, navel-gazing, soft, middle-class activity and irrelevant to their lives. Some of this antagonism is justified in that a lot of therapy shows an inadequate awareness of class issues – the so-called bread-and-butter issues of poverty, hunger, cold, homelessness, etc. – and fails to address issues like the cost, language, style and assumptions of therapy that effectively exclude most working-class people. Yet I do believe that therapy and counselling can play a valuable role in any liberation process. I see some working-class criticisms and antagonisms as buying into the lie that it's unnecessary for us to think and reflect on ourselves and how we feel, that it's indulgent to take care of ourselves physically, emotionally and spiritually. I know these feelings well because I felt this way myself for many years.

Because of these antagonisms, I knew that not many 'ordinary' women would be likely to come to a workshop at the Centre. This concern for other, more exploited women has been raised at every workshop so far and I think that it's right that it should be, except that sometimes it reaches a point where some women become so guilt-stricken that they risk getting nothing out of the workshop for themselves. At times I've had to remind myself and other women that depriving ourselves of nourishment in whatever form is an old story and does not automatically mean that other, more deprived women will thereby benefit. As an 'educated' woman myself, it's important to me that I use the slack or reserves that my 'privileges' have given me to make myself stronger and more resilient so that I can continue to be effective in my feminist activities and my work to change the mental health system.

It is also important for me that we don't trade-off one woman's experience and struggle for another, that we don't get bogged down, as we have in the past, in creating a hierarchy of oppression rather than keeping our attention firmly fixed on how to free ourselves, other women and all people. That's not to ignore the fact that some women are more oppressed but to say that women who are less oppressed are often well placed to play a vital role in empowering others. And we need to give this support from a sense of love rather than one of guilt or patronage.

Although I am the sole author of this chapter, I shared the running of the four workshops at the Centre with two other women. The first two I led with Jill Brown, a middle-class woman, and the latter two with a working-class woman, Christy Adair. In addition to working with women individually, Jill and Christy were there to think about me and what I needed to run the group well. Jill's presence also gave women the chance to work on any feelings they harboured towards middle-class women. Jill was born of a working-class mother who died when she was eight, and although she described herself as middle class, her position highlights a dilemma about which class women who have one working-class parent belong to. Given the confusion of identity which can occur for these women, it is very important for them to decide themselves which class they belong to, or wish to be known as belonging to, and for their decision to be respected and supported without criticism or cross-examination.

All the women who attended the workshops were white – this is an important point to remember throughout the chapter. However, all the workshops attracted women from countries outside England, the most noticeable being first- or second-generation Irish women, who were by far the largest single racial group, sometimes being over a third of the group. Being among Irish women gave me a lot of safety. I am very aware, from my own life and family, of the grief, shame, anger and rootless feelings that many Irish people carry.

If any age predominated, it was women between 25 and 35, though more interesting than the age composition was the fact that many women described having had almost two lives, one where they lived according to others' expectations of them – as wives, mothers, unskilled workers – and a later life where they strove to assert their independence – through becoming educated, changing jobs, leaving husbands, moving cities, etc. In terms of sexual preference, I suppose a quarter to a third of the women who attended were lesbian and this also helped me to feel at ease. Finally, none of the workshops attracted any women with any disabilities.

## Settling in and Introduction to the Day

The timetable looked like this:

Settling in and introduction to the day.

Introductions.

Information about oppression and especially classism.

Exercises – reclaiming our heritage.
           – reviving a dream/reclaiming powers.

Drawing the workshop to a close.

Going through these points often took a while, because they all stimulated feelings that needed attention. For example, collecting outstanding fees often revived feelings of concern about poor women being excluded from workshops of this kind. Women often raised these issues for reassurance, because they didn't feel safe in surroundings like the Women's Therapy Centre that have a smart, middle-class appearance about them. I've found it quite important to stay on these issues until women feel more relaxed and ready to move on.

At the beginning we describe how we work. Far from being a distant facilitator, I find it vital to throw myself wholeheartedly into the process of the group, leading from a feeling/thinking standpoint. This means opening myself up to the feelings the women are expressing, and discharging them through crying, yawning, etc. so as to keep my thinking clear. In re-evaluation co-counselling terms, I model openness and expressiveness, creating safety for the group members in that I can be seen to survive my feelings and theirs, which encourages them to get in touch with their own pain.

It is important for the leader to use all her resources of warmth, understanding, knowledge and wit to generate an atmosphere of trust and acceptance. Our approach is to share time more or less equally among all the women, rather than let a few women take the time as they want it. This has the advantage of encouraging all women to find their voice and to see their input and experiences as equally important. As women, many of us feel uneasy about taking up time or being the centre of attention. These insecurities are often intensified for working-class women, because a lot of our silence is about feeling stupid, feeling that we have nothing to say of importance, that we cannot think properly or communicate our feelings as we wish to. For these reasons, I think it's very important that every woman is given the time and encouragement to describe her life in her own words. If the majority of women found this easier to do in small groups, we split into two groups of six, with Jill or Christy running one group.

In the first two workshops, we spent some time explaining Jill's role within the group as a middle-class woman. Jill's presence invariably provokes feelings of resentment at what's seen to be a violation of some women's space and sense of safety within the group. However, when Christy and I were doing the workshop together as two working-class women, quite a significant number of women mentioned in their workshop evaluation sheets that they would have welcomed the opportunity to work on feelings of resentment, anger, bitterness, etc. with a middle-class woman present.

*

## Introducing Ourselves

We originally began doing this with a list of questions for each woman to answer, but in time it became clear that it was better merely to ask each woman, including ourselves, to say something about her life and what she would like to get out of the workshop. In the last two workshops, these introductions have grown in importance and taken up the whole of Saturday morning and sometimes part of the afternoon. Some of this is because I have, if permitted, counselled each individual woman as we've gone round the room. Almost every aspect of working-class oppression is described and felt in these sessions, which makes it a very emotional experience and gives an extraordinary sense of closeness to women in the group. At times women have said they were surprised at the experiences they have focused on. For me this highlights the importance of allowing women to introduce themselves in an unstructured way. For example, many women cry for the losses they've suffered, for those who have died, for the people who just couldn't carry on, who gave up their lives rather than suffer more – in whatever way. What also sticks in my mind is the extent to which women recall things that have happened to their mothers, brothers, sisters or friends before relating what has happened to them. It can feel safer to focus on another person's pain, particularly when we feel overwhelmed by our own, though it also confirms for me the view that it is very painful for us to watch other people being beaten or mistreated in any way. Sometimes, too, when describing someone else's pain, we are talking about something we have also felt and perhaps cannot yet own.

What comes up as we scan our lives in this way is the degree to which we internalise negative messages about ourselves, other women and all working-class people, and the confusion and conflict this brings.

It shows how privileges have been used to divide us, to dispossess us of our heritage and to confuse us about the extent to which the vast majority of working-class people continue to be mistreated, humiliated, exploited, dehumanised and dispossessed of basic civil liberties and the right to be treated with respect. Scanning our lives also exposes the sense of powerlessness and despair that we feel about ever being able to end this injustice.

But what also comes up during these introductory sessions is how courageous and determined we are as working-class women – despite all the harm that's been done to us, we still carry on, perhaps a little more mistrustful but still able to share, to love, to communicate simply, to see the world from an uncluttered and unpretentious viewpoint. We only developed our patterns of mistrust, shame, blame, envy, resentment and powerlessness in order to survive, and we will let them go as soon as we no longer need them. This will happen all the sooner if we remember that even our most distressed behaviour is not our fault but a measure of how we've been hurt, that all wounds can be healed and that we deserve to be unconditionally loved through our changes. I once captured these thoughts in a poem.

WE WILL LEAVE NONE BEHIND . . .

As women we are capable of anything
Time and again, throughout herstory
We have shown
That no matter what obstacles
Have been manoeuvred
To hinder our progress
Most of us do come through
Still human . . .
Still loving . . .
Still hoping . . .

Let us grieve for those we've lost
Whilst we lend a hand to those of us
Who are still reeling from the pain
And let us wait for those of us
Who have for this moment given up
Who have forgotten the reason for their struggle
And their importance to us

And through our commitment and love
May we discover ourselves and each other
In a way never dreamt possible
Sharing and celebrating with generosity
Our successes and disappointments
Yet always remembering
That ours is a revolution
Too radical for measurement
Because it touches peoples' lives
In a thousand silent ways

# Classism

After our introductions I give a talk about how I see oppression, particularly classism, drawing on the experiences that women have already shared. Afterwards, I go round the room again, asking for any comments or additions that women wish to make.

In this discussion I raise issues about the external world. I see the economic and social oppression of working-class women as part of a system which keeps a very few rich at the expense of the many. I talk in some detail about this, drawing on the experiences that women in the group have already described. It is important to be able to make connections between unhappy and discouraging personal experiences and the social world we inhabit.

Exchanging information in this way is, I believe, quite different from the approach taken by most workshop leaders. I do it because one of the ways that oppression works is to deny us access to the truth, to accurate information about ourselves and the nature of our oppression. Through repeatedly having our hurtful experiences ignored, we are effectively denied an acknowledgment of our oppression, which leaves us doubting our own version of events or even our sanity.

Without this understanding of our oppression, we're left to heal old wounds while we gather new ones, or we're left divided or diverted off course into complaining about or blaming the wrong people (e.g. our parents) for injustices that are initiated at a much higher level in the actions of governments and other institutions (e.g. the legal system, housing, health and educational establishments). We've learned to live with mistreatment to the point where its guiding principles are accepted as given, as natural to human beings. It's like seeing the world through a filter, an invisible film that blurs and distorts our vision and limits our expectations and dreams.

One such blinker that distorts our vision and contact with other people is the view that it's somehow character-forming and in a child's best interest to be reared within an atmosphere of conditional love, instilling within us a fear of rejection or punishment as we're moulded into being or doing what others want of us. I think it's hard for us to imagine what it would be like to live in an environment in which feelings of criticism or rejection from people around us were replaced with a sense of encouragement, appreciation and respect. That's not to say that we cannot offer each other loving challenges. One of the challenges that lies before us is to open ourselves up to each other, so that we can be cherished in our shared struggles to change ourselves and eliminate oppression.

Another distortion says that we are all fundamentally different and have little in common with each other. While it's true that as women or men, black or white people, working-class or middle-class people we are reared differently, this does not mean that we cannot understand each other's struggles. I do not believe that there is a distinct body of feelings that is unique to working-class people or women, or is the monopoly of any oppressed group. All oppressed people carry, to varying degrees, feelings of anger, resentment, bitterness, humiliation, fear, mistrust, inferiority, powerlessness and pointlessness, and the sharing and politicising of these feelings can be a source of great unity between different oppressed groups. However, when, how, where and with whom we experience the impact of our oppression is unique to each individual, and so we all react differently.

Because oppression is initiated at an institutional level, some common distresses emerge. For example, poverty intensifies feelings of shame, while physical, sexual and/or emotional violations often heighten feelings of self-blame. Oppression begets oppression unless lovingly interrupted.

Oppression can be seen as taking two forms, both overlapping in an intricate weave. On the one hand, there's the external oppression of laws, institutions and other social structures that reinforce the principles of inequality – namely that certain people are inferior and therefore deserve less than their 'betters'. And on the other hand, there's internalised oppression in which we come to *believe* in our own inferiority, worthlessness and powerlessness, both as individuals and as a group. Whenever we act out negative messages against ourselves and each other, internalised oppression is at work.

In running a workshop for working-class women, we are always dealing with at least three oppressions, adultism, classism and sexism, all of which overlap a great deal, so that it's not always clear which is dominating. Adultism, that is the oppression of children and young people by adults, is rarely recognised as a major oppression but deserves special mention because many of the most painful experiences that women describe take place in early childhood. Violence, both physical and emotional, dominates these experiences. Women describe the brutalities they've received or have been forced to watch as their mothers, sisters or brothers were beaten, bullied and humiliated into submission or into believing in their worthlessness. As children, we have all experienced the impact of adult power at some time, irrespective of class backgrounds; so much so that, for me, this is the foundation on to which all other oppressions are overlaid – sexism, classism, racism, the oppression of the elderly, disabled people, lesbians and homosexuals, and people of minority religions or cultures. I've listed all these forms of oppression because they are all concentrated within the working class. This was brought home to me during one workshop where four out of the twelve women present had a mentally or physically handicapped close relative.

For classism to work, we need to be convinced, from the earliest age, that we are lesser people and deserve poorer homes, jobs, health and social service provisions. It isn't hard to believe this since class divisions taint everything we do: how we speak, who we know, where, what and how we eat, where and what we learn, the kind of job we do, the type, size and location of our home, etc. It is more than economic deprivation; it's about constantly looking up or down at each other to see who is superior or inferior to us. It affects everyone since it's impossible for anyone to escape its impact, but the most devastating blows fall on working-class people.

Yet this level of our experience can be ignored by others if we're seen to succeed or to acquire middle-class traits such as higher education. Through the use of these privileges we're divided off and disinherited from our class. For the majority of women who attended the workshops, myself included, the first privilege came when we went to grammar school. This experience, while providing new opportunities and a chance to learn and achieve, was not without its pain, particularly when it meant being separated from childhood friends or no longer feeling accepted by our family and friends.

Some of our parents also experienced this estrangement and loss when they aspired to a better-paid or more prestigious job, which for them was a source of great joy because it indicated success or a way of ensuring that their children would have a better chance in life than they had had. Sometimes this drive to aspire is confused with a rational desire to be competent, skilful, appreciated and successful. Because privileges mark a turning-point in some people's fortunes, it's easy to forget that it's not a privilege to be treated with dignity and respect but a civil right that everyone is worthy of from birth onwards.

Given the negative characteristics that are frequently ascribed to working-class people – that we're stupid, shiftless, mindless, unambitious, ignorant, crude, rude, untrustworthy, dirty, violent, cruel – it's hardly surprising that some working-class people are desperate to separate themselves off, in whatever way they can, from their class. I see the drive to aspire as acting out an illusion. I see my class like an invisible colour that lies within me for all time. I inherited it from my parents and so too will my son inherit the same class from me, no matter how he lives his life. The more we are able to reclaim our successes as working-class women, the more we will reclaim our culture in all its diversity, richness and changes. It's a lie that we can't be whatever we want to be – successful, creative, articulate, educated – and still be working class. The truth is that no human activity is the prerogative of any class. For example, one person may garden for a living while another does it as a hobby. It isn't gardening that belongs to any class but the social status associated with that activity.

## Exercise – Reclaiming our Heritage

In this and the following exercise, we sometimes split into two small groups, depending on what women want. To help women to get in touch with their feelings, we ask the following questions:

What do you most appreciate or like about being working class?

What can't you stand?

What do you never want to hear said again of working-class people?

Virtually any issue can come up during this session, and I describe certain experiences or feelings here rather than elsewhere merely for convenience and to avoid repetition.

This exercise helps to draw out both positive and negative feelings, in particular the way in which classist values have affected how we feel about ourselves – all the ways that we're locked into measuring ourselves against other people. It also exposes all the ways in which we've been cheated and robbed of our dignity and unity, and the wealth we create through our labour. The cruellest irony comes when we're blamed for our poverty, poor housing, unemployment, inadequate education, health care, etc. Our response to this oppression may be one of anger but it's more likely to be a feeling of powerlessness, since we've learned from the earliest age that fighting back can lead to further mistreatment. Hence our anger becomes locked into self-blame and self-disgust; or we find some comfort in blaming others, bearing grudges, complaining or fantasising revenge. None of these responses satisfies the rage we feel inside, nor do they bring positive changes, though exposing the feelings can be an important first step in moving away from self-blame.

One of the reasons why we've become afraid to express our anger is because we're afraid of being further humiliated, we're scared to expose ourselves in case we might look stupid or be made a fool of. I think that more than anything else, the fear of being humiliated stops us from acting powerfully, because it locks us within feelings of shame and secrecy that lead to loneliness and isolation.

I have found for myself and from working with other women that expressing anger is a most liberating and healing experience. It not only helps to clear out past hurts but also pushes us to give up being a victim and to take charge of our lives through setting boundaries, stating limits and saying 'No' to further oppression. Unfortunately, it's hard for women to give full vent to their anger at the Women's Therapy Centre, because this would disrupt other workshops. I therefore encourage women to bang something or to scream or shout into a cushion. This is often effective in disarming defences so that women can let down their guard. I begin by asking women to shout something simple and relevant like, 'No', 'Get off', 'Leave me alone' or 'Stop'. The aim is to encourage them to fight back, to believe in their own strength and that no mistreatment is deserved.

Expressing anger in this way can be terrifying, as can crying, for women who've been punished for expressing their feelings, through threats like, 'If you don't stop crying, I'll give you something to cry about,' or 'One more word out of you and . . .' But it is particularly frightening for women who've been beaten a lot. For totally understandable reasons, women can be very reluctant to own that they've been beaten or violated in any way. I don't push them to reveal such things unless they clearly want to, but I am nevertheless aware that these are major hurts that need some thought, because the deep internal fear can affect how safe women feel in the workshops. Sometimes women have blocked out what's happened and now don't remember, but I have worked a lot with women who have been beaten and can read it in their eyes and the way they hold themselves, in the fearful way that they search my face, as though trying to read my mind so that they know what's coming next. Sometimes it shows up in women finding it hard to sit still, as though they're on guard, ready to jump out of the way if anything unexpected, like any sudden movement, happens. Less often, it appears as aches in the body, like rheumatism, or in women talking a lot as a way of taking control and staving off attack. When counselling women on these experiences, I've found it healing to remind them that they are now safe, that no one will harm them here, that these wounds can be healed, that the worst is over and they'll never be beaten again in that way. These words usually bring lots of tears or sobbing, and if it seems right, I like to hold women very close to me as they cry. When anger or terror is being released, our bodies can shake uncontrollably. Again I try to get women to hold me tightly as they shake.

For one reason or another not many women reach the point of expressing great grief or anger, but this doesn't matter, because what's important is to encourage women to release whatever feelings they can. So, if they feel too embarrassed to shout, this feeling plus its history is what needs to be looked at. Laughter can be a very important and contagious release for women working on lesser fears or anger.

Somewhere along the road most women feel the need to grieve – to cry about all the little and major losses they've endured over the years. This may centre on the death of parents, children, brothers or sisters, friends and relatives, but a lot of the grief expressed is much vaguer and more confused – perhaps the loss of a dream or hope for some way out of suffering. For women who have had some education, their grief is often about losing childhood friendships or a closeness with their family, relatives and neighbours as they moved off to take up their privileged place in some grammar school or university. Loss, withdrawal or denial of love also brings many tears as women struggle to unravel the confusion they have felt at being trapped in the push/pull of conflicting messages that said 'Be like me/Don't be like me', 'Get away/Stick around', 'Get an education/You'll do all right without.' These experiences have left most women feeling that whichever way they turned, they would not be able to get it right or feel good about themselves. In the face of material and emotional deprivation they have felt overwhelmed by feelings of 'what about me?' that yearned for attention.

During this exercise, nearly all women focus on their relationship with their parents. Some of this is because of the mediating role that parents play in teaching us what they see to be right and wrong behaviour, which in some ways is inadvertently teaching us to accept rather than resist our oppression. As parents we want the best for our children, but don't always know what this is or how to get it. Consequently, most of us enter adulthood with many unresolved feelings about our parents. The following is a scan of some of the issues, first in relation to our mothers and then to our fathers.

We are angry with our mothers for allowing themselves to be mistreated and for not protecting us from the oppression that they knew so well. We blame them for not handling our fathers better, for not defending us at school, for not showing us how to belong, for

failing to prepare us for life or for scaring us as to its
before we even set foot in the world. We are bitter th...
childhoods too soon when we were asked to 'mother' our mothers or
brothers and sisters, and we are sad for ourselves and our mothers that
we couldn't have a life without poverty and hardship. We are
disappointed that she couldn't be the 'ideal' mother in the 'ideal'
home, waiting for us with outstretched arms as we skipped or slumped
through the door after another long day in the wilderness, and we are
disappointed in all the ways that she couldn't live up to the promise of
powerfulness that we once saw as tiny, dependent children. And we
are sad for our mother's losses – for her loss of spirit and hope for life,
for the joys that weren't shared, the skills and effort that went
unnoticed, the emptiness that went unnourished, the love that wasn't
returned, the views that weren't respected, the sacrifice that wasn't
appreciated, the emotions that were ignored or mocked, the loneliness
that consumed her and all the work that went unpaid.

And just as our thinking about our mothers brings up painful
feelings, so too it arouses enormously deep feelings of love and a sense
of amazement at how well they managed, given their situation and the
limited resources available to them. Many women in the workshops
also express very painful feelings about their fathers. We may be angry
with them for being bullies, for doing nothing to ease the load that our
mothers carried, for removing themselves from us and wasting money
on alcohol or gambling that should have been spent on food, clothes,
holidays. We despise them for earning too little or for leaving our
mothers to worry about how to make ends meet, and we rage inside
from all the physical, emotional, verbal and sexual abuse that we've
seen inflicted on women, our mothers and ourselves, by them or other
men. We fear their strength and power yet loathe their weakness for
not being strong enough to withstand the onslaught of their oppression
better or for not protecting us from the anguish of being treated as
inferior in a thousand settings.

And we are disarmed when we glimpse how these bullies came to be
bullies or how our fathers came to be locked in a fear that led them to
become weak, indecisive, anxious and over-dependent on our mothers.
We are sad when we see written on their faces or in their eyes the
anguish of being bullied and humiliated to the point of numbness by
those who had power or authority over them. And, as their lives draw
to a close, we feel bitter that they too have so little to show for a
lifetime of toil and struggle, and we wonder at the end of the day
whether they really ever had much male privilege and if they did,
whether this could ever be enough compensation for having been

denied the right to feel, to show their emotions and to enjoy being connected to themselves, their families and other human beings.

For many women, recounting what actually went on within their families is itself a very liberating experience, because it contradicts deeply rooted feelings of shame and secrecy that they've held on to for years. For some women, secrecy is the only way they have known to protect themselves and their families from further humiliation and criticism. This was certainly the case for Jay, who had not spoken of her childhood for years. Jay was a single woman in her early thirties whose mother died when she was young, leaving her to care for her four or five brothers and sisters with little money and an absent and cruel father who left all the work to Jay. Quite early on, Jay realised she was clever and saw education as an escape. As soon as she could she left home and class behind her.

Doing this exercise was very painful for Jay, because she could see absolutely nothing good about being working class. Her anger was very much to the fore, as were feelings of bitterness and even hatred towards her father. What was less available to Jay was any sense of grief and anger about the death of her mother. Because of the abuse she'd experienced, Jay was not able to release her feelings beyond talking about them, which she did very openly, despite feelings of mistrust and fear. Somehow, I sensed that Jay's body was very sore and I wanted to hold her very closely, but every message told me that this was not possible. Instead, I listened very closely, and eventually Jay began to cry about how lonely and pointless she felt her life to be. Since she was a child she had fantasised about committing suicide when she felt that she couldn't go on any more.

Jay's story stayed in my mind because her childhood had been so deprived, both materially and emotionally. Her description of the poverty she and her sisters and brothers had experienced was one that many women were able to relate to – situations like having no money for food or living off toast for weeks at a time, living with no heating or lighting, a whole family sharing one room with the constant threat of eviction if a child was noisy or mischievous, being mocked at school for being dirty, having no money for school funds or trips away, never having the right uniform or never living in the right neighbourhood that could save you from being picked on by teachers, the police, anyone, always worrying about what was happening at home or who was going to get beaten next, whether at school, in the street or at home.

Thinking about Jay's experiences, my own and those of other women reminds me that it's a measure of our courage that we are prepared to expose our feelings so openly given all the shame and mistrust that we carry. While it's true that as a class we've been taught other people's rules, we've also been taught crucial skills of survival – resilience, determination, quick-wittedness, humour and courage. We learned these mainly from our parents, particularly our mothers, who were often central in passing on a sense of working-class culture and heritage. Some of this sense I once saw written in a poem; unfortunately, I don't know the author, but whenever I have recited it, women have wanted me to write it down.

> I swear it to you
> I swear it to you on my common woman's head
> This common woman is as common
> As a common loaf of bread
> And will rise.

## Exercise: Reviving a Dream/Reclaiming Power

Describe a dream you once cherished or some goal that you'd like to achieve. What's the first step in achieving this? Who could help you?

These questions focus on how hard it is for us to act to change our lives when we feel bad about ourselves and have so little confidence that we can get what we want. It's hard to put into words these feelings of inferiority and inadequacy because they seem so much a part of us.

Our feelings of inferiority and worthlessness come out in the feeling that we and other working-class people are stupid, crude, ugly, etc. and that we don't belong anywhere, that we're always in the wrong place, outsiders who don't know the rules about how to behave or what's expected of us, particularly in middle-class company or settings. What's also revealed is a sense that we must earn our acceptance through working hard, giving out to others, putting ourselves last, never showing our ignorance or lack of knowledge for fear of being punished, humiliated or dismissed. These insecurities come through in our desperation about 'getting it right' and when we repeatedly trust middle-class people's thinking more than our own.

One of the major ways in which we've been held back has been through people having low or no expectations of us; this comes through in phrases like 'Don't bother, it isn't meant for the likes of you,' or 'It was never possible anyway,' or 'Give up now, then you won't get disappointed.' It is hard not to assume that we will fail, hard to trust our successes or achievements. Low expectations are also used as an excuse for working-class people to be starved of the resources and money we need to live with dignity – the notion that 'those people live like pigs because they like it that way and don't know any better.'

Asking women to describe their dreams can bring forth some unexpected and poignant responses. Years ago I asked a group of homeless women what they most wanted in the world and one woman whispered, 'A bicycle.' That was all – not a home, not a job, not some money or decent food and clothes, but a bicycle. I wish I knew if she ever got her bicycle or whether she was returned to the mental hospital, where she had spent most of her life.

One of the aims of this exercise is to encourage women to see middle-class people as potential allies and to give them the opportunity to look at any feelings of resentment or bitterness they may have, something that women did more when Jill was present. Middle-class people can play a vital and liberating role in supporting us, by encouraging us to take charge of this relationship, by being on our side, listening and learning from us about what we need to act in our interest. Running alongside the negative feelings, there is also a sense of safety that many of us get from middle-class people, and hence our attraction to them, because they are not caught up in the same distress. We hope through our contact with them we will be given the same status and respect.

Thinking about middle-class women or men in this way also brings up many feelings of mistrust. Trust is a major issue for all oppressed people and, sadly, many of us dismiss options that could have been enriching, or even liberating, for fear of being let down again or of becoming dependent on something that may disappear. Or, rather than seeing mistrustful feelings as an expression of our oppression that yearns for healing like any other hurt, mistrust is used as an excuse to reinforce divisions or as a reason for giving up. If mistrust is felt towards middle-class people, it will also eventually come up around working-class people, so to work on feelings of mistrust is also to work towards unity.

To ask women who have suffered a lot in their lives to recall their dreams and ambitions can seem a very 'wet' and somewhat irrelevant thing to do. I remember asking an older woman about her hopes and dreams. Her response was one of frustration, bordering on anger, at being asked such an irrelevant question, given all the other issues that overwhelmed her. I encouraged her to give vent to these feelings, which in time drew her to speak very honestly and fully about her bitterness and resentment of men and middle-class people who 'had everything'. I recall asking what was her first memory of feeling bitter and resentful, and she replied the birth of her brother. It then came to light that as the eldest child, the birth of every one of the seven or eight children that followed meant that Ros became increasingly deprived both emotionally and materially as her parents struggled to survive. For Ros, the loss of a dream indicated the loss of hope. When older, Ros saw that she either had to get stuck into that struggle or leave home. She left, and then decided never to have any children or to marry; instead, she decided to get herself trained in some skill so that she could earn her own living and live independently, which she had done after a lot of hard work and sacrifice. Eventually, Ros found a dream: she wanted to be a writer. We spent the remaining time working out what her next steps would be, namely, to borrow a typewriter from a friend, to ask another three or four friends to help her by constantly referring to her writing, and to join a writers' group.

Although Ros was unable to cry, and hadn't done so for years, she released a lot of her feelings through laughter and talking. This exercise often brought up lots of laughter, which released some of the fear and embarrassment that comes up when sharing secrets like our dreams and ambitions. I've found it very good to get women to exaggerate whatever they say. This helps to counteract the feelings of worthlessness that show through when women settle for little rather than going for the lot. Equally, when working out who could help them achieve these goals, I encourage women to be outrageous and demanding and to state very clearly what they want out of the relationship in terms of support, love, appreciation, validation, etc. On a couple of occasions I've asked women to stand on chairs during these sessions to counteract feelings of unimportance, and this usually brings peals of laughter from the whole group. Asking for help is often confused with weakness and not being able to do it. To get at these feelings I have, on occasion, asked women to plead for help in their most pathetic and helpless voice. In many ways this is a good exercise to end on, because it revives hope and reminds us that we're much more likely to get what we want if we believe it's possible and that we deserve it.

## Drawing the Workshop to a Close

To draw the workshop to a close, we spend about an hour summarising some of the main issues that women have raised and listening to what women feel about the day. More recently, we've given time to working out what, if anything, women want to do next; sometimes this has involved women meeting up in couples or threes or as a group. We have sometimes led a follow-up day some months after the first workshop and more recently a network of women who have attended these workshops has been set up. This meets monthly in London.

I've described in this chapter some of the feelings and experiences that are common among working-class women. My aim in doing the workshops has been to empower women by sharing with them whatever knowledge and insights I possess so that through our connection to each other we can begin to fight back.

The aim of taking a direction that is positive and hopeful is to free ourselves of all the negative, powerless, fearful and debilitating emotions that stop us from being ourselves in all our dignity, courage and compassion. By reclaiming our anger rather than blaming people, we acknowledge our powerfulness and our right to be free of all oppression. By surrounding ourselves with as many allies as we need, we go against feelings of weakness, worthlessness and unimportance, and we remind ourselves that we need not struggle for our liberation alone. By sharing our triumphs and disappointments and by inviting other women to do the same, we are laying aside feelings of isolation and shame, and pushing for a stronger, unconditional connection with ourselves, our class and other human beings. And in this, as in all things we do, we can enjoy and be energised by our journey towards powerfulness and liberation.

I'd like to end with one of my poems and a thanks to all the many women who've shared their wisdoms and loved me through my doubts about ever finishing this chapter. In particular, I'd like to thank Sue Krzowski for her constant encouragement and Jill Brown, my lifelong companion and journeywoman, for her love and belief in me.

A POEM FOR MY SISTERS ON THEIR JOURNEY

Would we be foolish or arrogant
If we saw ourselves
As travellers
On a 'journey without maps'
Steering a course without compass
Searching for ourselves

Each other
And for safety
In this beautiful but invaded earth.

And if we're caught
Should we too leave a marker
To say that failure wasn't possible
Since the pleasure and triumph
Was always in the journey itself.

1986

# 5
# Black Women's Workshop
Janet Hibbert and
Dorann van Heeswyk

Our workshops are for us to come together and take pride in our blackness and our womanness. Our publicity sheet states, 'This is a workshop for us to get together as black women, to share ourselves, our feelings and our experiences. An opporunity to stop and take stock of what happens to us as we grapple with the double oppression of racism and sexism and start working towards reclaiming our real power and potential, particularly looking at the way internalised racism and sexism prevent us from being as close and supportive to each other as we know we can be.'

As black women we are the majority group in the world, though living in a white, male-organised society makes this reality hard to hold on to. The workshops were set up in response to the request of a black woman who, having attended several workshops at the Centre, came away feeling that there had been no place for her blackness. As the only black woman in a group of white women, this essential 'her' had had to be put aside. This is a common experience, and rather than resign herself to the situation, this black woman spoke out and the workshops were set up. Despite often operating in isolation, many of us black women take our responsibility of being representatives of a majority world group seriously and speak out. This takes a lot out of us and it's important to get together and take a break from this public service and be free to feel all we feel without double- and triple-thinks, without 'seeing round corners' – recognising racism and sexism and assessing the appropriate response.

We need to come together, we look forward to coming together. Then, when we come together, we face head on all the hurting, back-biting and criticism that goes on between ourselves as black sisters, e.g. 'Who has sold out?', 'Who has the true black consciousness?', 'Who has the right social and political analysis?', 'Who indeed is *really* black?', etc. The list is endless, as anyone who has tried to organise among their own group will know; 'in-fighting' is not peculiar to black groups.

Racism and sexism are *real*; they are enshrined in the institutions of the land. We organise together to combat these oppressions. But what of the aspects of racism and sexism that seep into our very beings and lead us to accept – unwittingly – the worst definitions and spectres of ourselves and our people? This internalising of racism and sexism operates between us insidiously and is tricky to tease out. It gets in the way of our being close, for if in some way the information (or misinformation) of our intrinsically 'second-class' nature has seeped in, then spending time with others with that same second-class nature is bound to stimulate all our self-loathing and lead us to be suspicious of each other. Intellectually, we know that these thoughts and attitudes are incorrect, and in our everyday lives and in our roles as political activists, we fight hard against them and achieve a great deal by sustained hard work. (When we speak of political activist, we refer to all black women who, in whatever way they choose, assert their blackness and their womanness, whether as black parents, teachers, health workers, as unemployed, as young women, as tenants, as school pupils, as grandparents, etc.)

Our role as workshop leaders is to provide a haven from the pressures that prevent us giving airspace to our feelings, however 'off' they may be – space to deal with our internalised racism and sexism that is our self-invalidation, with self-doubt, isolation and feelings of powerlessness, and space to look at differences among ourselves. We believe that while actions have always to be justified, feelings do not, and feelings buried usually come out somehow, often in hurtful action. Feelings let out with the appropriate physical release – crying, laughter, shaking, anger, rage – in a safe place can leave us free to be flexible and creative in our actions; most importantly, free to be clear that what separates us as black women is not that she is lesbian, she is heterosexual, she is too educated, she is ignorant, she is light-skinned, she is dark-skinned, etc., but the *belief* that these differences are destructive, threatening and dangerous to our unity.

We learn the prejudices of light skin versus dark skin, educated versus less educated, gay oppression, upper and middle class versus working class, etc. from the time we open our eyes on our world. The society into which we have all been born breathes this nonsense into our very beings, and while some of us have had information and experiences to counter this, the effects of society as a whole are still there; especially since for most of us it was our very close ones who taught us the views that rank individuals according to sexuality, skin colour, accent, class background, etc. Why does this nonsense have such an impact? It does so because it comes at us at a time when we are vulnerable, that is, when we are children and looking to those around us to inform and protect us. Often, as mentioned above, it will be those we love most who will pass on these oppressive notions, they themselves having learned them in the way they now teach them to us.

In the workshop we start from the premise that *no human being is born with oppressive attitudes and behaviours, and no human being willingly takes them on.* Each person must first have been treated in an oppressive way and have had some of their power denied them before they would be prepared to settle for what is dealt them. We have only to look at the treatment children receive to see the many ways in which their power is denied, and the natural fight that young people put up when their rights are denied.

The so-called terrible twos (the name betrays the hard time adults have over the many confrontations and powerful assertions from two-year-olds) is a significant stand in this battleground. Unfortunately, in many cases it is also often the last stand. Young people do not give in easily, yet manifestly it does happen that our power is eroded at this time.

No girl readily internalises her oppression; no girl begins to think of herself as second-rate, inferior and stupid without putting up a fight. Several workshop participants had brothers whose job it was to knock a 'cocky' sister into shape. Afro-black parents have the legacy of bringing up children in slavery, where keeping in line was a matter of survival. Slavery and whipping may be things of the past but the notion that children need to be knocked into shape, because you love them and want them to survive, still prevails. A mother in one of the workshops spoke of her own struggle to bring up her children in a way that fosters their sense of self and power. She wanted them to be free to question her and others, and to stand up for themselves in all circumstances. She found this difficult not only because it went against the way she herself had been raised but also because there lurked the fear, 'Will they survive if they are open, free and self-confident?' This question goes to the heart of our internalised oppression.

Children in the playground act out on each other the bullying they themselves have experienced or witnessed. They begin to express and enact the prejudices they have known. As black girls we learn that black is inferior to white, girl is inferior to boy, and that to be a young child is inferior to being an adult. Each of us begins to move between being oppressor and oppressed. A black girl is herself oppressed, but she too can be an oppressor around someone younger, someone newer to her school, someone who doesn't speak English, someone with a disability. This chain of being hurt and then hurting others comes to be 'how the world is.' There is little time given to teasing out the chain of hurts, and without such analysis there arises the commonly held belief that human beings are cruel. That we behave cruelly is different from saying that we are inherently cruel.

As a young black girl our best and closest friend could very well be another black girl with a similar background. However, since we inevitably internalise the information (misinformation) that to be black and female is inferior, then within this relationship with our best black girlfriend there will be an element of distrust and contempt. As we grow older and learn that there are socially acceptable ways of discriminating against each other, e.g. heterosexual women against gay women, well-educated professional women against manual workers, those who speak the Queen's English and those who speak patois, we have a way to justify the feeling of distrust and contempt. The differences of skin colour, class background and sexuality become convenient hooks for the divisions among ourselves.

The oppressive prejudices and beliefs that separate us are not something for which we must blame each other but something we must expect each other to take responsibility for eliminating. We must air these differences and be clear that it is the functioning of our internalised racism that separates us. Being open about our oppressive ideas of each other allows us to move on to see each other for who we are – gloriously individual although commonly oppressed by racism and sexism. Exploring and airing these differences is the most liberating thing we, as a group of black women, can do for ourselves. It is an act of true defiance of our oppression to say, 'I will look at, face on, whatever it is that keeps me away from you, my black sister, and talk openly about it in the full knowledge that all the prejudice about you that I carry around with me has nothing to do with either you or me and everything to do with the oppressive society in which we both live.' Any change we hope to effect for ourselves and our relationship with each other as black women depends on our having the courage to do this, and it does take courage to be honest in this way. We do blame ourselves or each other for the separations between us and can get stuck in this blaming. In these workshops we offer the opportunity for each of us to take the time and make the commitment to look beyond the exterior, learned oppressive behaviour to the person who must first have been hurt and had her power denied her before she would have gone along with such nonsense.

We must each listen to our sister's story and tell our own, taking the opportunity to explore our pain and hurts so that we can be free of the restrictions these place on our functioning. We believe that it is the storing-up and repression of these hurts that block our full power, intelligence and compassion. Tackling internalised oppression among ourselves takes courage. Facing up to the fact that it even exists is in itself very difficult. The Grenadian US black writer Audre Lorde says:

> Often we give lip-service to the ideal of mutual support and connection between black women because we have not yet crossed the barriers to these possibilities, nor fully explored the angers and fears that keep us from realising the power of a real black sisterhood . . . We cannot settle for the pretences of connection, or for parodies of self-love. We cannot continue to evade each other on the deepest levels because we fear each other's angers, nor continue to believe that respect means never looking directly nor with openness into another black woman's eyes.

*Dorann:* I grow stronger with each workshop because each time I take the step of telling my sisters the ways in which I have felt hurt by them, I get closer to my most valuable resources, myself and my black sisters. I am a light-skinned, straight-haired black woman and had for years been too timid to make this step since I was 'not really black' and could be (and indeed was) attacked for this at any point. I felt all the pain I suffered was my own fault for being too light-skinned, and felt guilty about the preferential treatment light-skinned people get, and the way we have let ourselves be used by white people. All this 'not really black' feeling plus the guilt is an example of my internalised racism fed by my sisters' internalised racism and the resulting timidity is a certain way of keeping me powerless, in line, and out of touch with other black women, both light- and dark-skinned. Speaking out about my life and hearing from other women breaks through this.

*Janet:* I am a black, dark-skinned woman and from an early age felt there was a tremendous 'silent' pressure to assimilate (become invisible). As I could not achieve this through skin colour, my other choice was through education – being 'ten times better', which for me not only meant passing exams, but having 'intellectual' (usually white) friends who I could relate to, who would enhance my aspirations, which involved my trying to believe that if you had 'education' and good manners, then there was no problem in your skin colour being black. So in trying to achieve this, it meant for a long time denying the blackness of me, and holding on to my false expectations of the 'real' world.

In our experience, this 'not being really black' is one of the nastiest expressions of our internalised oppression, and in our most secret places we have found that many of us have tried to keep quiet about or alter who we are to fit more neatly into a position of easy acceptance. This 'not black enough' syndrome often has nothing to do with skin colour. It can be the factor behind the way we have come to deny ourselves access to a wide range of experiences. Some of us, for example, love classical music, opera, ballet, outdoor camping and hiking, dislike dancing and reggae, yet can't feel at ease with this. Those of us who grew up separated from other black people (perhaps in care or with white foster parents) can feel ashamed of tastes and habits we have acquired, and are left timid and unsure among our black sisters and brothers. One workshop participant reported how she spent time meticulously learning Jamaican patois and all there is to know about reggae music in order to 'pass'. There is a great feeling of unburdening when these things are shared, and we feel a sense of solidarity as we confirm the obvious – that the appreciation and enjoyment of any piece of human culture is not the preserve of any particular group of people, though it's certainly true to say that access to certain cultural forms is more readily available to the white middle classes of our society.

Racism has limited our access to many facets of society. The brilliant culture we have developed in response to these restrictions deserves to be seen as brilliant, but cannot be used as an imprisoning definition of all the culture we are entitled to. Putting each other down and buying into this is colluding with our internalised racism.

One woman in a workshop told of how her mother had been abandoned by her own mother because she was 'too dark'. Her mother's pain and bitterness had permeated the participant's own life and the workshop was a place for her to look at how this issue of skin colour had affected her own relationship with people. The politics and realisations of the sixties were very important for us in establishing black pride and a way forward; however, the extent and degree of the workings of internalised racism on ourselves was not realised and we developed a reversal of the skin colour positions. It became wrong to be light-skinned. Racism and, more importantly, the way we as black people have internalised it can leave those of us with one white and one black parent feeling there is no place for us.

In our workshops we encourage all participants to realise that every one of us is totally all the parts that go to make us up rather than to remain tyrannised by such offensive notions as half-caste. We do this by offering a participant the phrase 'I am totally black' to say out loud to the group. Saying this out loud in front of others gives the woman an opportunity to voice what she has always hoped to hear. That she herself is now saying it goes against her long-established feelings of being a nothing, with no group to belong to, no place to feel accepted. When we move on to ask the participant to map out the implications for how she would see herself and how she would live her life if she were able to identify completely with the truth of the statement, we see her begin to get in touch with a self that is grounded, that *can* be and *is* powerful, that has got rights. She can begin to relinquish the view of herself as a victim. One participant, who had been a member of an important black women's group, raged and sobbed as she repeated, 'I am totally black', and when asked what brought the anger and the tears described the indignities and slights she had allowed herself to endure because deep down she had never felt sure that she belonged. She had always known intellectually, as did the other women, that she did belong, but the internalised racism was running rampant in her feelings about herself, fed by the internalised racism of her black sisters.

Without a sharp understanding of the ways in which internalised racism and internalised sexism operate, our workshops would achieve little. Indeed, it is when no attention is given to the way internalised oppression is operating that our black women's groups fall apart.

We can always find 'good and objective' reasons for why so-and-so is at fault, lazy, uncooperative, etc. As workshop leaders we believe that it is internalised racism and sexism that keep us mistrustful, fearful and suspicious of each other, self-doubting and powerless around our own lives; that on many of the occasions when any of us feels intolerant of, ashamed of, not as black as, blacker than, better than, not as good as, afraid of, not cared about or not supported by another black woman, some aspect of internalised racism and sexism is at work. We also believe that the workshop is exactly the place in which to begin to grapple with it.

Looking at internalised racism and sexism is looking at ways in which we have habitually colluded with our own oppression, where we have been hurt/oppressed, been victimised and, most importantly, stayed victims. The knocks and hurts that come from the agents of our oppression, men and white people, while most significant in themselves, become less significant as we get older in relation to the knocks we give ourselves, e.g. 'I can't really because I am only . . .', 'I can't since they are so much . . . than me', etc. A welcome relief for all at our workshops is that within the framework outlined above, we spend little time and energy focusing on the agents of our oppression. It is a well-known phenomenon that as soon as we get together we let the very groups of people whose power over us makes it vital for us to get together in the first place dominate the subject-matter of our exchanges, leaving no space or time for just who *we* are, how *we* feel. Not so here.

As black women we can't, for obvious reasons, always hit back at the agents of our mistreatments, so we take our hurt and frustration out where it is safe – on each other. No oppressive white person can hurt me as much as a black sister, for no oppressive white person knows so well where to hurt me. Turn this around and it is a black sister's love and support that can allow me to soar, since her power and strength is a reflection of my own power and strength. It is this thinking and emotion that is the background to our workshop; our programme is to move from 'pretences of connection and parodies of self-love' (Audre Lorde, above) to the *real thing*. Black sisterhood is powerful, flowing from our very bellies rather than from shrill voices, chin forward. Whenever we are defiant like that, there may still be the victim tape playing somewhere in our heads. We are survivors, we are brilliant survivors like our mothers, grandmothers, great-grandmothers. We urge: let us move on beyond survival to ownership of our lives, our destinies, our world and, above all, let's have each other's.

When we first meet we share our names. What brings you to the workshop? Where are you from? What is your heritage? What do you want to get out of our time together? What's special for you about bèing in a black women's group? What experience do you have of black women's groups? Is there anything you'd like to share, e.g. how you spend your days, important relationships? Any fears, appre-hensions? What's special about you that you'd like us to know right at the beginning? This serves as a broad and opening introduction to each other. Some women have no experience of being in a black women's group but refer to sisters, cousins and close friends as a valuable resource. Some women come to make contact with other black women as they have been cut off from their black sisters through adoption, fostering, work, education. They want to affirm their identity as a black woman in the face of their everyday isolation – real or imagined. Our backgrounds in terms of language, culture and country of origin vary enormously. Some of us are second generation in Britain and some of us are immigrants, usually from ex-British colonies – from the Caribbean, South-East Asia, Africa, the Indian subcontinent. We also vary in our class backgrounds. Some of us were middle class in our country of origin and are now working class in Britain; some came from wealthy classes in our country of origin. However, the majority of us are working class. Some of us are mothers, some not; some are married, some single; some are heterosexual, some lesbian; some in paid employment, some unemployed; some with disabilities, some able-bodied. We cover the full range of possibilities, arriving together because we each of us define ourselves as black, and we are women. There is no 'test' for blackness and one of the most exciting features of the workshops has been to learn what each woman's blackness has meant for her, leaving no room for stereotypes of black womanhood.

A common theme in response to 'What brings you to the workshop?' is 'To gain strength and solidarity, to get a clearer sense of who I am and of my power.' This opening round never fails to move us all and takes some time. We often pair off to talk to just one person about what we want to share before going straight into sharing with the whole group. A quick loosening-up round usually precedes this, e.g. we each finish the phrase 'Right now I feel . . .' Sometimes we share one obstacle that had to be overcome to get to the workshop. This sharing pinpoints all the fear and anxiety that most women feel before coming and how often something crucial has had to be put aside before the commitment to come could be acted upon. Frequently, something crucial does come up to try to prevent us from doing something for ourselves, for, indeed, it goes against our very oppression to put ourselves first and to take a weekend for ourselves. To call self-examination in a workshop navel-watching and inappropriate for black women (we must always be out 'doing'), is to fail to acknowledge the courage it takes to go against our conditioning, which teaches us to serve others and to put their needs before our own. The fact that there are usually more women enrolled than finally show up underlines the courage it takes to come. Throughout the workshop we see fit to congratulate ourselves on having made the commitment to spend time together. As black women we so often take our courage for granted; we would hazard a guess that even Harriet Tubman did! We attempt in our workshops to interrupt this habit.

At the beginning we outline the groundrules. Confidentiality is very important. We also ask for smokers to smoke as little as they can, as we believe that smoking keeps feelings in check. While it is the safety that we workshop leaders manage to create that allows feelings to come out, it is also for each participant to steel herself to take risks. We see ourselves as demonstrating this risk-taking by participating in all parts of the programme. For both of us this has always been a powerful experience. One participant said that she was a bit taken aback by this at first but had valued this peer element of our workshop. Our most valuable resource for this work has been re-evaluation co-counselling, and here peer counselling is an essential element. We also encourage physical closeness, which can cause great embarrassment and bring out inhibitions. It is our encouragement and modelling that allow these to break down and/or be explored. One woman in a workshop felt strongly that she did not want to touch, and when touched felt intruded upon. We shared our observation that many children (and by implication probably many of us when we were young) took closeness to be a matter of course and that it was something we could reclaim. She was still adamant, and this was respected. Physical closeness is a rich part of our heritage and one which we both enjoy reclaiming and expressing. It has, however, to be used sensitively so as not to be an 'ought', as this would be a distortion of the connection expressed by physical closeness. While one of us as workshop leader counselled this same woman on her life-story, she spoke of her difficult relationship with her mother, and the counsellor sensed the importance of just holding the woman to give her a break from holding herself together. Knowing how the woman felt about physical closeness, the counsellor first asked permission and the woman held back. Somehow, however, this exchange had an effect, for as we ended the weekend, she welcomed our closeness and it was this reclaiming of closeness and the dent in her isolation that was her highlight.

Much of what we do in the workshop involves us dividing the time among us all so that each person has a chance to express herself with the whole group giving attention and one of the workshop leaders counselling. We actively encourage the sister to reach for feelings rather than intellectual descriptions and explanation; we listen to each other just for the sake of hearing and acknowledging and validating, rather than waiting for the right cue to jump in to agree or disagree and move in with our own 'truth'. This discipline of taking turns allows us to hear and learn from each other, and there is real excitement as each person takes a turn. Hearing someone talk about what is important to them when they are not expecting to be attacked or judged is exciting, for there is a quality of pride and integrity that comes over which grips us all. Without being rigid, we outline time-limits for each person as this gives space for those uneasy about taking 'eartime' and protects over-talkers from over-talking. We emphasise that the essential part of what we are organising is for each of us to have, in turn, the attention of all the rest of the group. In our experience, each of us has a great deal to say, even if at first habitual shyness or a retiring style might indicate differently, and this practice of dividing time, while awkward at first, never fails to work well. It also discourages the discussion format which parodies what goes on in everyday life, with attention paid to who is articulate, who has the 'right-on' views, etc. We want to create a break from that to look at what are our pains and our joys, what we dream of and what we usually keep secret because of various taboos. We say in the workshop, 'We encourage you to have fall off your lips what you have hardly dared think.' We cover the walls of the workshop venue with posters that say 'celebrate', 'explore', 'share', 'risk', 'love', 'power', 'soar', 'commitment', 'we are worth wanting one another'.

We aim to cover two basic themes. One, our life-stories, and the other, direct work on internalised oppression. The order of these two themes has varied. We also play games, often introduced by the participants, as well as singing, doing relaxation exercises or spon- taneously 'mucking around'. We always bring music (Sweet Honey in the Rock and tabla music have been favourites) and we always share meals together. We bring books that have been important to us and encourage the participants to do the same the second day. We exchange book-lists at meal-times. Overall, there is hard work in the context of celebration, and we as workshop leaders take responsibility for maintaining the balance and tone. When energy is low, particularly after a meal, we ask for games and songs to be volunteered and offer some ourselves. We have had cushion fights, played children's games from Sierra Leone and other home countries. We find that these light, lively activities free our attention for listening to each other's pain, particularly when that pain reminds us of our own.

Life-stories are important, for our backgrounds are so varied. In a racist society, black is a significant, single category. However, among ourselves our differences are vast. It is refreshing to experience ourselves and each other as not just skin colour, but as who we are as women: mother, sister, lover, worker, lesbian, wife, daughter, immi- grant, black born in England, etc. Those of us who have the dubious privilege of being considered exotic (a less obvious but none the less nasty form of racism) will often have been asked our life-story and would have told it for the sake of the listener. We have all had the task of informing and educating racist society of who we are. The life-story that we are after in this session is very different. It is the story that is significant for each sister to tell. Each of us tells it as it occurs to us, focusing on whatever details seem important at the time without aiming to be comprehensive or even chronological. So often we speak of loved ones we miss or of the emotional hurts suffered in coming to a strange land; of the pain of being the 'dark one' or the 'light one' in the family, or being the only black girl in such and such a situation; of the responsibility of carrying the reputation of our people on our shoulders, knowing that all black people may be judged by how we acquit ourselves. We speak also of our relations in the family, of the pain of seeing parents struggle against poverty and racism, of deep love and loyalty between friends and family.

Family is very significant. In a racist, antagonistic society, it is often our family to whom we turn for refuge and help. When this does not work out, our pain has to be dealt with silently or in other ways; often it is buried. Black children learn early not to complain to authorities. There have been families where the support is available, the support needed to deal with such nonsense as the phrase 'If you're black, stay back.' Grandmothers have often been key people, especially when they have been caretakers while parents were absent. Whole areas are opened up and there is a feeling of closeness and deep respect after this time together which can take all of a day. When dealing with life-stories, we often start with 'How was life for the young powerful (Janet)?' If she can remember a photograph of herself when very young, we ask what words could she hear coming from the lips of the young (Janet) in the photograph. This helps her get in touch with a young, often hopeful, full-of-dreams self. If the woman talks of painful times, we ask her who was there to turn to for support. This allows her to acknowledge a dear person, and if this person is lost to her, to express her grief. If there was no one, she has an opportunity to feel the hurt of this experience, the grief and anger.

When we counsel we aim to be a companion to the woman as she journeys into some part of her past. We usually sit close and ask other participants to do the same, and we may take the woman's hand. We notice which areas bring tears, hesitations, embarrassed laughter and evidence of fear. We put over that now it *is* safe to face head-on the full impact of a previous event in her life. We encourage her to look out at the faces of the women in the group in order that she can draw on their supportive and empathetic presence. They too can be companions, and together we can show that at last someone is there and notices. This is the exact opposite of the earlier experience when she may have had to face her pain on her own. Chronic isolation, this feeling that we must, in the end, do everything on our own, is something that we aim to knock sideways in the workshop. Good attention, particularly from people whom we suspect understand more easily than most what we are talking about, gives us the safety to let go. For many of us it is a shock to realise how much grief and rage is tied up in incidents we have grown to accept as just part of our past.

We believe that the release of pent-up emotional distress is necessary if we are to move beyond the blocks and inhibitions which set in at the time we were hurt. We don't offer sympathy or advice but notice what it is that the woman is talking about when she releases her emotions and encourage her to stay there rather than move on quickly. We may move nearer to her and/or ask her to tell us more and in greater detail. If at these times we ask questions, it is not to satisfy our curiosity. Our hope is to guide the woman to the cluster of feelings and experiences which constitute the block that prevents her from being free of the effects of the hurtful event in her past. Through our words, facial expression, physical closeness and the presence of the whole group, we all affirm the way each woman has dealt with the events of her life. This affirmation contrasts sharply with many of the responses she will have had from powerful figures in her life.

Many women learn to feel anything but pride in themselves and have spent years blaming themselves for not being more this or more that – more compliant, less compliant, more rebellious, less rebellious, more intelligent or too clever by half, etc. Our positive regard provides a contradiction to all those self-invalidating feelings and allows a woman being counselled to let herself off the hook and *feel*: to cry, rage, tremble, laugh with embarrassment.

One woman was seven years old when her mother walked out. She was in such agony she could not learn at school. No one in her life acted as though they noticed what she was going through and she was in constant trouble. At school she learned that she was stupid. She blamed herself, as did her teachers, and grew up believing that indeed she was stupid. We pointed out to her how right she was to put her attention on what was most important for her at the time – her mother leaving – and how sorry we were that no one had noticed. This contradiction to her view of herself and the acknowledgment of the double suffering she had endured – the pain of being abandoned and the failure of anyone to acknowledge that pain – brought deep sobbing. After this she was able to reach a true appreciation of her intelligence and strength, a foothold out of the mire of self-invalidation.

It is difficult to give sustained attention over a long period. Therefore we each take between two and five minutes, in pairs, to share the effect that the previous life-story has had on us. Out of our differences comes a sense of what we share; many women divulge things they have not shared before, and each person's session triggers memories: 'Yes, I am not alone after all.' There are many shared tears as one woman's story touches deep feelings in others in the group. We finish the day by sharing our highlights. This is validating for us all when we have risked opening ourselves in the hope of getting closer to each other and to ourselves.

The second theme is internalised oppression. We talk about our understanding of this, and the insidious way it operates, as explained above. We tell the workshop that we believe that each of us fought, for as long as was possible, against information and actions that belied our inherent power, intelligence and beauty as black girls. Many participants are able to recall this struggle, and the pain and the confusion experienced at becoming aware that whatever they thought or felt, being black and being a woman are rated second in this society. In these sessions we, as workshop leaders, have spoken openly about ourselves and discovered the degree of shame and grief we feel at accepting our oppression and internalising it. This shame is part of the powerlessness that we experience in our everyday lives. Inside the tears, we find our rage.

The process of moving from tears and shame to anger is true for all participants. In order that each person may experience this we ask certain key questions: 'What has been good about being a black woman?', 'What makes you proud to be a black woman?', 'What are black women *really* like?' These simple questions have an astonishingly disarming effect; stumbling to respond we are compelled to contact our hope and faith in each other and ourselves.

It is precisely because we do have this hope that we feel disappointed and hurt by each other. We hold out the viewpoint that in reality we never gave up on each other, though we often behave as if we have and even persuade ourselves that we have. Not all participants agree with the viewpoints we offer, particularly the one that 'If all circumstances were known and taken into account, we have always, at each moment of the past, done our best and deserve neither blame nor reproach from anyone, including ourselves.' We do not go into lengthy discussion, or invest time or energy in persuading participants to adopt these viewpoints for ever. Rather, we ask them to experiment with the viewpoints for the time being, i.e. 'If this were true what then . . .?' The viewpoint is a useful device for allowing the participant to shift out of habitual patterns of self-blame and self-doubt. As workshop leaders we aim to counsel each woman with full appreciation of who she is, however she feels about herself. Few, if any, of us maintain a sense of our inherent goodness.

We counsel each woman with the full expectation that underneath the hurt she *is* proud of who she is, and has hopes and dreams that can be reached, however well hidden or embarrassing they seem. It is our appreciation that allows each woman to feel completely awful, and in reaching for pride, to feel and discharge her self-loathing. This is an interesting phenomenon. If someone, a counsellor, is reflecting back the goodness and integrity that each of us knows, or at least hopes, are there, then we are free to break down and feel pain and self-loathing. There is no energy being spent defensively holding ourselves together. We have only to suspect that someone believes us to be worthless and we stop mid-way and backtrack with remarks like: 'Well, I'm not so bad . . .'

A counsellor, holding out for our good self, allows us to go the whole way and feel the grief and rage at coming to see ourselves as second class. This is the core of the effects of racism and sexism. It is moving to see a black woman share her grief and rage as she tells of experiences of selling herself short ('What are black women *really* like?' is the question that brings this out); of her fear of really not being good enough, that maybe it is true that she's second class; of the energy that goes into being twice as good all the time to be half-way good at all; of wanting support from other black women, starting sometimes with mother, only to be cut down to size; of physical and sexual abuse – a litany of experiences that eat away at her power.

Through the mantle of self-loathing, each woman can make her way to her supple, early pride. This pride is radically different from the defensive pride that many of us display for survival. As counsellors/workshop leaders, in this as in all sessions, it is the extent to which we have been counselled and been through our own tears and rage that enables us to appreciate fully each woman's struggle. It is useful for one of the workshop leaders to be counselled first. When each woman has established a base of identity and pride, we can move into the area where our minds are usually working in overdrive.

However, it *is* vital to provide the base first, for without it this subsequent part can become a rehearsal of a hopeless person's catechism. (There is a difference between being aware of how awful things have been and so feeling hopeless, and being aware of how awful things have been, recognising that there are resources available to combat the injustices and ceasing to feel hopeless.) With the sense of pride in ourselves, we move on to 'What has been difficult about being a black woman?', 'What can't you stand about other black women?', 'What do you want your black sisters to know about you?', 'How have you been hurt by other black women?', 'What do you want black women to never do or say again?'

These are powerful sessions and the learning about ourselves and each other is immense. It is a relief for many of us to let rip. We have permission to offload all the times we've been let down, sold out and hurt by each other. Amidst embarrassed laughter and tears of hurt, we can share what makes it hard for us to be among our own people. The things we can't stand about each other are, of course, the behaviours that result from our oppression as black women. Perhaps the most common thing we can't stand in another black sister is behaviour that suggests that she is lying down and taking what is dealt her without fighting back. This keys directly into our hopelessness and highlights the way each of us needs the other for inspiration, role-models and soulmates. There is a lot of laughter: 'Can't stand women who press their hair, who think they're better than the rest, who forget about their people when they're a success, who . . .'

After one session on internalised oppression we noticed that heterosexual women were making remarks that were oppressive to the lesbian sisters. Remarks like, 'It makes no difference to me if she's a lesbian, I treat everyone the same,' the implication being that there's no difference and what's the fuss; plus others in the same vein, subtle and polite. In discussions on relationships, there was an absence of discussion about lesbian relationships, the underlying assumption being that women had relationships only with men. This needed to be interrupted, so we divided into two groups, lesbian and heterosexual. The lesbian group looked at the following questions: 'What is good for you about being a lesbian?', 'What do you find difficult about being a lesbian in a heterosexual society?', 'What would you like from heterosexual women?', 'What do you want heterosexual women never to do or say again?', 'What do you call upon heterosexual women to do as your allies?'; the heterosexual women considered: 'What is good for you about being heterosexual?', 'What were you told about lesbians when growing up?', 'What would you like from lesbian women?' We then came back together to share the experience of meeting together and to share our answers. This gave everyone the experience of how oppressive behaviour among us could be interrupted, without accusation or defensiveness.

A third component is the conscious celebration of who we are, who we know ourselves to be. As stated earlier, celebration is part of the overall tone of the workshop. We set aside time at the end to celebrate, in whatever form makes sense (a song, a drawing or a dance). Usually it takes the form of something visual on paper, in many coloured feltpens. We ask each woman to present her true self, encouraging her to err on the side of boastfulness and to question all the oppressive messages she may have received: e.g. 'You, an artist?', 'Too big for your boots', 'Always fancied yourself', 'Pride comes before a fall', etc. In our experience, there is still a great deal carried around in our black culture that says 'Being black makes you a target enough without your having the audacity to think well of yourself, *and* proclaim your talents.' This position, perhaps once a must for our survival, has had its day. This exercise goes against any pull to live out the message 'If you're black, stand back', and is great fun to do and share proudly. Sharing proudly is important, and as workshop leaders we push for this, again amidst much laughter and embarrassment. With each workshop we see that many of us are brilliantly proud already.

We close the workshop with highlights. A recurrent highlight for participants is the realisation that 'I'm not alone.' The isolation we each carry around seems consistently to take a denting. A renewed sense of power is another common highlight. One woman said that she felt hopeful for the first time that she could remember in her life. Her face had opened up in the short time we had been together. The depth and breadth of sharing leaves the group feeling very close. We often go round and have each woman give an appreciation of each participant in turn. These are like gifts for each of us to take away. We always make up an address-list and send this out after the workshop. Two groups have met after as support groups, and other participants have gone on to learn re-evaluation co-counselling in a class together. There is always a call for further work, given that what we do is very much a beginning. Part of the call for further work, however, reflects the difficulty we all have with endings and farewells. Having come so close, it is always hard to say goodbye.

*Dorann and Janet:* We have been friends and work-partners since meeting in May 1981. We enjoy working together and share similar outlooks and viewpoints, though different backgrounds. Janet was born in London, of Jamaican parents. Dorann came to England at 13 years of age from Guyana, and has lived here since then.

We are both committed to black liberation and in particular to the empowerment of black women. Our work at the Women's Therapy Centre is an excellent way of expressing this commitment and we have learned a great deal through our work there. We have learned that we can be vulnerable, not know the answers and still lead successful groups.

Our emphasis is on the process rather than on lengthy discussion, elaborate theory and the use of techniques. We aim to create an atmosphere where each woman wants to offer herself generously. What we achieve together, the change in ourselves that we experience, is due to our generosity in offering ourselves as models and resources for each other. We aim together to unfold the powerful reality of black sisterhood.

# 6
# Lesbian Workshop
## Pam Trevithick and Joanna Ryan

'As lesbians we have often been very powerful in making ourselves visible and raising issues about sexuality and sexual choices. In challenging lesbian oppression, however, we may often fear unacceptability or that we are not good enough lesbians. We can feel confused about our needs in relation to other women or experience disappointment and resentments that are hard to cope with. We will explore these feelings in areas where we find it difficult to be powerful – for example, in close relationships, at work, in coming out, around our parents and/or children. We hope to extend our sense of lesbian identity and sisterhood around these different struggles. Lesbian-only for this workshop.' This was the programme description for our workshop.

## Becoming Involved in the Women's Therapy Centre and Running Workshops

*Pam*: Looking back, it's not easy for me to identify how I came to be involved in running workshops of this kind. I suppose one milestone was when I contacted the Women's Therapy Centre in 1980 for help with a paper I was writing on feminism and therapy. Some time earlier, I'd met Sue Krzowski and Sheila Ernst, who offered to help me in whatever way they could. This contact with Sue and Sheila was very important to me, because I felt a great warmth and sisterhood flowing from them that in time encouraged me to look at therapy not from an intellectual standpoint but from a personal, emotional part of me. In some ways, I had begun this process by becoming involved in re-evaluation co-counselling, which I'd chosen because of its strong emphasis on oppression and liberation issues. Then, as now, my interest lay in trying to see how the wisdoms of therapy and co-counselling could nourish me emotionally. I needed a new viewpoint that could explain my confusion, inject some hope into my involvement in the women's liberation movement and revive a dearly held sense of sisterhood that was beginning to slip away from me and other women I knew.

As I look back over these years, I now realise that I was looking to therapy and co-counselling to give me a place where I could focus in a different way on my internalised oppression – that is, on the negative feeling that I was still harbouring about myself and other women. In the past, consciousness-raising groups had provided this personal and political insight, but after being involved in about six of these groups over a 10-year period (some of which were lesbian-only), I felt I'd reached a block – a point where I knew that I needed to do something different if I were to be free of a deeply rooted fear and lack of trust in other women (and men) and feelings of inadequacy and insecurity in myself.

In many ways, I hoped that running a lesbian-only workshop at the Women's Therapy Centre would bring together bits of myself – my feminism and lesbianism – so that I could look again at some of the unresolved issues that I still harboured as a lesbian, feelings of not being a real woman, of not being a good enough lesbian because I'd never chosen to be one, feelings of being unable to reconcile the influences of my Irish Catholic upbringing that had drawn me towards loving women at an early age.

Though I harboured some fears that I would be attacked by some other lesbians for daring to do a therapy workshop, I also knew that I had a lot to gain and to give. I wanted to share with other lesbians some of the personal and political wisdoms that I'd picked up from many years of active involvement in the women's liberation movement and around feminist and lesbian issues. In particular, I wanted to look at how internalised oppression operates for us as lesbians – to keep us feeling bad about ourselves, separated from other lesbians, and deserted and misunderstood among other women/feminists.

I can't quite recall how Jo and I came to decide to do these workshops together. What I do remember with great affection is our occasional evening conversations where we shared our stories – our journeys towards feminism, our thoughts and experiences of the women's liberation movement and our dreams for women. I think that in time these conversations formed the basis for our workshops, so that running a lesbian workshop became almost the most natural next step in our friendship and journey together.

*Jo:* I had been involved peripherally at the Women's Therapy Centre for many years, running groups and workshops on various issues. During this time, I had become surer and clearer about my lesbian identity. For me, this process was slow and complex, with many hesitations and confusions. Although I was working in a very supportive feminist context, I felt isolated and invisible as a lesbian – I did not know any other lesbian therapists and the distance between certain aspects of lesbian feminist politics and therapy seemed enormous. So eventually meeting Pam, and then other lesbian women interested in therapy, represented a real coming together of fragmented bits of my life.

It also became clear how little the Women's Therapy Centre offered specifically for lesbians, despite the generally supportive and unstigmatising attitudes of its staff. Too many lesbians had the experience of going to workshops and finding themselves isolated, invisible or marginalised, pushed into either hiding or over-asserting their identity. It seemed obvious that some lesbian-only space was needed, and also that a greater consciousness among staff and workshop leaders about lesbianism, and about their own feelings and attitudes towards lesbians, was necessary.

Running lesbian-only workshops was also wanting to share the benefits I felt I had got from therapy, and that I felt were too often not available to other lesbians, or were not perceived as being available. I did not necessarily feel that they had to be 'about' being a lesbian or about lesbian oppression – after all, there are many other issues in the lives of lesbians – but I think inevitably, given the context, that is how we set them up, and indeed there is a vast amount of need for this. As well as the always present issue of visibility – coming out again and again, or deciding not to – I was particularly interested in exploring relationships between lesbians. I feel we really are just at the beginning of knowing and understanding the dimensions, dynamics, contradictions of lesbian sexuality and intimacy.

*Pam:* In many ways Jo and I could seem to be unlikely sister-travellers, since we came from very different class and cultural backgrounds. Also, in terms of therapy, we came from very different experiences, mine being based more on re-evaluation co-counselling and various women's groups, and Jo's being based in a much more complex involvement in different therapies, including Red Therapy, Battersea Action and Counselling Centre, and the Women's Therapy Centre, with an increasingly psychoanalytic orientation. I think that in many ways, the success of our workshops lay in these differences between us, because they meant that we brought to any issue before us two different but overlapping perspectives, which allowed us to take the best from both and to draw up an exciting series of exercises.

However, we did have a couple of differences that I think showed up more in the first workshop than in the later two. One focused on whether we should use some time in the workshop to give information about how we see lesbian oppression operating, inside ourselves and in the world. For me, the importance of doing this is to remind ourselves that our oppression is real – that we live in a culture that is, for the most part, hostile to us and that this has implications for how we feel about ourselves as lesbians and women. Jo's concern was that this more 'heady' input would pull us away from looking at our feelings and from developing an emotional dialogue within the group. I agreed with this and in the end we decided to have some input and discussion about how we experience our oppression but to keep it brief.

Another difference was how we shared time within the group. I prefer to give every woman more or less the same time, because it encourages less confident, quieter women to be the focus of attention and it puts some boundaries or limits on those women who feel compelled to work in front of the group or who are very practised and familiar with group settings of this kind. Jo's orientation was to a much looser, more spontaneous approach which encouraged women to take the floor if they felt they wanted to, at the same time as maintaining an awareness of the whole group and its dynamics. Since both approaches have their strengths and weaknesses we in the end amalgamated the two – we went round the room at the beginning of the day, allowed spontaneous feedback from some of the work done in pairs and, when we split into small groups, organised it according to how we and the group wanted to use the time.

*Jo:* For me this difference in how we worked was initially very difficult – it posed a real challenge in how to share leadership and control without just abdicating responsibility and becoming passive. I felt Pam's generosity helped this enormously.

*Pam:* At one time we felt concerned that in doing a lesbian workshop at the Women's Therapy Centre we would be reinforcing the myth that lesbianism is a disorder and something that needs to be worked on. Also, as the first lesbian-only workshop at the Centre, we felt quite wary that our workshops should not be used as a token gesture towards lesbians nor an excuse for other workshop leaders to ignore the issues of how to make their workshops more directly relevant to lesbians. Our answer to these concerns was to plan to take them to one of the workshop leaders' day workshops, but unfortunately neither of us have managed to get there so far.

Another of our concerns was whether our workshops would be seen by some lesbians as a way of 'de-politicising' lesbians, of diverting them/us from developing solutions to our oppression. In answer to this, I would say that it's important to extend the choices open to us as lesbians, not to confine them to political dogmas of 'shoulds' and 'oughts'. It is mythical to suppose that we have to choose between exploring our feelings and campaigning or working for change. We can do both. In fact, I've learned that I need to do both if I am to continue to be effective and successful in pushing for change.

*Jo:* This is a very common fear, by no means confined to lesbians. It relates to the feeling that to do therapy is to be self-indulgent, weak and dependent, not the coping, strong, concerned and independent women we are supposed to be. This attitude really is a projection on to therapy of the parts of ourselves we feel to be most unacceptable.

## The Workshops

### Who came

The workshops that we're about to describe ran from 10.00 a.m. to 5.00 p.m., stopping at some point around midday for a shared lunch. Each workshop was attended by 11 or 12 women. All were white, mainly of English origin, with quite a wide class mixture, though working-class women dominated slightly. To our surprise, some women travelled quite a long way to attend. Most women were between 25 and 35 years old, though there were a couple of older women in each workshop. A few were mothers and they were joined by an even larger number of women who had regular contact with the children of friends, sisters, lovers, etc. None of the women attending either workshop had an identified disability.

## Workshop Timetable

The following gives an idea of how the workshops are organised and some of the issues that come up.

## Settling in

Here we give a brief outline of the day, in terms of content and how we plan to work (i.e. in large and small groups, in pairs), the layout of the Women's Therapy Centre, lunch arrangements, payment for the workshop and how the heating, ventilation and seating arrangements can be improved to give the greatest comfort. We also stress at the beginning the importance of confidentiality in creating an atmosphere of trust and acceptance. Confidentiality is always of paramount importance in any therapy, but for some lesbians it has a very specific importance – they may not be out in any areas of their life.

## Introductions (1 hour)

These introductory questions are designed to give us some basic information about everyone and to encourage us to open up to each other. They also give women a chance to introduce changes in the timetable. Beginning with ourselves, we spend five minutes each, going round the room using the following questions as guidelines:

1.  Give your name and a brief summary of your life. What occupies your time (e.g. children, waged work, living relationships)? What is your living situation? What do you enjoy?

2.  What has been an important influence on your life (e.g. religion, class, childhood experiences, etc.)?

3.  Why did you choose this workshop and what do you hope to get out of it? Is there anything you can identify that gives you greater safety (e.g. small groups, close contact, etc)? What does it feel like to be here now, talking in front of the group?

## Guided fantasy on coming out (approx. 1½ hours)

*Pam:* Before beginning the fantasy, I spend a little time talking about coming out and reminding the group that this is an important issue for all lesbians, no matter how often we have come out, because it touches on our fears of rejection and unacceptability. It is also rarely a one-off event but involves the dilemma of how to stay visible as a lesbian in a heterosexual world that's wont to forget us or to ignore our lesbianism and its importance to us. I also remind women that there is no one way of coming out and that whether we do it little or often, we frequently come away feeling bad about how we explained ourselves. Yet, despite these difficulties, most of us have been very imaginative and determined in finding different ways of being open and visible about our lesbianism. And our numbers are continuing to grow – in fact, there are probably more women who are now openly and proudly lesbian than ever before in history. Equally, there are probably now more heterosexual women than ever actively making the choice not to be lesbian, which for some of us brings up enormous feelings of disappointment and rejection.

*Jo:* I ask women to sit or lie as comfortably as possible, close their eyes, and take notice of their breathing; then to deepen their breathing somewhat (breathing out from the belly) and observe any feelings of discomfort, tension, pain, etc. in their bodies, and try to relax this a bit. Before starting any guided fantasy, I always make a point of saying that this is not a test of any kind, there is no such thing as a good or bad fantasy, and that what is important is that it is *their* fantasy. Also, that if they find themselves blanking out or losing concentration, simply to notice this fact, rather than blame or criticise themselves.

## The fantasy (spoken with suitable pauses)

*Choose a scene that has other people in it. This can be anywhere – at work, at home, at a social event or meeting, with family, friends, strangers, etc. Focus on a particular scene, and if you have difficulty choosing, just decide arbitrarily on one. Picture to yourself who is in this scene, what they are doing, what you are wearing, what you are feeling like, how you are relating to the other people there, what you are wanting.*

*You decide to tell these people, or some of them, that you are a lesbian, have sexual relationships with women, have fallen in love with a woman, or however you want to put it. Picture yourself doing this: whom you tell, the words you use, how you feel doing it. What is the reaction you receive? Picture what the other people (person) say(s), what they seem to be feeling. How does this leave you feeling and what do you say?*

*Now, imagine that you leave the scene and go for a walk by yourself. You go to a park, and sit on a bench. How are you now feeling, about yourself, about the people (person) you have told, about being a lesbian?'*

*Then I ask women to gradually open their eyes, sit up and come back into the room.*

## Feedback

We ask women to tell others their fantasy in two stages, firstly in pairs, using a co-counselling format, and then in the larger group (the first time we split the whole group, the second we didn't). The first stage of feedback allows women to go over the content of their fantasy in some detail and to notice any feelings, memories, etc. associated with this. The second allows for further work on issues arising from the fantasy and for general discussion in the group.

In the fantasy itself, some women revisited previous experiences of coming out, but most created new scenes, often involving parents, especially mothers. Others chose people with whom not being out was a constant source of tension, e.g. colleagues at work. One recurrent experience of the fantasy was rejection, with very high levels of fear and panic surrounding this; the dread that to come out as a lesbian might involve never being allowed to go home again, never feeling relaxed or comfortable with one's family; one might bring upon oneself the full force of someone else's disgust, pity or incomprehension. Certainly, there were no anticipations of pleasure or positive support. This tremendous fear of loss and rejection is what makes it so hard for most of us to be open with families or friends. The last part of the fantasy, the walk in the park, often brought out the loneliness of being a lesbian – that however close our immediate relationships, or however accepting our family, lesbians so often feel and are outsiders to the mainstream of heterosexual life.

In the discussion that followed, actual experiences of coming out were mixed with fantasy ones, with some women recounting how they had survived the experiences others most dreaded. There were some lighthearted anecdotes about how hard it is to assess who you should tell, when and how. One woman spent years not telling her mother, whom she was convinced couldn't take it, only to find out that her mother had known all along but was waiting for her daughter to broach the subject. Some women described building themselves up to this great coming out revelation only to find that the person hadn't understood, or had forgotten or felt too overwhelmed by the experience to say more than something like, 'So what' or 'Oh, really.'

Because of these and other more negative reactions, we often come away feeling that it's all our fault, that we bungled it in one way or another. Similarly, some women felt that no matter how positive the response, it never felt enough; it's as though in some silent way we're hoping for a response that would contradict all the internal, negative, messages that we've been carrying about ourselves as women and lesbians for years. This desperate plea for approval in a hostile world can lead us to feel very disconnected from ourselves, so that sometimes we feel trapped in the non-option of whether to be victim or martyr, i.e. to be terrified and lonely as invisible, or unwisely and unsafely visible. And a lot of the time, we feel too ashamed or embarrassed to share these dilemmas with other people.

*I have come out – like a martyr, without support and without checking on how safe or wise it was to be out at that time, in that place. I think I did so because I wanted to be noticed, for someone to recognise that being a lesbian is not without its trials and tribulations, particularly in a world that ignores us, or treats us as revolting, men-hating child molesters.*

Several women also talked of how hard it was not so much to come out but to stay visible as a lesbian; that once having told someone, how hurtful and frustrated we can feel when the person forgets it or neglects to take on board all that it implies. It can seem too trivial or be too painful to keep reminding them. Most women felt that the choice about whether or not to come out or how to stay visible depended largely on how financially secure and independent they were at that time. Similarly, most women felt that it was almost impossible to be openly lesbian at work, particularly if working with children or other women.

At the other end were the highs – the excitement and freedom we'd nearly all experienced after coming out to people who could cherish our secret and how important this had been to us in developing a sense of identity and connection as lesbians.

*Coming out for me is about being true to myself in as many situations as I can safely do this.*

## Self-image
The second major exercise we do is on self-image. Our aim is to draw out some of the internal, negative messages that we carry about ourselves and other lesbians. The exercise focuses on four questions:

1   How do you feel good about yourself as a lesbian?

2   How do you feel bad about yourself as a lesbian?

3   What do you like/love about other lesbians?

4   What can't you stand/dislike/hate about other lesbians?

We ask women to answer these questions in pairs for five minutes each, and then we ask for feedback in the large group.

What immediately struck us about this exercise was how much time women spent describing negative emotions, particularly in relation to themselves. It is sad that so many of us are still loaded down by harsh and at times totally incorrect negative judgments about ourselves and other women.

For us, this highlights the depth and range of our oppression – what we once experienced as blows from outside now has a life within us, eating away at our confidence, our sense of importance to each other, our ability to trust and to make changes in our lives. Time and again, women described in different ways not feeling good enough as a lesbian: because they felt they weren't out enough, or physically attractive enough, or hadn't been in the women's liberation movement long enough, or hadn't been a lesbian long enough, or didn't orbit in the right feminist circles, or didn't feel political enough, or hadn't had enough sexual relationships, or the ones they'd had didn't count, or because they felt that they still wanted and needed to work things out with men – their husbands, fathers, sons, etc. – or because they didn't wear the right clothes, live in the right area, or have enough . . .

*Pam*: Again, I think it was useful to hear each other's fears, because it showed very clearly how much we see our lesbianism as being dependent or conditional on being able to fulfil certain, often imagined, expectations. For me, this estrangement from other lesbians begins when we're taught as little girls to compete – to always measure or compare ourselves up against other girls. Whether we come off as inferior or superior to others, both leave us feeling isolated and wounded that we've been placed against each other as rivals rather than friends and companions. From these experiences, we come to see differences as threatening rather than as signifying diversity.

In terms of what we enjoyed about ourselves and other lesbians, common answers focused on how committed we are to women and the central role that many of us have played in campaigning against women's oppression. There was also a sense of how exciting it still is to come across other lesbians, particularly in unexpected places, and how proud we feel about each other's achievements, especially in the different ways that we have shown that there is no greater or more important activity than loving and caring for other women.

These positive aspects to our lesbianism proved hard to sustain and many women drifted back to earlier discussion on the conditions, expectations and judgments that are made about us in our lives as lesbians. For many women, these unresolved and painful issues originated in their relationships with their mothers, and this led on (with different formats for the different workshops) to an exercise on mother/daughter relationships. This took the form of a guided fantasy:

*Pretend you're your mother, describing you, her lesbian daughter. What feelings does your lesbianism arouse in her? How do you feel about your own lesbianism when you're with your mother? How desperate do you feel for your mother's approval? How close, physically and emotionally, can you feel towards your mother and still be a lesbian?*

This was a very emotionally charged and poignant part of the workshop. Time and time again, women described how scared or terrified they were of their mother's rejection and how impossible it felt to be a lesbian and be close to our mothers, physically and emotionally. To varying degrees, we all harboured some anger towards our mothers for failing us, for being so conditional in their love. At the same time, there was a sense that if we did become close to our mothers, we would be swamped, eaten up, overpowered or suffocated by feelings of responsibility to take care of our mothers – to ease her misery and fill her neediness and emptiness.

Many of the feelings and dilemmas women experienced in relation to their mothers were, of course, common to other women, whether lesbian or not. Lesbianism seems to heighten and deepen our sense of having disappointed our mothers, to intensify the anxiety about not being fully or unconditionally loved, and of being too threatening or disturbing to the family.

## Jo: Postscript

I subsequently ran a third lesbian-only workshop on my own, using many of the same ideas and exercises. This confirmed for me, as had the previous two workshops, the immense value of a lesbian-only space in allowing both our most positive and our most painful feelings to emerge. Once again the issue of coming out was a major one to every woman there. And once again we recognised how hard we have to struggle with our internalised oppression, with the fear, more or less unconscious, that at bottom, being lesbian means there is something wrong with us, that we are quite unacceptable, at fault in our sexuality and love of women. These feelings tend to come out most strongly in relation to our families, because it is there that our sense of ourselves as lovable (or otherwise) is formed. A lesbian-only space allows us to come out of the isolation that so many lesbians still feel; it allows a temporary suspension of the judgments of the heterosexual world and thus an unusual kind of acceptance; and it reaffirms our respect and love for other women who dare to love women, and thus for ourselves.

# 7
# Agoraphobia: A Group Approach
Inge Hudson

Some of our most basic and fundamental beliefs and feelings about our relationship to the outside world are learned when we are very young, even before we have any words for them. They are transmitted to us by our parents and others in complex emotional and behavioural ways from the time we are babies and toddlers. We internalise in a largely unconscious way our experiences with our mother and her feelings about whether or not it is safe to go out into the world. We learn about her confidence, or the lack of it, about whether or not it is safe to venture away from our sources of support and security to become a separate and independent individual.

The world is in fact a frightening and uncertain place and, looking at it that way, it can seem almost surprising that any of us have the courage to go out, to board a train or plane, to mix with crowds of strangers in a department store, and so on. And yet most people, to varying degrees at different times in their lives, do manage to do these things. They seem to carry around within them an almost unreasoning sense that it will be all right, whereas others experience themselves as lost and overwhelmed by a sense of threat. It is because these feelings and attitudes are laid down so early in our lives that they are experienced as so powerful and so unreasoning. An agoraphobic woman who steps outside her front door only to be assailed by a sense of panic for which there seems neither an adequate explanation nor a means of control, feelings which she may not even be able to put into words, thereby communicating her distress to others, not unnaturally thinks to herself, 'I must be going mad.'

Agoraphobia represents an impairment in our relationship to the outside world in a very fundamental way. It is the name given to a group of related anxieties often found together: fear of going out, being out of doors, being in public places, especially crowded ones, travelling away from home, etc. Fears which commonly exist in conjunction with these are the fear of being shut in, the fear of social situations and the fear of being alone. Most people agree that agoraphobia is not a true phobia of particular situations but rather a form of separation anxiety, i.e. an anxiety about moving away from a secure base, usually one's own home. Behind this fear of leaving familiar surroundings there is most commonly a fear of panicking while out, becoming ill, collapsing, of becoming helpless or out of control in some other way, or even of dying. Sometimes there is a fear of becoming lost or even of losing one's own sense of self. The fear of being shut in and trapped is likewise associated with anxiety about being unable to get back to familiar surroundings and with being helpless and not in control. Agoraphobia, or for that matter any phobia, is a means of dealing with anxiety by the avoidance of what makes one anxious. Thus the anxiety is reduced, but the problem remains.

The National Association for Mental Health estimates that there are 500,000 people in Great Britain suffering from agoraphobia at any one time (Factsheet 8, 'Agoraphobia and Other Phobias', MIND, London), and it is generally agreed that the vast majority of them are women. In a survey of 1,200 agoraphobics carried out in Britain in 1970, 95 per cent of the respondents were women. In a survey carried out in 1977, 88 per cent of agoraphobics were found to be women.

My own involvement in groups for agoraphobics arose in the following way. I had been involved in giving individual help to agoraphobic women within the NHS and this had made me realise several things: first, how very widespread the problem was, so that groups seemed a more realistic and economical way of getting help to the people who needed it; second, how very real the fears of agoraphobic people are, and how incapacitating; and third, that help was quite possible. By contrast, agoraphobic women I had come across in the course of my work often suffered from a sense of despair regarding their symptoms and the possibility of change, as well as a sense of isolation and frustration at the difficulty of conveying to a non-phobic person the reality of their difficulties and generally of getting anyone to take them seriously. Very few of the women I had come across had ever met another agoraphobic person and nearly all were keen to do so. This seemed a further good reason for trying to set up a group. It also seemed to me that a group might have some advantages over individual help in yet another way. Agoraphobic women are most often demoralised and lacking in confidence. They are in touch with their weaknesses rather than their strengths, which they often believe to be almost non-existent. A one-to-one situation of therapist and client can unwittingly reinforce this, in that, though it is made clear that the client is the one from whom the work and effort has to come, the situation is still an unequal one where it is easy for a woman to see herself as weak and helpless while the therapist appears to be the source of strength. In a group things can be more equal: it can be strengthening in itself to realise that you are one of many others with the same problem and are not alone in the world. Encouragement and support have a different quality when they come from someone who shares the problem rather than from a professional: 'If I can do it, so can you!' is more powerful than 'You can do it.' It is sometimes easier to see strength in others than in oneself, and it can be more powerful to have the strength in oneself pointed out by another phobic person than by a therapist. The experience in a group that no matter how many problems you may have, you also have something to contribute, that having a problem is not shameful but a common part of the human condition, and that asking for help and beginning to do something about one's problems can be seen as a strength rather than as a weakness – all can be confidence building.

These were some of my thoughts at the outset, but there are also difficulties and drawbacks about groups for agoraphobics which soon became evident. One of the difficulties which needs to be taken into account is that the very act of coming to the group is nearly always a source of great anxiety in itself for the agoraphobic woman. At the beginning of each workshop or group the sense of fear, helplessness and anxiety which almost tangibly fills the room can be very powerful, so much so that the group leader herself can somehow get caught up in these feelings and temporarily experience herself as having lost her skills. The effort of helping the group to contain such intense feelings of anxiety can also be quite draining for her. For this reason it is a very good idea, in a led agoraphobic group, to have a co-leader to enable both leaders to provide each other with mutual support. It also helps to pay close attention to the setting of the group and to make this as reassuring as possible, e.g. by always meeting in the same room, by providing comfortable chairs, making sure the room is warm enough, etc.

A related difficulty is that an agoraphobic group more than any other, in my experience, will have to deal with such problems as lateness, absence and group members either dropping out or never turning up at all. All these are inevitably connected with peoples' fears about coming to the group at all, but they can be disruptive to the group's sense of cohesion and security. How one deals with them depends partly on the available resources and the setting in which the group takes place. It has to be faced that there are some people who are so phobic that they cannot get to a group at all. In some settings it may be possible to provide transport for such people, and getting to the group on one's own can then be made a goal to be worked towards. As the group becomes established members can ring each other up before setting out in order to give and receive encouragement, travel together, give each other lifts, etc. Alternatively, if all else fails, potential group members can be encouraged to seek some individual help first, coming to the group being seen as a future goal. Drop-outs can be encouraged to try again when they feel ready rather than seeing themselves as failures.

## Factors in the Development of Agoraphobia

In arriving at an understanding of how agoraphobia develops I have found John Bowlby's ideas on attachment and separation (see *Attachment and Loss*, vol. II. *Separation: Anxiety and Anger*, Penguin, Harmondsworth, 1975) as well as D. W. Winnicott's ideas on human development (see *Playing and Reality*, Penguin, Harmondsworth, 1975; and Part One, 2, 'The Capacity to be Alone' in *The Maturational Processes and the Facilitating Environment*, The Hogarth Press, London, 1976) most useful.

Bowlby stresses the need for a secure base and access to sources of help and support to enable the development of self-reliance and confidence in exploring our environment. This is true throughout life, but is a particularly urgent need for children during their early development. Winnicott describes how, in order to develop a secure sense of self, the capacity to be alone, the capacity to play and explore and to be creative, young children need the reliable presence of another person (usually the mother) who is available but not intrusive, and from whom they can gradually separate at their own pace.

Bowlby describes the child's growing confidence in exploring her environment with the knowledge that people on whom she is dependent for support (attachment figures) continue to be reliably available. If a child, or for that matter an adult, has insufficient confidence that her attachment figures will be accessible, responsive and able to cope, she will develop a strategy of remaining in close proximity to them to ensure that they are available. Bowlby describes this condition of insecurity as anxious attachment. In the developmental history of an agoraphobic, it is likely that during this phase of learning to be a separate person there has been some disruption or failure in the person's developing confidence that it is safe to venture away from sources of support and explore the environment. While it is the parents' task to allow the child to learn that the world is by and large a safe place to venture into, it is common, in the history of agoraphobics to have had parents who did not feel particularly safe about their own ability to go out into the world in a confident and independent way. Common fears experienced by agoraphobics are that something terrible will happen, either to themselves or to those on whom they depend for their security, while they are apart. One of the most common patterns in the life-histories of agoraphobics is of parents who, because they felt insecure themselves, used one of their children to make them feel safer and less isolated. This means that instead of having parents who are confident models for them, whom they can embody and draw upon for their own strength, these women have the additional burden of having to provide reassurance and support for their own parents – an inversion of the healthy parent/child relationship. The experience of separation is frequently associated for them with anxiety and guilt rather than a sense of excitement and pleasure at their growing independence. Often this means that the individual is not able to separate at all, or only incompletely. In other cases, where the separation is apparently accomplished, there is the feeling that one can never go back for fear of getting enmeshed again, and so the person has the feeling of being adrift in the world without a secure base that she can orient herself by. There are, of course, other variants of these patterns.

Of course, it is likely that, in addition to early experiences such as these, later experiences, relationships and life events will have reinforced the original sense of insecurity. Finally, there may be a crisis or stress such as illness, family conflict, a move or other important life-change which precipitates the actual onset of symptoms. In other cases, the onset of symptoms is gradual and no particular stress can be discerned. The most common pattern seems to be for the agoraphobic person to experience her symptoms as having started suddenly and without warning in the form of an unexpected panic attack at a bus stop, on public transport or in some other public place, but for closer enquiry to reveal that the attack occurred against the background of some life-stress or transition.

How does this kind of thinking about agoraphobia shed light on the fact that most agoraphobics are women? The most obvious connection is the different attitude held by society about men and women as regards independence. Women are expected to be connected to others while men are expected to be self-reliant and independent. From an early age boys are encouraged to explore while girls are encouraged to be timid and cling. The mother, herself a product of these social attitudes, is likely to feel unconfident of herself as an independent individual and to see her daughter as someone like herself, who will remain partially attached to her, while in the case of a son, she is likely to see him as someone other than herself, who will move away and have a separate life. If she needs to keep one of her children close to her as an attachment figure for herself, this child is much more likely to be a girl, since being a caretaker is part of the girl's social role. An obvious instance of this is that it is far more often a woman than a man who devotes her life to the care of elderly parents. There is evidence that within our patriarchal society the needs of girls are *in fact* met less fully than those of boys, which is a further reason why they grow up to be less confident and secure. There are numerous social attitudes which continuously reinforce women's lack of confidence about their independence, e.g. it really is less acceptable – still – for a woman to go to a pub, the movies or a restaurant on her own; it really is less safe for a woman to walk alone at night. And, of course, society by and large expects men to go out to work but expects women to stay at home.

The pressures and expectations which keep women in the home are so common and numerous that the fact that a woman has not left her home for years can pass unnoticed. Perhaps she has a mother nearby who does her shopping, or her children are sent out on errands. It can happen that no one in the family actually labels this state of affairs as a problem until some change in their life-style, e.g. a move to another town caused by the husband's job, causes it to become one. In some cases the husband finds it reassuring for himself (perhaps because of his own unacknowledged insecurities) to have a wife who is always at home – and so the system is perpetuated.

## Strategies for Change

It is helpful to think of human functioning in terms of three aspects: behavioural, cognitive (thinking) and emotional. These occur simultaneously and are in continual interaction with each other. What we do affects the way we think about ourselves and the world, and this in turn affects the way we feel, and vice versa. Furthermore, the way we behave, think and feel affects our relationship with others, and this in turn affects the way we feel, think and behave. Because of this complex interplay of factors, I believe that behavioural and psycho-therapeutic approaches can often be usefully combined, and can be more useful in combination than either can alone in dealing with agoraphobia and some other forms of phobic anxiety which involve coping with anxiety by avoidance. For change to occur, people need to face their anxieties in practice, but in order for this behavioural change to be consolidated and carried further, it is helpful to achieve some understanding of the meaning of one's anxieties in terms of one's current life and relationships as well as past experiences. If a woman gains confidence that she can face her fears in practice, this also increases her feelings of strength and confidence that she can face underlying issues and feelings to do with separation and independence. This newly found confidence and strength in turn affects her behaviour.

Behaviour therapy usually involves the graded exposure to feared situations with the support of a therapist. The woman is taught relaxation and is asked to construct a hierarchy of situations ranging from ones which make her only slightly anxious to ones which may seem impossible, the only proviso being that they are situations which she actually wants to tackle. The woman is then encouraged to enter these situations while relaxed and gradually work her way up the hierarchy as the easier situations are mastered. Relaxation and other anxiety-management techniques are important because they give the woman tools to enable her to feel more confident about remaining in control of herself.

Behavioural techniques thus have an immediate value and relevance in that they encourage women to face difficult situations and learn that they can deal with them. A danger is that symptoms may be dealt with only to the limited extent that they have become inconvenient to others and that the woman may gradually resume doing chores like the shopping without ever thinking of what independence could mean to her and what she would like to do with it for herself.

A focus on feelings about ourselves and our relationships helps to consolidate behavioural change and facilitate further change. Without such a focus there is a danger that change will be limited in both its extent and its duration. Behavioural change may involve important changes in our relationship to others and to the outside world, changes such as increased independence in a wider sense, increased sense of confidence in oneself as a separate individual and an increase in one's confidence in owning and expressing emotions in areas of adult life such as assertiveness and sexuality. Changes on this level are bound to raise anxiety in oneself and others, and are not accomplished without pain and struggle. Help and support are therefore needed for accomplishing and consolidating them.

## An Agoraphobic Group in Practice

At the start of each group, especially during the very first meeting, the first and obvious task of the leader is to help the group bring down its own level of anxiety. I don't start with relaxation exercises, because of the problem of latecomers which, in my experience, can never be completely solved. It is very disruptive to a relaxation session to have people walk in half-way and, in any case, it is probably the latecomers who need the relaxation most. Often I find it is most helpful for people at the start of the group to simply talk quietly about whatever is uppermost in their minds. Talking and sharing helps to build up trust and confidence so that people can begin to use the group as a secure base.

In the early stages, before people have got to know each other, it can be useful to divide people into pairs to tell each other why they came to the group, their hopes and fears, what their main problems about getting to the group were, what they feel right now, etc. This is then followed by sharing some of these same things in the larger group. Talking in pairs can reduce the anxiety about being in the larger group and serve as a preparation for using it.

Very early on, the basic principle is introduced that the only way to overcome a phobia is to face one's anxiety rather than avoid it, but that this can be done in easy stages and does not have to be done all at once. It is often useful to remind people that anxiety can be a positive thing rather than a state to be avoided at all costs. It is possibly a symptom of the era within which we live and of the predominance of the medical approach to emotional problems that people often see anxiety as something akin to an illness, something which must be got rid of, instead of a useful indicator that there is a difficulty to be faced or a problem to be solved. In the group, people are encouraged to see a certain degree of anxiety as a positive rather than a negative sign, an indication that they are beginning to face and work on their problem rather than avoiding it. Even panic, a state which most phobic people not unnaturally dread and view as a precursor to some sort of ultimate loss of control or even madness, can be viewed in a more positive light. In the group, people are encouraged to view panic as what it is, a natural bodily state which, although unpleasant, is not harmful and will eventually come to an end if one simply waits for the feelings to pass. People can be taught, or can teach themselves, not to fuel their anxiety by adding to it with further frightening thoughts, e.g. 'I am anxious . . . It's bound to get worse . . . I will probably panic, pass out, go mad, etc.,' but rather to substitute more reassuring and realistic thoughts, putting a more positive meaning on the anxiety, along the lines of the above.

A fuller account of this approach to phobic anxiety and a behavioural approach to agoraphobia is to be found in *Agoraphobia, Nature and Treatment* by A. Mathews, M. Gelder and D. Johnson (Tavistock Publications, London, 1981), expecially the 'Ten Rules for Coping with Panic' from the clients' manual, which people nearly always find very helpful:

1   Remember that the feelings are nothing more than an exaggeration of the normal bodily reactions to stress.

2   They are not in the least harmful or dangerous – just unpleasant. Nothing worse will happen.

3   Stop adding to panic with frightening thoughts about what is happening and where it might lead.

4   Notice what is really happening in your body right now, not what you fear might happen.

5   Wait and give the fear time to pass. Do not fight or run away from it. Just accept it.

6   Notice that once you stop adding to it with frightening thoughts, the fear starts to fade by itself.

7   Remember that the whole point of practice is to learn how to cope with fear – without avoiding it. So this is an opportunity to make progress.

8   Think about the progress you have made so far, despite all the difficulties. Think how pleased you will be when you succeed this time.

9   When you begin to feel better, look around you, and start to plan what to do next.

10   When you are ready to go on, start off in an easy, relaxed way. There is no need for effort or hurry.

During the first session of the group, after the initial warm-up and introductions, each person usually makes a statement about what their problem is. It can be useful to go around the group with each person taking five minutes to do this. There is usually quite a diversity of problems, e.g. one person's main difficulty may involve going into supermarkets, whereas another may find it impossible to travel on buses or the tube, etc., but it is also evident that there is much in common and group members nearly always express relief at having met others who suffer in the same way. Group members are encouraged, usually in the form of homework, to make a list of the things they are afraid to do and then to arrange them in a hierarchy from the easiest to the most difficult. Sometimes it is useful to have two or more lists to do with different themes, e.g. travel and social situations. They are then encouraged to start practising on the easiest item and to keep a record along the following lines. (They are asked to rate their anxiety on a scale between one and 10, where one means virtually no anxiety and 10 means panic. In the comments column, they are asked to write any other relevant remarks, especially what made this particular situation easier or harder.)

This record can then serve as a basis for discussion in the group as well as being a way of recording progress. It will be more relevant and useful to some group members than others. The expectation is that, with repeated practice, anxiety will reduce, but sometimes this does not happen. Sarah complained that although she repeatedly practised facing difficult situations, they remained equally frightening and unpleasant each time. I suggested to her that she should stay in situations, if possible, for as long as it took for her anxiety to go down rather than leaving them while she was still anxious. I reminded her that the feeling of anxiety would almost certainly pass if she was able

| Date and time | Place reached | Time taken | Anxiety | Comments |
|---|---|---|---|---|
| 2.2.88 10 a.m. | Local shop | 25 mins. | 5 | Went early – so no wait, which made it easier. |
| 3.2.88 4.15 p.m. | Lincoln Rd, by bus. | 20 mins. | 8 going, 3 coming back. | Caught bus to Lincoln Rd (two stops). Walked back. |
| 4.2.88 11 a.m. | Supermarket | 45 mins. | 6 | Went at quiet time with Jane. Just walked around. Did not attempt to buy anything. |

to stay in a situation for long enough. In this way she would not be 'rewarded' by a reduction of anxiety when leaving. Sarah subsequently spent the whole of one afternoon in a department store with her boyfriend and confessed that although she had been anxious initially, it got rather boring in the end. The experience of having been in a department store without anxiety increased her confidence on subsequent occasions.

I feel that it is important for the pace at which each woman wants to confront her fears to be her own autonomous choice. The homework or tasks are therefore not imposed but initiated and worked out by each woman for herself with the help and encouragement of the group. Responsibility for carrying out the tasks is likewise left to each individual. There may be discussion in the group about the extent to which people are facing rather than avoiding their fears. This may include an examination of what the difficulties were – perhaps the task needs to be broken down into smaller steps or more support is needed. It may also include an element of gentle confrontation, but at all times it is clear that the choice of pace is the person's own.

There is also some general discussion of how much help each person will need to carry out the graded practice and who an appropriate helper would be. The idea is put across that there is nothing wrong with asking for help but that support from a helper should be seen as a temporary step on the road to achieving the task independently. Sometimes group members can act as helpers for each other.

In some groups it is helpful, and fun, to plan a group task and for the whole group to carry it out together. This is possible even if there is quite a variation in people's problems, e.g. in one workshop we planned to go down into an underground station. For some people in the workshop getting to the station by bus or on foot constituted the task. For others going down into the station using either the stairs or the lift was the important part. At the end of this exercise everyone felt that they had achieved something, especially since, for one woman, it was the first time in 12 years that she had been down into an underground station, and we celebrated the occasion in a pub.

After the introduction of these basic concepts, ideas and strategies in the initial one or two sessions, subsequent groups usually have the following elements. There is usually some kind of warm-up. This may simply take the form of sharing feelings and the experiences of the past week, or it may be useful to have some exercises or games to get the group awake and started. Next there is usually a discussion of how people got on with their homework tasks, as well as setting future goals and planning strategies for achieving these, with all group members contributing to this process. The relaxation training or exercises constitute another element of the group. They can come either at the mid-point of a session, thus providing a bridge between the more practical and task-centred part of the group and the latter part where group members talk in a more free-flowing way, or right at the end. If they are left till the end, they can be useful in reducing people's anxiety about actually separating from the group.

There are a number of useful methods of relaxation training based on controlling one's breathing and on progressive relaxation of the muscles (e.g. those described in Sheila Ernst and Lucy Goodison, *In Our Own Hands*, The Women's Press, London, 1981, or those used in ante-natal classes). If the relaxation comes in the middle, it could be followed by a short guided fantasy or exercise to facilitate subsequent discussion, e.g. focusing on experiences of going out with one's mother in childhood, on experiences within the context of current relationships, etc. Some groups flow more freely and some need more exercises and structure, so this aspect depends on the particular group.

Part of the group is taken up with general talking and sharing of problems, feelings, etc. This may include talk about both current and early relationships, and will usually focus particularly on issues of separation and independence. It can be interesting to think about the attitude of husbands or partners towards these issues. How secure and confident are they? Men seem more secure and confident in relation to the outside world, but their insecurity can be partly hidden because of the support they receive from women in the home who are creating a secure base for them. Agoraphobic women often describe their husbands or partners as supportive but are unaware of how much security they themselves provide, perhaps by their very dependence.

I think it is useful to make links between current difficulties and early experiences and relationships, especially early experiences around separation. In asking group members to focus on early experiences of going out with their mothers, all sorts of interesting and relevant questions are raised. How did our mothers (and fathers) feel about being separate and going out? In what way did they present the world to us: as a safe or a dangerous place to venture into? What were some of the issues and experiences around separating and becoming independent in our families? This usually leads to a lot of sharing about family relationships, especially relationships with mothers, right from early memories to actual current difficulties. There are some common patterns and I think this realisation is strengthening in itself as it lifts one's experience from an isolated and individual to a shared and social problem. The most common experience that emerged from groups and workshops in which I have been involved is one of having felt in some way responsible for one's own parents and realising that one's own mother had difficulty in going out herself and in being left alone (again partly masked by the dependence of her children, leading to subsequent difficulty in allowing them to separate). The mother of a woman in one of the groups had actually taken over one of her daughter's children as a companion and was now clinging to this child and having difficulty in letting it go.

There is also a focus on social issues connected with women and independence. Why are these such difficult issues for women? Society, as it is currently constituted, certainly has difficulty in coping with women's independence and assertiveness. It is less acceptable for women to express anger, and this anger, if not expressed, can be turned inwards and experienced as anxiety or depression or projected outwards so that the whole world seems a more threatening and frightening place. Such linking of individual and social issues represents a further level of consolidating and integrating change which can lead to a sense of some power over one's life on a wider level than the individual.

In summary, each group or workshop has three main components: a task-oriented or behavioural part, the relaxation training and a time for sharing feelings and thoughts about the meaning of symptoms and difficulties within the context of present and past experiences.

If the total number of sessions is to be quite limited, more structure and longer sessions will be needed. In a more ongoing group continuing over a longer period of time it would be possible and appropriate to let the different aspects of the group merge into each other in a less structured way. I now feel that an ongoing group is probably more useful for agoraphobic women than a time-limited one, as such a group allows women to separate from it in their own time and in a more natural way.

The aim of any group is to provide a setting where members can give each other support on both practical and emotional levels and thus begin to set in motion a process of behavioural change within a context of personal growth.

## Acknowledgments

I am grateful to my colleague Ron Wood, who used to run groups along similar lines in the West Essex Health District, for discussions I have had with him, to Pat Land for her help and to all the women who have shared their experiences and ideas with me.

# Part Three
# The Inner World

# 8
# Running Groups on Depression
Vin Gomez

I've found this chapter harder to write than anything else in years. I get up, sit down, write a page and cross it out, write three pages and start again. I often find writing hard, but this has sometimes seemed to border on the impossible. No accident, of course, that I happen to be writing about groups on depression. Just under the surface of my mind lurks the confusion of anger and dread that the word depression touches off in me. As I write, the same kind of muddle and blankness assail me as people bring to the depression groups. And as I struggle with writing, I'm reminded of how people in the depression groups have struggled to face those aspects of themselves that are the hardest to face and share.

The first thing that struck me when I began to run these groups was that not many of the people who came were what I'd have called depressed. Rather than going into the theoretical definition, I want to look here at how in practice people use the term depression. Depression means different things for different people – guilt, resentment, confusion, loneliness, anxiety, a feeling of emptiness or unreality. But what prompts many of us to use or to acquiesce in the rather impersonal label of depression seems to be the conviction that whatever our feelings are, we can hardly cope with them. Surely, we may feel, experiences or feelings that are so painful, frightening, shameful or so unlike how we normally view ourselves cannot just be a part of ordinary life? Surely we shouldn't have to put up with or learn to come to terms with them? We can easily begin to think of them as an 'it', like my writing, that we fight against and are afraid of being defeated by. We may say to ourselves: 'Is it an illness? Would drugs get rid of it? I can't go on like this; and I don't think I can cope with it on my own.' People who come to the depression groups often come to share what they feel to be a rare and shameful disability, reaching to the edge of their ability to cope.

I have run groups on depression at the Women's Therapy Centre several times a year for the last few years. Each group contains about 10 women and meets for three Sundays, from 10.00 a.m. to 6.00 p.m. The participants have been aged between 20 and 70, and come from all backgrounds, though most are in their thirties or forties, white, though not necessarily British, and broadly middle class. When the opportunity first arose for me to run a group on depression, I was attracted by the challenge. I thought that a group specifically on depression could go directly to what I see as the core of therapy: finding our way towards accepting and coping with what we find most difficult in ourselves. Simply coming to a group on depression, I thought, would mean admitting that there is something one finds hard to manage in oneself – and that is the first step towards managing it and accepting it as part of oneself.

Apart from the professional challenge, there was also a personal challenge. Running a group on depression offered a way for me to use the experience of a very difficult period in my early twenties. At that time, I felt generally at the mercy of a muddle of fear and dread and anger that I was too afraid to admit to. My feelings felt like assaults from outer space, and for a long time all I wanted was to be rid of them. What made the difference was not that my feelings disappeared, but that with the help of my first therapist I slowly stopped feeling they were alien to me. Now I see them as aspects of myself which I can usually cope with and can use in a number of ways – some very enjoyable, like writing, when it is going well. Those four years when dread and anxiety reigned supreme appear to me now not as a catastrophe but as among the most fruitful and formative years of my life. Without them, I might never have faced and acted on such basic questions as: Is my own individual life worth living, worth struggling to create and recreate?, Are other people really worth getting to know?, Is happiness ever more than a dangerous illusion?, Is there anything good or solid or real about me or about the world?

It was during these years that I decided I wanted to be a psychotherapist, but it was more than ten years before I was ready to start training. I needed to continue learning to cope with myself, and I had to establish a place for myself in the world. Even after much more therapy and two training courses, it still felt like a leap in the dark to finally declare myself ready and start working as a psychotherapist. Though a lot has happened in the last 14 years, I am still grappling with accepting my feelings, my strengths and my needs, and using them to live my life. This struggle is the backbone of my work as a psychotherapist, as well as what led me to it.

Running groups where people can share their most difficult

feelings, conflicts and questions has been one way for me to give back some of what I have received during this time. What I work towards is helping people to tolerate a bit more of their feelings or their experiences, however difficult or contradictory they may be. It can be hard to affirm that we can be both sad and happy, mean and generous, confident and afraid, because life is simpler if we see things in black and white. It can be painful to acknowledge how much we may pretend to others and ourselves about what and who we are; and sometimes the sheer intensity of our feelings or our conflicts can seem overwhelming. Yet if we can accept that what we feel is what we feel, we are well on the way towards coping with those feelings, rather than leaving them to manage us. We often begin to find that instead of simply hating them, we can begin to value our difficult feelings, as they become more an aspect of our whole selves and as we find more ways of using them.

So I try to help people in the depression groups to face what they need to in themselves, and between each other and me. Many things may be hard to confront: feeling happy when we thought we were depressed; admitting to strengths when we see ourselves as weak; being honest about disagreeing or criticising people we are afraid of; and finding the courage to communicate all our feelings, because isolation makes everything worse. My aim is not to help people get rid of their feelings, much though they may want to at first, but to help them to let their feelings enrich their personal identity and increase their responsibility for themselves and their lives. In every depression group I have led, this process has also deepened in me. No group has been easy, personally or professionally, but each one in a different way has been moving and rewarding.

## Account of One Depression Group

### Day 1

Eleven women had booked for the group, but by 10.00 a.m. only six had arrived. I decided to start by 10.15 at the latest, feeling irritated by people's lateness. It often happens at the start of a group, and I haven't found a good way, for me, of dealing with it. I'll make sure it doesn't happen *after* today, I thought. I was excited and daunted at the prospect of the next three Sundays. What would they bring? What kind of a group would it be? I noticed that some of the women had already introduced themselves and were chatting, instead of sitting in frozen silence, as often happens. Good sign, I thought; I won't have to do all the work. On the other hand, I thought, maybe I'll feel redundant. After all, no one's talking to *me*, and it's not my job to be one of them. Sometimes it's lonely being a group leader. Like many women, I've had to struggle to accept and use both the power and the responsibility the leader role brings.

Feeling a bit out of things, I noticed that a few of the women had come to other groups I'd run. One had come to several and always got into a push–pull, love–hate battle with me. I was touched that she'd come to another of my groups, but I didn't fancy a fight straight off. There were three older women of over 50. I always respect those women who have the courage to come to what is in general a group of younger people. It is easy for the rest of the group to see them as the older generation, as mother; and it can be a pleasure to help both the older and the younger women to see past these barriers and realise that whatever our age, we often share the same issues and concerns.

I'd decided to refrain from packing in too many structures or activities. When I started running groups, I hadn't the confidence to leave too many empty spaces. I hadn't enough trust in the natural process of the group, or in my own ability to tolerate doubt and confusion, so I often came up with quick solutions in the form of structured exercises. Since then, I've learned how much a group can do for itself, and how much more appropriately they can do it than I can with even my most brilliant plans and structures. I've learned to listen to the group more carefully, and I see my role as helping them to express their underlying concerns and the feelings that go with them, rather than solving them in advance. This often achieves far more than too much planning, though it's hard to give up the role of rescuer and problem-solver.

By 10.15, all but one of the women had arrived. We started with a game to learn everyone's name and the usual introductions. Everyone said a bit about what had brought them to the group, what they hoped to gain from it and whether they'd done any kind of therapy before (about half had). I spoke about the importance of committing themselves to every session of the group or of letting the group know if they had to be absent; the importance of talking about difficulties in the group, even if they felt like leaving; about confidentiality; and a little about why I had chosen to run depression groups and why I thought they were useful. There didn't seem to be anyone in the group who might be too fragile or too disturbed to benefit from it – occasionally, very distressed people find a group too much to cope with. There were a couple of people, however, whom I felt I ought to be careful not to push. It can be difficult deciding how much or how best to work with people who already feel quite shaky, especially in a short-term group. It is tempting, as leader, to take either too much or too little responsibility for such people. There is often only a fine line between challenging someone and putting too much pressure on them.

For part of the morning we talked about what it was like to come to a group specifically on depression. A wave of relief swept over many people as they were at last able to admit, openly, to their anxiety, their despair and especially their loneliness – the main themes that had emerged from the introductions. Many people had been struggling to carry on outwardly successful lives, while hiding what they felt to be their shameful secret of depression. I felt suddenly thrilled to realise once again how powerful simply sharing our feelings can be. The group began to be less a collection of strangers and more travellers on a common road. I guessed, at this point, that contact and communication would be especially important for this group, so many of whom felt isolated in their lives. I would lead the group with that in mind.

At 11.00 a.m. the last person arrived, with a brief apology. I felt annoyed; we made some brief introductions and I asked the group to fill her in on what I'd already said about commitment and confidentiality. Her arrival must have jarred the group considerably, as well as being hard for her, and I think I let my annoyance stop me from realising both these things fully. As we continued, the group seemed to move into a different phase. The warm relief at finding shared company withered away; we had a wistful time wishing there were magic solutions to our problems. If only we had not lost that relationship; if only other people would offer us comfort and support when we are too afraid to ask for it; if only depression wasn't such a stigma. The group was beginning to want to find someone to blame for how they felt, society or partners being the prime candidates. They would have liked, even, to consider themselves as abnormal, because surely no one ought to have to cope with such horrible feelings or difficult conflicts, as they did. After feeling quite a part of the group, I began separating more and more from them as I opposed their wishes to dump responsibility on others or to see themselves as odd or ill. I felt that I was steadily and drearily dampening all their hopes and becoming in the process less and less a part of the warm circle that had grown up earlier on. We would always feel sad, or anxious, or angry sometimes, I was saying. What counts is not to abolish those feelings, which is impossible anyhow, but to find ways of managing them. Only then can we begin to feel differently about them. Even I felt disappointment as I spoke. The issue emerging was: what can therapy actually *do*? What could I, as leader, offer the group? It seemed precious little, at least of what they wanted. I couldn't bring back lost time, lost relationships, lost feelings of belonging. I couldn't even stop people feeling anxious or sad. All I could do was to help the group to listen, to communicate and to feel with each other as we tried to face the truth about ourselves. There was no magic solution, though we might offer each other limited help. Everyone knew all this really, but they were angry about it, and so was I. There were uncomfortable silences as it sank in, silences broken usually by me. People insisted that they were silent because they didn't want to seem greedy: someone else might need to speak more than they did. On the one hand, this showed the difficulty many women have in feeling they have a right to voice their needs; on the other, I felt that the silences also spoke of anxiety and disappointment. Things went on in an unsatisfactory-feeling, bitty way; I had a couple of half-arguments with people as I stuck to my guns and they to theirs. But by lunchtime the hope for a magic solution was thoroughly quenched. It had become clear that what people would get out of the group would be largely up to them.

I thought the group was going reasonably well but I felt drained and dejected in the lunch break. As well as coming up against my own wishes to magically cure all ills, I think I was also feeling the isolation that many of the group had spoken of. Sitting alone in the little room down the corridor, I felt light years away from what I found myself picturing – a cosy group sharing food.

When we started again after lunch, the latecomer had disappeared. No one, it transpired, had seen her during lunch, and no one had filled her in on what I'd said at the start of the group. Her leaving was a shock; we talked about it for some time. At first, people spoke of feeling guilty that they hadn't done more to help her feel part of the group. They realised how out of things she may have felt, and they all knew only too well what it was like to feel excluded. Then one brave soul owned up to feeling angry: not only had she interrupted the group by arriving late, she'd rejected us all as well, and pretty quickly too – or so it felt to her. I felt the same mixture of feelings and I pointed out to the group that not one of us could now see ourselves as 'not mattering' to the group (I'm sure they didn't realise I was speaking to myself as well!). Everyone was at least as much a part of the group as the latecomer had been, and everyone could feel the impact of her disappearance. They couldn't, either, continue to blame other people for being uncaring or insensitive for not seeming to realise when they themselves were feeling low. No one had gone out of their way to help the latecomer integrate into the group (we were assuming that this had contributed to her leaving), although that didn't mean they didn't care; they would have been glad to help if she had asked. Her leaving convinced the group, as no structure could have, that it was up to everyone to take responsibility for what they needed and to ask for it. They couldn't now authentically blame anyone else for not realising what they needed if they did not tell them. But asking was a risky prospect for this group, as it is for many women. They felt it might almost be tantamount to stealing: an aggressive, demanding, selfish thing to do which could well result in other people criticising or rejecting you. Or it could be a way of blackmailing people into doing something they didn't really want to, because, of course, you couldn't expect anyone to openly say 'No'.

You're using her disappearance in a pretty lively way, Vin, I thought. I was enjoying myself and certainly not feeling dejected any more. But the question remained as to how much the group and I had helped ourselves to feel *in* at the expense of the latecomer being *out*.

The plan was to spend the afternoons mainly on individual sessions. Here was another opportunity to continue the theme of taking responsibility for our own needs. I asked everyone to take some time to decide whether or not they wanted time for individual work that afternoon. This was real torture. To ask for time was scary, because of having to expose more of oneself and because it would be 'selfish' – other people might need the time more. But not to ask would simply ensure that one wouldn't get it and could make one appear cowardly. The whole group was gripped by this agony of decision-making. They knew me too well, by now, to seriously think I might make their decisions for them, though one or two people tried to get me to. Finally, four people asked for time. But I felt that the difficult, exposing process of deciding had itself been the group's main work so far. They were 'in it together' after that. I felt pleased and warm about the group's work and my own. Taking the time to follow through the latecomer's disappearance and the process of decision-making were things I could easily have skimped on or even avoided altogether. I probably would have done if I had been more anxious about the group holding together, or more arrogantly sure I could 'help' people through formal sessions. The group, meanwhile, had really begun to realise the importance and the difficulty of decision-making in all areas of their lives. It is an aspect of being 'real' and committed in one's life that is especially hard for many women. People saw that they could use the group to practise this.

The individual sessions carried on the process of group cohesion; but still that shared, agonised few minutes of making a decision seemed the focal point of the day to me. The day finished with the feeling that we had faced a challenge and had come through the ordeal.

## Day 2: A week later

As the group started – promptly this time – we felt like a band of pioneers who might have been together for months. I decided to stretch people's responsibility for themselves a bit more and asked the group to consider what they would like to achieve from the day, and how they could go about achieving or getting it. People came up, a bit unwillingly, with various plans: continuing the ideas from last week of using the group to practise asking for support, communicating how they felt and making decisions. It was harder this week for people to see asking as pure greed. It was obvious that those who had shared most about themselves last week had given us all a great deal. It was also becoming plain that the whole group was grateful rather than resentful to whoever broke the silences; I wasn't bailing them out this week and was quite prepared to sit them out for as long as it took. No one really believed this time that they were as powerless to take charge of themselves as they'd felt the week before, and so there was more aliveness in the atmosphere. I felt correspondingly active and assertive rather than excluded. But it isn't easy to begin to take charge of oneself more than one is used to, and I didn't expect the morning to be all plain sailing. It wasn't.

After a little while, the group clearly began to get fed up with my more challenging and less helpful stance. Someone spoke, at last, of what a difficult feeling *resentment* is to cope with, and many agreed, relieved that the subject had been broached, for the undercurrents were growing. I was pleased too. Nevertheless, anger was something that the group, like many women, felt very threatened by. There seemed to be little chance of anyone expressing anger or criticism openly or easily, except when it was directed towards people outside the group. In fact, I said, anyone brave enough to take that risk deserved our support. The group had to agree. And slowly and steadily, the undercurrent of anger began to be directed more and more openly towards *me*.

Once, when I asked people to notice how they were feeling, the predominant feeling for some people was resentment that here I was, bossily telling them to expose their feelings while I got off scot-free; I only shared what I wanted to. A bit later, people felt that rather than directing operations too much, I wasn't directing them enough: I was leaving them to make too many decisions without clear guidance or instructions as to how to make them. With about half the group, there was a general feeling that my position as leader was unwelcome and divisive; I was doing either too much or too little. The other half of the group was only too glad that I was there to take care of the group rather than get lost in my own feelings – they felt that having me as leader gave them more freedom. I pointed out that having someone in charge is a mixed blessing. However matey I might be with the group, and however much I might feel with them, the fact remained that they were paying and I was being paid; we were all bound to have various feelings about that. Although it was a bit unnerving, I was glad that this issue had come out into the open. Apart from being an important issue in most groups, it showed that people were now finding the energy and confidence to begin to protest about what they didn't like – a far cry from the subdued hopelessness that many of the group had arrived with the week before. It has taken me some time to be more or less comfortable about facing the group's resentment towards me as leader, especially as their criticisms are usually at least partly justified. And though I found this part of the group energising, it wasn't all easy going. As the group continued touchily finding fault with me, I started wondering: am I really jumping down people's throats, ignoring them, minimising what they say? I probably was, a little.

That afternoon, we had more individual sessions. Deciding whether or not to ask for them was far easier for the group this week. And it seemed that now I was clearly defined as the leader, for better or worse, people could use me as such. Several people explored, deeply and movingly, their aloneness, their pain and their disorienting anxiety following the break-up of important relationships. I was touched, and pleased, by how much trust people were able to put in me, as well as in themselves and the group, as they let themselves dip into regions of their feelings that were unfamiliar and frightening to them. What came out in several sessions was that it had been hard for them to feel fully themselves in those relationships; often they had played second fiddle in many ways, accommodating themselves to what they thought the other person wanted. The break-up of these relationships, though confusing and appallingly painful, seemed to offer a chance for the women to rebuild their shattered lives on a more autonomous basis.

I felt that the group had faced the challenge of the morning: instead of seeing themselves as victims of fate, and me as an unhelpful authority figure, they were beginning to take more of their problems into their own hands, using me as a midway supporting person. In the last session, one woman involved us all completely. She slowly entered into rivers upon rivers of despair, taking me and the group along with her. It seemed that she was expressing years of loss and sadness, and she was still crying deeply as 6.00 p.m. neared. I felt torn, but I knew I had to stop her, to give the group time to finish the day and prepare to leave on time. Overrunning the time would have felt like letting all our feelings manage us, instead of the other way round. Still, I felt, and seemed, mean.

## Day 3: A week later

This last day was taken up above all with ending. Meeting that morning felt almost like a funeral. Many of the group were astonished at how important it had become to them in the short time that we'd been meeting. This week, we had individual sessions in the morning, to leave the afternoon free for finishing up, going over what people had learned and planning for the future.

Several people that morning consolidated the strengths they'd gained in previous weeks. Some had already begun to put into practice in their lives what they'd been trying out in the group. Others took risks they wouldn't have believed possible a few weeks earlier. A woman who had spent her life listening to others now found the courage to ask us to listen to her. People were able to tell each other when they felt frustrated or annoyed or envious, rather than reserving all the negativity for me. The group felt strong enough to face and grow from challenge and confrontation, as well as support. Everyone's communication felt stronger and more convincing than before, and there was a glowing closeness between us. We all felt proud of what a wonderful group we'd helped to create.

The afternoon was thoughtful, sad and difficult. People moved between edgy anxiety at the prospect of losing the group and pride and appreciation at what they'd given to it and gained from it. They determined to continue to take charge of their lives, their feelings and their needs; they felt they would remember that they had taken part in transforming a collection of shy, nervous strangers who felt they were failures into this strong, warm, courageous group. They also looked at what they *hadn't* got from the group. One woman told the group in no uncertain terms how pleased she'd be to have her Sundays free again –

and most people had to agree, nostalgic though they felt. As usual, everyone's feelings were mixed. The subject of suicide made its appearance as the minutes ticked by. I think it was a way of saying how much it mattered that the group would in a sense die, although nobody really wanted things different. Most people had had thoughts of missing this last day, so as not to have to face the ending.

I asked the group to take some time, near the end, to decide on small, specific ways they could put something they'd learned in the group into practice in their lives outside, and a number of plans took shape. They varied from joining a dancing class to finding the time and the courage to speak openly to a partner or friend, to arranging further therapy, to beginning to plan a new career. We all said a little about our feelings as the group finished. I felt the effort, and the pleasure, of containing and feeling in me all that had been expressed through the group: the bitter anger of the suicide theme; the empty thought of next Sunday without the group; the pain of saying goodbye to this group of women I'd come to feel so close to; and the relief of getting the group over and done with. I felt that I had got to know a little more of the pain and loneliness of leading a group, as well as the pleasure and exhilaration – the same loneliness and the same excitement that we all feel as we define ourselves increasingly as autonomous individuals, responsible for ourselves and for how we contact the people around us.

Writing about it has been like going through the group again. I haven't felt so unwilling to write anything for years, nor been so close to feeling I would not be able to get anything good enough down. Now this chapter feels that it has come from me; it doesn't feel alien any more and I don't feel pushed around by it. So I appreciate myself for not giving up on it; and, like the group, I'm sorry to stop as well as pleased to be finished with it.

# 9
# Women and Creativity
## Gabriela Muller

Writing this chapter has been a challenge. Again and again I find myself wanting to arrive at a definition of creativity which would be neither too theoretical nor too simplistic. The task seems as difficult as getting a bird singing happily in a tree to sit on one's finger. However difficult it is to define creativity, it certainly involves both conscious and unconscious exploration. Indeed, there is no such thing as creativity, just a creative process in which we engage. This chapter is therefore about freedom of expression in all areas of our lives.

In the workshops I have led at the Women's Therapy Centre since 1981 my aim is to sensitise women to their creative abilities, to find out how they feel blocked and how they feel they may be able to develop their hidden potential. Often women come to the workshop because they feel they have some potential but don't know what this is. The exercises are taken from various creative therapies: music therapy, movement therapy, art therapy and psychodrama. I also use a variety of other techniques like guided fantasy, brainstorming, etc. Most exercises take place with non-verbal communication and interaction, as talking can often be a defence against undesired feelings and thus detract from the experience of what is actually taking place in a creative process.

I usually start the workshop by introducing myself, briefly talking about how I came to be involved in this kind of work. I painted and drew a lot as a child, partly for pure enjoyment, partly to escape from the pressures of family life. School diminished my self-confidence; art college nearly destroyed it. This was followed by 12 years of working – in a film developing factory, in film editing, in a young children's day centre and in other forms of community and counselling work. Finally I trained as an art therapist. Only then did I begin to value my creativity again and I became involved in painting and other art forms on a regular basis. This is now an important part of my life. Needless to say, it has all been both painful and rewarding .

After introducing myself I ask women why they have come. Many women say something like: 'I've done some good things, I've got a good job, partner, children. I shouldn't complain, but somehow I haven't done anything creative for a long time. I often feel tense and tired and haven't got much energy.' Having a job and family often demands a great deal of discipline, routine and self-denial. But it doesn't necessarily lead to a feeling of fulfilment. Women tend to blame and criticise themselves in addition to being put down by others, and often end up feeling, 'What I'm doing is nothing compared to what I should be doing. I'm just not creative!' Other women come to a workshop to retrieve some lost sense of spirituality – they use less clearly defined words like happiness, inner magic or energy. Finally, these workshops also attract some women with quite deep-rooted unhappiness in their lives. A creativity workshop may be their first step on the way to individual psychotherapy; for many people it seems much less threatening than, for example, a workshop on depression.

The workshop attracts women from a variety of cultures, as language is not the main focus. Most women are white and middle class, certainly by education, but many are of working-class origin. There are usually a few younger and a few older women, the majority being between 25 and 40 years of age. A quarter travel to the workshop from outside London, sometimes from as far away as Wales, Ireland and Scotland. There are usually a few women who have been to art school but have not been able to maintain their creative ability under the pressure of art production and constricting ideologies and treatment by art teachers (usually male). Some women have young children and are interested in aspects of playing and creativity or how to get some space for themselves.

Women's socially recognised creativity is often narrowed down to giving birth. Once having fulfilled their supposedly natural creative needs, they are left with the everyday invisible struggles: how to make a baby laugh instead of cry; how to stop children fighting; how to look after a home and everything that goes with it, and at least a little bit after themselves; how to cope with working inside and out of home; how to manage with lack of money and domestic facilities, unemployment or too much work and responsibility; how to cope with isolation or issues such as birth, illness and death. The list is endless. This is where a large chunk of our everyday creative energy goes.

Having a baby may be a very gratifying experience, but it is not the only way of expressing one's creative urges. Lisa came to the workshop feeling very creative and announced: 'I want to *make something*. I'm glad it's not a baby this time.' We do not always have to express our creative energy in relationships. Most women with or without children or partners find themselves in demanding nurturing roles, catering for others' emotional needs while their own are neglected. Whether they are holding down a job at the same time or are unemployed does not seem to make much difference to how this everyday creativity is taken for granted without being validated. This assumption about women's natural creativity (and responsibility) is held not only by society in general but is also internalised, and it affects the way in which women see themselves. I therefore find it most useful to begin by asking the group how women *are* creative, what they feel they are creating and making. Later I ask how they would like to be more creative, what their underlying assumptions and fantasies are.

Even if women are working creatively there may be many conflicts in what creativity means for them. Jane, a young white woman talking about a painting she had done in the group, spoke about her struggle to become a writer.

*This is my parents' house. I am standing far away from the others. I left a long time ago. I am a writer but I get totally stuck quite often. No one in my family was creative. I feel really guilty about wanting to lead a creative life. I come from a big family; my parents were always busy working to make sure we were all right.*

She stopped and held her breath. When I suggested that the process of working on everyday tasks might have swallowed up all her parents' strength, including their creative energy, she told us that she came from a working-class family but had managed to get herself a middle-class education. She felt guilty for having escaped from her family, particularly her mother. Although this had enabled her to become a writer, she felt angry that it had been so hard for her, and impossible for the others. After these feelings were aired, she remembered her mother's singing and story-telling, and her own pain about separating from her mother in an attempt to have an independent identity and different lifestyle. By appreciating her mother's creativity in everyday survival and in the songs and stories she told, she was able to see herself as a creative person with roots in her class background and her mother. She felt relieved of the oppressive thought that she had either to relive her mother's life or to repudiate it completely.

Women from working-class backgrounds often have to adopt certain middle-class values and assumptions along with education. In terms of creativity this may mean 'making an art product', often with a physical quality that presupposes having the money to buy the stone for the sculpture or the canvas and oil for the painting, or the money for dance-classes, etc. Women from well-off families, on the other hand, who have had to undergo training in a creative skill, are often angry about this being almost the only measure of creativity allowed. Their playfulness and wish to explore more freely were given little reward or interest. Claire, a woman from an upper-class background, came to the workshop because, in her words, 'I was always the one who wasn't considered creative in my family. I had painting lessons and learned to play the violin, but my greatest sense of joy and achievement was when I disobeyed and broke the instrument.' Her notion of creativity was thus hampered by having had to conform, perform and produce a 'product' of creative skill which could be valued by others on their terms. She was very angry about not being allowed to play for her own pleasure. Her obstinate refusal to identify with her family's cultural practices and values became the beginning of her search for her identity.

## Moving into the Creative Self

The lack of validation of women's contributions, creative and otherwise, can produce a sense of 'bodily invalidity'. Marianne Wex, in her book *Let's Take Back Our Space*, illustrates with photographs how e.g. eight women fit into the space of only six men – in this case, on a park bench.

Since feeling creative is also a physical experience I use a relaxation-movement exercise to explore the issues of external space, bodily expression and communication and its relationship to women's internal space. The exercise begins by shaking out individual parts: hands, arms, feet, and so on, and ends with a shaking, kicking and stamping about of the whole body. I ask the women to try and sense in which part of their body their tension is located. I then ask them to explore through movement the area around this tense part – not the part itself – while I put on some music. The music I have edited together contains clear high, medium and low moods to allow people different kinds of explorations. It begins slowly and melodically and becomes increasingly rhythmic and complex.

I urge women to stay with their tense part, to keep on breathing, smelling and staying in touch, with their feet on the ground, until they feel ready to move gradually into their own dance. I try to keep my own movements as simple as possible as I am aware that I provide a model for those first, often quite embarrassing moments when I have stopped giving instructions. The tensions which are released after the relaxation exercise usually return, and women explore their bodily movements and fears of taking up all this space. I can always sense my own anxiety at the beginning of this exercise, but as I explore those oncoming blocks I eventually feel more relaxed and in touch with my body. As Caroline put it: 'I felt so inhibited . . . and clumsy at first when I saw others watching my movements. I haven't danced like this since I was a teenager, but I really enjoyed it in the end, especially when Sylvie and I copied each other's movements in turn.'

Implicit in this exercise are various challenges: first, the experience of being alone and separate in the presence of others without verbal communication; second, taking up space; and third, communicating through movements within a group of women.

## Self-image

The movement exercise focuses mainly on how we feel ourselves physically. The self-image exercise, which derives from art therapy, concentrates on how we see ourselves. The women are invited to paint any image they like to represent what they feel about themselves and their lives.

The materials I use are large body-size pieces of paper, which I prefer to stick on the wall but floor-space will do; plenty of thick liquid paint (such as Ready-Mix, fingerpaint or powderpaint); and big household brushes. (The exercise takes between two and three hours.)

I reassure women that this painting is about feelings and thoughts explored and expressed in the process of painting and will not be judged in terms of a 'good' or 'bad' product. It's most important to try to stay with the feelings and to observe one's creative process, rather than attempt to produce an artwork. It is up to the women how they use the materials, and whether they paint figuratively or choose marks, shapes and colours in a more abstract representation. Again, this exercise calls on women to explore and expand their boundaries, their 'real size' as opposed to how they 'should be'. At first women often feel overwhelmed by the huge pieces of paper and the plentiful paint available. They have been so conditioned to keeping themselves small and invisible that this can arouse a lot of anxiety and fear! 'I felt it was impossible to fill up this space. I thought I had nothing to put there. My art teacher always said I was useless.'

Art teachers can show children how to create their own sanctuary but they can also do a lot of damage. Paintings are often images of a child's internal world and show how she copes with the inner and outer world and resolves conflicts. Usually the child is not conscious of this. Therefore to be criticised or assessed can feel like an attack on your very existence. 'I can't paint' therefore often unconsciously means, 'I can't show you how it looks inside me.'

The internal space that appears in women's self-images can express an enormous pressure of dangerous feelings, being experienced as 'too full'; on the other hand, it can be painfully lonely and 'too empty'. Sometimes it is the space around women which for a variety of reasons occupies most of their time while painting; by attending to others and things outside, they avoid dealing with their inner selves: 'I simply didn't get around to painting myself with all these people in my life.' One woman realised: 'Looking at this picture, I can see that I feel quite all right, but what's around me isn't.'

Some women prefer to work on 'what women have got' and explore how they feel about owning their identity by focusing explicitly on the vaginal area of their body. Others choose to paint themselves naked. This nakedness is not a passive nudity in which women are the object of the observer/painter. In these self-images the nakedness exposes itself to itself, making a woman's internal feelings visible and valuing the strength of self-expression. To realise how powerful one is can be very scary too. One woman remarked, looking at the glowing figure she had painted of herself, 'It made me realise how much energy is dying to come out. I feel really overpowered by it.' Some images show a war going on inside the body.

When contradictions which have been internalised are fought out on paper and seen and shared with others they no longer occupy the same internal space. The struggle for a self-defined identity is hard and the women often feel exhausted after this exercise. It arouses so many contradictions, feelings and ideas that are contained in their bodies and ways of seeing themselves. The more anger and conflicts can be acknowledged, the more energy is set free and made available for creative use.

Art therapy can be a useful way of coming to terms with loss. Carol came after a miscarriage, still mourning her baby. She later wrote a long poem about her experiences at the workshop. This is a short excerpt which speaks for itself:

> ... we talked of the fantasy
> of being all colourful
> of being a colourful,
> creative person
> dressed in wild colours
> like a clown
> happy, joyous
> and we sat there in the gloom
> in the darkened room
> with the light falling, falling
> and people sobbing
>
> me sobbing
> as I danced for my dead baby
> lifting it up to my shoulders,
> laying it on to the floor
> giving it a piggyback
> loving it
> crooning over it
> before putting it back where it belongs

Although the self-image exercise might seem relatively easy, it does require someone who has had enough training to be very aware of her own imagery and visual associations; otherwise she may project these on to other people. She also needs to be able to reflect on the emotional content of the image as a whole. It is usually unnecessary to focus on individual bits. 'Why did you put this here?' generally evokes a defensive answer, such as 'I can't paint.' If you find yourself asking a lot of questions about individual parts or making value judgments (this is pretty, ugly, etc.), it may be worth finding out why you need to do this.

## Collective Painting

If the individually creative process is about one's inner relationship with oneself, the collective creative process is about human communication and sensitivity with others. In the non-directive collective painting exercise I will now describe I ask women to paint together on one large piece of paper without using any verbal communication. I give as few instructions as possible. Usually, by the beginning of the painting, there has been no agreement as to how women are going to relate through painting. This is not the only way of doing a group painting, and it could be very threatening when working with people who are in a fragile state. However, I choose this non-directive exercise as it makes group dynamics more clearly visible than a structured exercise would do.

As in any other group, there is often an initial hesitation about who will make the first leap. Then, when everyone has joined in, women usually stay in the space they have started to paint in and become fairly self-absorbed for some time. When the initial territory has been painted in, they gradually become aware of their own and others' boundaries. How to connect now? We see many different ways of painting, use of colours, shapes and space. Some women take up little corners, others may risk entering the centre of the paper, which is often left until last. We see symbols emerge which have special significance to women: moon, triangle, snakes, cat, flowers, etc. A collective language emerges.

Still, how are women going to speak to each other through these images? And is it all right to paint into each other's territory? Anna and Carol have begun to paint little dots into each other's spaces. Gradually they become more curious and paint into the centre space. Some other women watch this process. Do they approve or have these two gone too far? A bit of Sarah's sun has been painted over by Angela. Was this deliberate? Sarah withdraws by walking around the painting. Fiona repairs the sun and adds a red outline around it as if to protect it. A short while later Sarah paints a bird into Fiona's tree. Angela now watches the others paint, hesitant to enter the painting; she adds some slim, almost invisible lines on to an already existing patch of grass. A lot of things are going on at the same time. Three women seem to engage in decorating a bit of empty space in one part of the painting. Pink, purple, green. They seem to be quite excited about having rediscovered the old suffragette colours and being able to play around with them. A figure emerges, a woman; finally she becomes an Indian woman dancer. Every woman seems eager to paint something on to this image. What does this mean? I ask myself. Is she the collective symbol of creativity in an all-white women's group? Are women expressing a desire to explore creativity other than within Western concepts? Have they found so much within themselves that they wish to share this with women outside the group? Or is it simply another form of re-creating a racist stereotype? Have the women got in touch with their sexuality only to project their new-gained excitement about themselves into the idea of an 'exotic' idealised woman, therefore denying her reality? Or has this image emerged because women in this group feel more validated and therefore more able to validate the contribution of an Indian woman dancer to women's creativity?

The women in the group seem slightly surprised themselves. There is a breathholding silence as we all stand back and look at the image.

'I really wanted to put something into your space but I didn't want to intrude on you.'

'I wasn't sure about this either, when I painted some of your house. Is it all right, then?'

'Oh, yes, yes. I was hoping more would be added to it. Was it all right to put these stars on to your sky?'

'I really liked it. I wish I could have thought of it myself.'

'I felt quite possessive about my territory. I felt really scared someone would destroy my painting, particularly when my sun got painted over. I nearly cried, but then you protected it with this line around it. I was really pleased you did that.'

'Thanks also for putting the bird into my tree.'

Reality is being tested; assumptions looked at; fears of being destroyed, envy, jealousy, appreciation, anger and so much else is being expressed.

No one mentions the image of the Indian temple dancer. 'This is an all-white women's group with various origins,' I say, 'yet we have an image of an Indian woman dancer in our midst. What does this mean to you?'

'To me, she is a symbol of beauty, a goddess.'

'Aha, she is not very real then, and very different from you. How about your own beauty and creativity?'

'I still find this very difficult to believe in. I suppose I am quite envious really.'

'I am a bit sad that we can't share our experience with women from other cultures.'

'Can you tell us more about this?' I ask.

They then begin to reveal fantasies and attitudes towards black and Asian women, and explore issues about white awareness, culture and some of our own differences. I wonder whether this should have been our starting-point or whether it is simply that when these women have been able to look at their own oppression they begin to see, consciously or unconsciously, how they relate, sometimes oppressively, to other women and also how they use other women, like the Indian dancer, to oppress themselves through idealisation. Obviously, racism and other forms of oppression among women need far more attention and this short treatment can in no way do justice to the subject.

As women we grow up in a world that has produced many great white male artists and scientists, but has acknowledged the contributions of very few women, especially black and Asian women.

Creativity is about feeling free to play and being open to oneself and others. As children we may not have had an environment that allowed us a reassuring parent whom we could internalise and who thus gave us the strength to explore ourselves and the outside world freely. The workshop begins to give women a chance to experience such an environment and to give the little girl within permission to play. The following poem emerged as I was reflecting on what women want from the creativity workshops.

CREATIVE DESIRES

when you can see
your creativity
emerging
from those open
spaces within
my imagery
I like you
to leave
me
and be
by yourself
trusting me
to be with you
in your brightest
lightest
darkest
warmest
moments of creation

and in those moments
when you fear the

thunder of your
own destructions
I will hold your hand
and walk with you
through fire
not getting burnt

as you emerge
in those new lands
where you can build
the home you wish
to live inside

I will say goodbye
and anything you give me
I will keep for ever
and if you call me
I will be there

Gabriela Muller
13 February 1987

# 10
# Leaving a Relationship
## Gill Martin

The idea for this workshop came out of my own experience and that of many women I know. We seem to arrive at a point when, struggling to resolve difficulties in a long marriage or partnership, we get stuck. Often this happens when we are on the brink of leaving and moving away; sometimes it happens after the separation. The desire to separate is there, but the strength to carry through the desire deserts us. At the same time it seems impossible to rebuild anything with our partner. We feel stuck in a kind of limbo, neither moving clearly towards each other nor apart. A vicious circle can develop where we begin to despise ourselves for our failure to carry through what we want to do. This loss of self-respect diminishes our power. The trap lies in the fact that our ability to move through the difficulties in our relationship, either towards or away from our partner, is dependent on how much inner strength we have and on how positive we feel about ourselves.

The workshop is structured around the themes of self-image and loss. There is usually an introductory session on one evening, a further evening a week later and a full day on the following weekend. The structure allows space for members of the group to reflect on what has been shared at the workshop and on how their experience there can be used in their day-to-day lives.

When I thought about the theme of the workshop, I began, I suppose, with my own experience of having spent several years picking through the wreckage of my own marriage and, in the process, building a very different life for myself. I had originally felt suspicious of psychotherapy, but the crisis in my own life precipitated me beyond that suspicion and into beginning to try to understand myself a little better. I knew, from that time of personal change, that the crisis could be an opportunity to move. I also knew that, in the middle of it all, I did not feel positive and hopeful; I felt helpless and caught in a contradiction. I appeared to do all the things I had done before, but inside I was overwhelmed by the chaos of my own feelings.

There were several years between that point and the decision to run the workshop. I felt that I had learned something about separation and also about retrieving and rebuilding for myself. This gave me the confidence to use my understanding in working with other women in the workshop. In addition to my personal experiences during that time, I had done a four-year training in analytic and humanistic psychotherapy. With the perspective which the training gave me, I could see other women's experience as different and separate from my own.

Despite the title, the workshops I run do not focus strongly on the particular relationship each woman has, on the specific events or on what the partner did or did not do. It is most certainly not about woman as victim. The workshop mirrors the struggle we all have in close relationships: can we sustain our identity living closely with another person?; what is left of that identity when we separate from that person? Essentially, the workshop is about trying to retrieve the forgotten strengths of each woman. It is also, of course, a place to share the regrets and pain. Leavings are never unambiguous. There is rarely a relationship so appalling or so meaningless that the leaving is not tinged with regret or sadness. Generally, the women who come to the workshop are acknowledging that they cannot find answers for themselves by moving immediately into another relationship. They come because they want to struggle with their fear of being alone.

At the beginning of a workshop there is a great deal of apprehension. Most women seem to come with the fantasy that everyone else is 'all sorted out'. They will all have left tidily and be clear about what they want. It never seems to strike anyone that, if this were the case, why would the others have wanted to come to a workshop. During the introductory session, when people are describing what brought them along, there is usually an enormous sense of relief in finding that other women are involved in painful endings and struggling with contradictory feelings. Finding out that other people have messy lives too is painful and funny and a source of comfort.

I never find it easy to walk into a workshop, sit down with a group of people who are mostly strangers to one another and encourage women who are perhaps feeling very raw to talk about themselves. I am caught in the tension between knowing that time is short, only three sessions, yet that it is important to take time with beginnings, to allow space for introductions rather than rush into 'making something happen'. I am aware that many of the women are feeling very bad about themselves and very vulnerable. Difficult separations test our security and sense of our own worth to the limit. The longer a woman has tried to make a relationship work, the more likely she is to find the 'failure' devastating. She feels she can no longer rely on herself and has lost trust in her own perceptions and judgment. During the introduction each woman is asked to say something about herself and her reasons for coming to the workshop. At the beginning expectations are high; perhaps there is a hope that the workshop will be a magic panacea. It is part of my function as a workshop leader to keep both my own and the group's feet on the ground. A single workshop can do no more than raise a few questions for women to take away and explore in their lives. I can only offer a structure which might help these questions to surface during the limited time we have together.

I am always amazed at how different each group is and how utterly different is the 'animal' which each group creates and becomes. In each session we spend time talking about each person's day-to-day life, talking about our conscious existence. It is important, however, to reach beyond that to areas of awareness which are more difficult to control. The various exercises I might use in a workshop are intended to reach beyond words. If we draw, move our bodies, use our imagination, we are still saying something about how we feel but speaking in a different way, without words, and perhaps because of this we are able to reach deeper feelings than words alone allow. At the beginning of a group, few people feel safe with the idea of sharing what they may discover with more than one other person, but gradually, as trust grows, there is more willingness to talk with the whole group.

I often begin a workshop with a life graph, literally a drawing of our lives in the same way as any graph, mapping the high and low points of each woman's life. By seeing the ups and downs in front of her, the pattern of her life, a person can reflect more clearly on how she came to be at the workshop. Significant events and emotions from the past emerge, and the graph often has a prevailing mood which will mirror the woman's feelings at the present time. For instance, someone who is feeling isolated currently in her life will frequently emphasise, quite unconsciously, the other times in her life when the same feeling of isolation has been strong.

I try to move away from words in the second session, and may use drawings which speak to us in a rather different way. I have used drawings for myself for some years and I know that I cannot completely control what I express through drawing. The images which have emerged have forced me to acknowledge feelings which I might otherwise have slithered away from. Throughout the workshop I use relaxation and simple movements to heighten body-awareness. The relaxation also helps the flow of images. One example of such an exercise is to draw the five petals of a flower and in the petals to represent our five most important relationships. It is not important to be able to draw. In fact it is probably a disadvantage; somehow the drawing will take shape and reflect something in the quality of colour with which the woman can communicate. If the workshop is large enough I might suggest that the drawings be discussed in small groups of three or four, in which everyone helps each other by probing and questioning further. I also learn something from the way in which the drawing was done: the quality of the colour used, how much space is taken up by each petal, whether the drawing was completed quickly or never finished, where the petals are placed in relation to one another. I move around the groups as a resource if anyone needs extra support. I might use what I see to offer suggestions, to highlight a particular quality in the drawing, but only the woman herself can grasp the meaning from what she has drawn. Other people's perceptions and interpretations may be accurate, but if she is not ready to hear them she will become more defensive. We can offer what we see, but if we push our own image on to someone else we cease to hear them and we lose contact with the meaning of their communication.

So many thoughts and feelings can be generated by an exercise such as this that usually several women will talk further in the large group about what they learned from their drawings. At this point in the workshop, women usually feel more secure and able to trust themselves in the group to be more open about what they are feeling.

At the beginning of each session there is time to go round the group and for each person to talk about what has been happening in the intervening period since the last session. Perhaps someone may choose to look more deeply at her conflicts and the group will focus on her for a while. I try to remain flexible, to respond to what the group is saying and at the same time to keep in my mind the overall theme.

During the final, full-day session of the group the focus is on loss. Endings evoke powerful feelings and past endings re-emerge and can act as a barrier to facing present loss. Old wounds are reopened and need to be given attention in order to heal again. We move more freely in the present if the fragments of our past are not forgotten but gathered together as part of our history. Sometimes it is hard for some women to see the point of going back to other difficult times of bereavement or loss, and they may withdraw from the group, or become angry with me. For others, it becomes clear that feelings which they thought they had sorted out still colour their close relationships.

I may suggest that each person find an image, a simple form, to represent past loss. They draw the symbol and explore what it means for them. One woman, who had opened up a good deal during the sessions, shared rather shakily with the group her experience of being led back, through the image, to a time when her father had touched her breast. It happened on only one occasion many years before, but her loss was of her trust and that loss had remained with her, affecting her close relationships. She had never been able to tell anyone before how powerful this event had been in her life. Taking the risk of telling the group left her shaky but much relieved.

The closing, afternoon session looks at the transition back into the world without the group. We reflect on what we might need in order to give ourselves some support and nurture ourselves. For one woman, the need might be to slow down, to relax; for another, a decision to go to an assertion workshop so that she can find ways of reaching out to friends. Whatever the need, it is for each person to identify it for herself and suggest practical ways in which she can meet it.

## Self-image

Although each group is very different and no two people have the same experience, certain common themes have emerged during the workshops with which many women seem to identify.

We feel confusion about both asserting our independence and autonomy and also accepting the nurturing role which is part of the socialisation process of becoming a woman. In so many situations in everyday life, women nurture others. This can become a problem when the demands of others turn our attention away from ourselves and our own needs. When this happens, we do not differentiate clearly enough between our needs and the needs of others. Consequently, many women value themselves according to how much they are giving to other people; their own image of themselves is dependent on their relationships with the people around them, and they frequently try to overcome problems in these relationships by giving to others. Some women come to the workshop and describe how dependent they feel on their partner. When they talk about their lives and describe what actually happens on a day-to-day basis, they present a very different picture. They may be giving financial support to their partner, paying for the total cost of the household and giving a lot of time and emotional support to their partner. Their behaviour shows that they can be strong, but their own self-image is very different, and they cannot see themselves as strong women. It is difficult for those who hear their story and can see the contradiction to understand how dependent that woman feels. What seems to be happening is that the woman is trying to get her own emotional needs met by giving. Surely, if I give enough I will get enough in return. My own neediness will be satisfied, seems to be the unconscious statement.

The women in the workshop help each other in two ways: both by giving support and by being direct about their response to one another. They can say what they feel about the circumstances someone has described, being honest without being destructive in their criticism. If we value ourselves, our needs for emotional support seem quite legitimate and we can expect some recognition of these needs from our partner. If our sense of self-worth is fragile, we will tend to deny our own needs, and then we are in danger of being trapped in a vicious circle. The more we deny our needs the more overwhelming they may feel. It is clearly not legitimate to have overwhelming needs, and so we are more self-critical. The problem is a complex one and can take a long time to resolve. However, in the workshop it is possible to encourage a woman to accept some simple needs as legitimate.

Suzanne was a woman who found strength in the feedback she got from other members of the group. She had left her partner after a long relationship and was staying in a flat with a friend. She had her young son living with her. She was panicking about the need to find her own flat and critical of herself for not having found a job. She felt guilty that maybe her wish to spend time with her son was more to do with her own needs than with his. The group helped her to take the pressure off herself by saying that she could not solve all these problems immediately. In fact, she was less likely to resolve any of them if she attempted to do everything at the same time. Perhaps both she and her son needed one another during the time of change and she could allow herself to be with him. Their support helped Suzanne to see a different perspective on her problems; they encouraged her to be less self-critical with regard to her own needs and to accept that it was appropriate to feel so vulnerable.

Being sensitive to the needs of others makes us good carers. But care has to be appropriate both to the needs of the giver and the receiver, and the question which emerges for some women concerns boundaries. Where do I stop and where does my partner begin? Where is the demarcation zone between my partner's pain and my pain, between my partner's problems and my problems? It seems that the more a woman denies her own needs, the more difficult she finds it to sort out her own boundaries in relation to her partner. Of course, an enormous threat of which she is barely aware lurks in the background, the threat that if she were to assert her needs in the relationship she may be forced to acknowledge that she will not get the warmth and the response she wants. She is then faced with a very unpalatable reality.

Alice came to her first group at the age of 50. She found it very difficult at first to contain her distress and both she and the group were afraid that she was going to end up in a helpless heap in the midst of us. It was my task as a group leader to explain that perhaps what she had to say would not be as frightening to everyone as she feared. I tried to contain her panic so that she was able to hear what other women were saying to her. Once these limits were set she was more able to talk about her life and less afraid that she was going to overwhelm us. She was going through a huge crisis. She had always seen herself as strong and coping, bringing up children, caring for an assortment of animals and supporting an alcoholic husband. She had survived by being the strong one. Her body had finally taken control and collapsed with a severe back problem. She had had to listen to the statement her body was making and she had decided to leave the marriage. Her distress arose from the effort she had always put into being capable; her self-image had been supported through being able to cope with every eventuality. If she was not coping, then she was nothing. She was overwhelmed by the shock of suddenly being aware of how empty she felt. The group was able to give her enough support to take the risk of acknowledging how she felt, rather than simply drowning in feelings. Slowly, during the workshop she began to see in her drawings another image, of herself as a child from a colonial background, left in England at the age of five and being forced to deny her needs for warmth, roots and belonging. She had become a strong, coping person through long experience of having to cope, but had pushed away her own neediness by making sure that there were a number of people and animals around her who needed more than she did, or so she believed. She felt unable to find the strength to rebuild her life. The workshop helped by giving her a different way of looking at herself, through the image she captured with the drawings of an abandoned child, and she began to think about how she could get long-term help to support her both through the practical changes and also through the exploration of this new self-image.

One of the topics which is discussed frequently in the workshop is the fear of being alone. A woman may separate but both she and her partner maintain contact without being quite sure why. The contact is not usually very satisfying; neither seems to know quite where they are going, but it is better than making the separation clear. Or is it? Women in this position often feel stuck and uncomfortable. Hearing about other people's lives helps to reassure the woman that she is not strange or abnormal in finding the separation slow and difficult. On the other hand, it is also important to look at what might be getting in the way which is preventing her from acting on the decision to separate. Perhaps there is still a hope that the partner will change. Often women come to the workshop wanting to try to work through the difficulties with their partner but the partner resists going for help as a couple. If the woman grows and moves, she will eventually be challenged by her own emotions into making a decision about whether to stay in the relationship. What will she do if her partner does not want to change their relationship, does not want to talk about the problems? She will ultimately have to take a decision for herself and keep some trust in her sense of what she needs to do.

Sarah had been aware of problems between herself and her husband for a number of years. She had tried to talk about her feelings of unhappiness but had resisted moving from her marriage, partly because her husband refused to talk about their difficulties and partly because she had two young children. She had only been separated for a few weeks when she came to the workshop and was very tearful and raw. She had had to face her husband moving to live with a new partner, but paradoxically she had surprised herself by finding extra energy which was released by no longer being so stuck. She had felt a strength she was not aware she had. She described well a pattern which seems common between couples. Each partner tends to adopt certain roles, and in the expression of emotions and feelings it seems that the woman is the more open partner. The women often describe their partner as having difficulty in sharing what they feel and also in accepting the woman's feelings. Both partners polarise, the woman becoming more and more emotional, until she sees herself as being 'out of control'. The man withdraws, rejects her, and her emotional energy is drawn into trying to provoke a response. The polarising pattern is not exclusive to heterosexual relationships. Lesbians have also described similar patterns between themselves and their partner.

In this pattern, neither partner is going to get the response they are seeking. They are caught in a ritual of provocation and withdrawal. A woman trapped in this will probably be feeling very bad about herself, have an image of herself as a screaming harridan. If she can look more coolly at what she is really trying to express, she has the possibility of transforming her words into something which might be heard by her partner.

She may have a long history of 'not saying'. Other women in the workshop can help by giving some feedback about the way she expresses herself, allowing her a kind of rehearsal so that she can try to say what she wants in a different way. Many women have talked about the difficulty they have in finding some middle path between hysterical, angry outbursts and saying nothing at all. Feeling physically more relaxed and solid helps us to be more assertive and I sometimes use simple bodywork exercises to explore how women hold themselves back, how they restrict their movements and their voices. The way a woman uses space with her body and the fullness of her voice tends to reflect the amount of space she allows herself to take up in a relationship. If we are under stress, we express that in the way we hold our bodies: we raise our shoulders, hunch our backs, tighten our necks. If these tensions continue over long periods of time, we can develop physical problems, illnesses or stiffness in the joints, for example. The release of physical tension and emotion can enable us to relax and respond more flexibly to difficulties in our lives.

Particularly towards the end of the workshop, when we talk about loss, some women express as a loss all that was never said in a past relationship, all the resentment still buried. Margaret, a woman in her fifties, began to talk about how angry she had been with her first husband. Her anger was not only with him but with herself. She had allowed him to define what gave her pleasure sexually. He had told her that she was abnormal to want to masturbate while making love and she had accepted that and carried the anxiety for a long time. She had resolved it for herself some time before, but she still had a sense of loss that something had been taken away from her. She took the risk to talk about sexuality in the group, which freed others to talk too. There was relief in the group; we laughed at the absurdity of taking our sexual identity from a man. But we had all done something similar in one way or another. Margaret was still carrying some resentment and anger because she had complied.

In coming to the workshop a woman has taken a step towards being more active in facing her difficulties. Perhaps in the past, she has accepted the passive, receptive aspect of being female and projected the assertive, masculine aspect of herself on to her partner. Listening to other women in the group is a forceful reminder that each woman has both qualities within her. She is capable of taking decisions for herself and she can touch a buried part of herself which feels a great deal and has a lot to say. She can begin to acknowledge new strengths in herself.

I find this workshop difficult to run. It is painful, but often very moving. It is also exciting, because it focuses on a crisis point, an opportunity for change. The change cannot happen in one volcanic eruption, but small beginnings can be made. Ultimately we have to learn to live with ourselves and our own fears, and that can take for ever.

Some women are in a lot of pain when they come, and part of my role is to help the group support and contain those very painful feelings. Learning not to be afraid of another's tears and anger is an important element of the workshop. Sometimes the work has been fruitful enough and the contact between the group members safe enough to encourage them to continue to meet together as a self-help group.

One woman brought a problem to the workshop which was rather different. She had lost a very important relationship, the best she had had, she said. She was a strong woman, had a satisfying life in many aspects, but her partner had felt overwhelmed by her emotions, by her expressiveness and power as a woman. Where did she go wrong? she said. What could she do? None of us could answer except with our support and recognition. It is dangerous to express such a full range of emotions. It disrupts an ordered world. We cannot deny our strength and power, but we may threaten what we most want – an intimate relationship. I do not know the answer to that dilemma. If I did, I probably wouldn't be running this workshop.

# Part Four
# Our Bodies

# 11
# Bodywork

## Birgitta Johansson, Amelie Noack
## and Viqui Rosenberg

In order to write this section we have looked at our different approaches to body therapy and have found a common core of understanding based on a feminist perspective and neo-Reichian theory, namely one which incorporates psychotherapeutic insight rather than dealing simply with the body, as is the case with the Alexander technique.

The shape of our body and its habitual posture store information about how we feel and about our early experiences. Physical awareness and its ensuing loosening of chronic tension can release emotion and help to re-establish a sense of well-being. Women often have a specific range of physical sensations which bear the mark of their culturally determined role. Exhaustion, depression and disconnection from the body are the most common complaints from women attending our programme.

As workshop leaders we are often expected to respond to the high expectations of women to be seen, heard and given attention. But these expectations may also be accompanied by a paralysing fear of what might happen: 'Will I be able to feel anything?', 'Do I have to reveal everything?', 'Can I allow another woman to touch me?', 'Will I like touching?', 'What will happen if I can't stop being upset?' The group has to become a safe 'home' where these fears can be shared and overcome in order to allow an exploratory attitude towards oneself and others.

The workshops that we each lead reflect our different trainings and also our different experiences of how our own fears and expectations have been met in the past. For in working with the body it is essential to have participated in everything we ask other people to do; and also to be sure of our ability to deal with the problems that may arise when long-held tensions begin to dissolve.

Exercises which introduce bodywork to a group should not be presented at random but should arise from the therapeutic situation.

It is necessary to keep in mind the physical and psychological needs of the participants as well as the particular stage of individual and group development. The group leader needs to anticipate the sadness, anger, surprise or relief that may be triggered by a certain exercise and be prepared to give time and support to every woman who needs it. Any connection between body and psyche that group members become aware of should be talked about so that the experience can be understood and digested. To leave a group mystified or fearful of their bodies is a counterproductive experience which only reinforces already present blocks.

Very strong emotions sometimes emerge when muscular tension is released. Hyperventilation may occur as a shallow breathing pattern is modified. This can be frightening and occasionally dangerous if the group leader is not emotionally available as well as technically equipped to contain the distressed person and ground her back into reality. As a general rule, the sort of movement and exercises that are best done in a group with no specific skill in bodywork are those which depart the least from everyday adult experience, such as running, dancing and massage. Situations that are likely to recall childhood experiences and thus to unearth buried feelings should not be attempted without an experienced leader. Deep breathing should not be encouraged except when it comes as a spontaneous response to increased energy expenditure.

The work described in this chapter aims at creating an understanding that will integrate intellectual, emotional and physical levels. Emotion and physical experience always go hand in hand. Emotion is always felt in the body. Our intention is to offer a language and a matrix where physical experience is not just tolerated but invited, elicited and encouraged to find expression. Speech is also used, but it often comes later as a mediator and communicator of meaning. Bodywork functions very much on a pre-verbal or non-verbal level. Experiences are difficult to put into words; this chapter is an attempt to find words for what happens, but we are aware of the limitations. However, to some women body workshops provide an experience that becomes part of their personal history in a more vivid and tangible way than words ever could.

## The Value and Relevance of Bodywork

Bodywork offers a good counterbalance to the normal over-emphasis on the mental life of Western women and men. It helps one to live 'in the body'.

Our attitudes to touch and physical contact are primarily connected with the very basic experience of how our mother touched us when we were babies and how we felt about it. As women, our early relationship with our mother influences not only how we feel later about our own bodies but also how we feel about ourselves as women. Conversely, our relationship with father provides the basic experience of the 'other' and everything that is strange and foreign to us. Since the experience of our bodies is so closely connected with mother, bodywork brings us back into contact with mother, not only our personal mother but also our capacity to mother and nurture ourselves. In this way we can learn to like and to love ourselves.

Bodywork also therefore puts a person in contact with feminine values. This is as much the case for men as for women, since men are mainly brought up by women too, and also learn for the first time in this early relationship how to feel about their bodies. However, nurturing and mothering describe only one aspect of the feminine qualities inherent in bodywork.

Another aspect is provided by the wisdom of the body: if one learns to listen to the messages of the body, a whole new realm of experience opens up. The body's intuition tells us very distinctly how to respond to a particular person or problem. To illustrate this we could mention one basic model of body therapy, which differentiates the body into the three areas of head, heart and belly: if you find a person intellectually stimulating, you respond on the head level; when you fall in love, you feel touched on the heart level; and when a person attracts or repels you, you respond physically with your belly, on a gut level. This may seem a simple model but it helps us to differentiate between people we like to be touched by, and in what way, and those we don't. Recognising our impulses helps us to find out what we want.

A third aspect of bodywork is to find the key to unlock the power, strength and energy which is contained in our physical impulses. For example, many people repress the impulse to strike out when they are angry. We don't suggest that they actually hit someone but that they allow themselves to feel the energy in the impulse rather than repressing it. In the workshop we may well suggest that they hit a cushion in order to experience their own strength. In this strength is contained our full potential and our creativity, and it provides the fuel and driving force for action. By using this energy we can learn to express what we want physically and verbally and to act upon it.

The fourth aspect of bodywork is the body's quality of uniqueness and wholeness. No body is like another. Everybody's body has its own beauty and ugliness. Every body is complete in itself – a balanced unity, even when compensating, e.g. lopsided hips with opposite lopsided shoulders. The body in this sense is an image for the completeness and wholeness of a person.

All these aspects also have a dark, threatening side. The sensations of the body can become overwhelming and terrifying: hunger can turn to greed; the feeling of bodily individuality can change into one of being distant, alone or abandoned; our impulses can become destructive or lead us compulsively in directions we don't want to go in. Working with the body reveals the meaning of these attitudes and helps to change them if we want to.

## Our Bodies Reflect our Past

Not everything we feel is acceptable to others or to ourselves. This creates conflict and is a problem, particularly in childhood. A child experiencing angry feelings and destructive fantasies cannot easily distinguish between the relative safeness of the fantasy and the danger and violence of acting it out. Imagining that we were attacking mother was then virtually the same as having killed her. It was threatening to her and to ourselves. We preferred to stop feeling in order to avoid fear, pain and guilt.

Wanting too much, needing something different from what is offered, the desire to devour or to reject – are all feelings experienced by a child as intrinsically destructive drives that should be suppressed. Emotions are expressed physically: crying when we are sad; starting when we are suddenly frightened; hitting and kicking when we are angry. In order to avoid feelings, we try to keep the body under control.

Breathing becomes a very important instrument of this control, due to its unique relationship to the nervous system. On the one hand, breathing is a totally spontaneous and involuntary function similar to the heartbeat; it happens independently of our consciousness. On the other hand, we can produce changes of rhythm and depth at will; we can even stop breathing voluntarily in the same way as we consciously manage our movement and speech functions. Breathing is also a unique bridge between the inside and the outside of our bodies. When we breathe in, we take air from our environment into ourselves; as we breathe out we let go of it. Reducing this action, or slowing it down, has the overall effect of diminishing the exchange between the inner and the outer world. It helps us to feel less and to express less. It constitutes a trend towards shrinking and contracting, and freezes the traffic of being alive. As a natural consequence of this process, there follows a restriction of movement and sound.

The reduction of breath also affects other areas of the body. These areas are usually functionally related to the emotion that we were seeking to suppress: e.g. the arms may become stiff and weak as an avoidance of experiencing the need to hold and the desire to grab; or we may develop a tight jaw that closes the mouth to counterbalance the wish to bite and shout. In this way whole sets of muscles and tissue become rigid and therefore starved of oxygen. These areas of the body are then unavailable for sensation and incapable of any free movement.

Over the years these holding patterns get frozen into characteristic postures and gestures, like an armour of muscular tension surrounding the body. Flexibility and responsiveness still lie beneath this heavy coat, but they are very often perceived as alien and dangerous, since they are still unconsciously associated with fears experienced during childhood. The process that has affected the body runs parallel and is in every way equivalent to what has happened to the psyche: protective patterns have been established in order to avoid pain; they have eventually become mechanical and are no longer related to the initial originating cause. In this process the physical and the psychic levels reinforce each other in building defensive blocks. For example, for a person who feels she has always to stay in control, even letting her head drop can feel like a frightening loss of control.

Thus the most traumatic experiences of childhood seem to be mapped out in the body as well as in a person's attitude in dealing with the world. A person struggling with unresolved and suppressed fear reacts very often to situations as though they represent a threat. The body posture may include eyes wide open, hunched shoulders, a pale complexion and difficulty in breathing out: as though the person is permanently startled by danger that no longer exists. Another person who experienced early sexual feelings as frightening and undesirable may have developed a rigid pelvis with unexplained adiposity around the hips and a difficulty in giving or receiving sexual tenderness.

## Restoring the Link between Sensations and Feelings

The body-therapeutical approach focuses on the blocked flow of energy in the body. The aim is to resolve barriers and release blockages in two main ways. First, by increasing the charge in a particular area or in the body as a whole in order to energise the whole system. This is done until the process reaches a climax which leads naturally on to a discharge of energy: a kind of explosion. Exercises like the bioenergetic stress positions are designed and can be used in this way.

The second way is to try to make a person aware of their personal way of taking in energy, containing it, building up a charge and finally letting this energy flow into self-expression: a model of pulsation. It follows the rhythmic process of organic life and facilitates the natural movement of physical and emotional expression. Expression will occur when the person is open to letting it out. It is a self-regulatory process which is brought forward, and put into movement spontaneously, when the time is ripe for it to happen. For example, a person who is angry could become aware of the impulse to strike out and contain it consciously to discover that it changes into a desire to reach out.

The first way aims at discharge and the freeing of emotion; the second aims at the intake and new orientation of energy in a way which fosters internal growth and doesn't show in a dramatic outburst of energy. Breathing exercises can be used in this way. Full and regular breathing adds to the vitality of the body. It feeds the body with energy. This energy can be directed into any part of the body. Tension and pain can be released through the nourishment of the painful area with fresh oxygen. This can happen through exercises on this area of the body, like massage, movement or shaking.

Another way of raising the energy level is to support the breathing process by consciously directing our awareness into the respective area. This is done by thinking about the movement of the air through windpipe and lungs, the transfer of oxygen to the blood and its transport to the particular part of the body. Changes take place in corresponding parts of the nervous system, and at the same time circulation in the area is increased, i.e. fresh oxygen is brought there and more waste products can be taken away. This is often accompanied by tingling sensations.

If the intake of air is increased, some people may have feelings of sickness or nausea, especially those who have a block in the neck area. Here a very careful and gradual approach has to be used, teaching these people to allow their breathing to become more full step by step.

Breathing especially affects the stability and posture of the spine, since the main muscles of the respiratory system are connected to the cervical and lumbar vertebrae. Back trouble is therefore very often connected with tension in the lower back due to insufficient breathing.

Deep breathing is then needed involving the movement of the diaphragm and the lower belly. One deep breath here can by itself bring up feelings of pleasure or resentment or disgust connected to childhood experiences of a too rigid toilet training or repressed sexuality.

Another way of restoring the link between the physical and the emotional are relaxation exercises. During relaxation breathing becomes slower and deeper and the mind gradually becomes freer from concentration on outer events. The activity of the brain changes. It shows the brainwave pattern called the 'alpha' state, a very calm but alert state of mind and body. During relaxation the sympathetic nervous-system, which deals with outer activity, the day's work and emotions, is at rest. The parasympathetic nervous-system now directs the work of the inner organs of digestion and slows the organisms down. Such a relaxed state allows a reconnection between the inner and the outer world. Experiences can be processed and rearranged as in sleep, but this happens now with some kind of awareness. Through the connection of outer and inner, relaxation also provides a means for regression. Childhood experiences and memories may come up and corresponding feelings be re-experienced. In this way we can begin to remember our conscious selves with parts that seemed to be long lost and forgotten. For example, a woman started to cry during a relaxation exercise. She experienced feelings of utter loneliness that she remembered from her childhood and a new sense of being with somebody while this was happening.

Bodywork as a whole is a facilitator for the self-regulatory processes of the body and the psyche. It reconnects us with our past, our feelings and our energies, and teaches us to go with the flow of these energies so that we can learn to rest when we are tired and to dance when we are happy.

## Our Experience in the Workshops

We would like to show how we see these ideas working out in practice in our workshops.

First, Birgitta will give a general picture of the way in which childhood experiences emerge in adult behaviour, using examples from her workshop. Second, Amelie will present her Relaxation and Movement workshop, including an account from a group member. Third, Viqui describes her Bioenergetics workshop, followed by a detailed account of the mirror exercise she uses in the workshop.

*Birgitta:* Writing this, for instance, I feel tension and restlessness in my knees. Knees and ankles are very much in focus for a six-year-old child as she jumps, climbs and learns to keep her balance. When I was put in a classroom at the age of six and had to sit still, I was forced to give up many of my physical needs. I still feel restricted today whenever I have to sit still for a long time.

Another example is the baby sucking at the breast or bottle but feeling frustrated or insecure due to circumstances between her and her caretaker. In the workshop, there may be women whose cheeks feel loose and dead and who have a constant look of sadness on their faces. We decide to work with it. I explain about early frustrations around feeding and feeling insecure during the first months of life. The group is then encouraged to remember what they have been told about their early feeding. We then touch our own cheeks and pull faces. If we feel safe enough we can allow some of that early sadness to come to the surface – by holding our cheeks or by being touched on the cheeks by another woman in the group.

Let a year pass and the baby is a toddler who wants to investigate her home and her family through touching everything with her hands. Perhaps she is stopped from touching anything but her own toys. Years later this woman might be in a group. She has developed extreme tension in her hands, combined with a feeling of fatigue and powerlessness in her arms. It's as though her hands and arms are saying, 'I want to touch and find out, but I shouldn't – it's bad.' Her hands are still fighting with the impulse to touch and hold. The tension in her fingers expresses the conflict between wanting to reach out and having to hold back. The powerlessness in her arms can be understood as giving up trying altogether.

We talk about this in the group. I point out that in general girls are stopped more from using their arms than boys are. We do exercises on pulling and pushing each other in order to become more aware of our hand and arm muscles. Massaging another woman's hands is also a good way of focusing on lost opportunities. It allows the hands to be sensuous and alive again.

Another important example of lost opportunities can be traced in the legs and feet. For a small child it's such a nice sensation to start standing up, to stand without support and to walk in the direction she chooses for herself. Imagine the child's frustration if she is lifted off the ground and carried around at a time when she is struggling to stand on her own feet. She may also have been confined in a small space for too long and too often. And perhaps she was constantly pushed in a pram, because the grown-ups got impatient with her slow pace. Exercises like firmly standing on the ground are very useful here. Feeling well planted on the ground also gives you the confidence to manage a task alone and to face any situation without immediately wanting to run away.

These examples may seem obvious. The point I'm trying to make is that particular parts of our bodies are in developmental focus at certain phases in our early life. It is very important not to interfere with the muscular learning processes while they are happening. The role of a body-therapist is to stimulate a general body-awareness, as well as to help a woman connect her tension or slackness to a specific phase in her past. If you are aware of what you missed earlier, it's easier to complement that today.

At this point in my writing I get restless again, so I go into the garden and clean out the drains. I have to eat and I also drink constantly while writing. Mapping out developmental ideas seems to trigger off endless needs for distraction. Is this a clue to what happened to me as a small child? Was I distracted too often when I needed to sit by myself and concentrate? It seems to be such a familiar theme among women: to be distracted and interfered with without any regard to our need to develop in our own time.

But let us go back to a very early age. Between five and eight months of age we start to lift the neck really high and roll over on to the stomach. This allows a new experience of space and depth. The back now becomes important. Before, most of our needs were satisfied from the front of our bodies. But now, if we have been satisfied and feel safe enough, is the time to flick over without anxiety. Through rotating the back the baby is also preparing to start crawling and walking. Knowing that so many women complain about tension and pain in the back, let us have a look at its psychophysical meaning.

The back may show signs of stress, aches and involuntary tension or slackness. For instance, a woman with a very stiff posture shows that she is holding herself up at any cost. In her way of carrying her back you can sense that she is trying to control and that she is doing this with intimidating efficiency. This woman cannot relax or relate to others on an equal level. She cannot give in to pleasure easily. Her back is carrying and expressing all her losses, setbacks and unfulfilled needs from earlier phases in her life. Now she is determined not to be overpowered again and not to feel what she has lost – perhaps she is trying not to feel at all. If the muscular system in your back becomes tense and aching – due to inhibitions, fear and other constraints in early life – then movement and feelings become inhibited too.

On the other hand, a back may feel like collapsing and look jelly-like with no will to hold you up. The world seems too heavy a weight on your shoulders, you cannot keep up with the pressures, your head drops and your back slopes. Those of us who have worked in or visited mental institutions, old people's homes and prisons are surely familiar with this physical expression of total hopelessness. The resigned neck and back tell us about a person who has been fighting for mental survival for years, but has met too many disappointments and setbacks to feel any impulse to continue the struggle.

One way of approaching the problem and helping backs which have suffered like this is to start again like a baby. In the group the women are asked to lie on the floor on their back. They gently rock from side to side until they feel the impulse to roll over to one side or the other and then back again. The goal is to create a sensation of safety at a tempo which suits each person. Another very relaxing exercise is to sit with your back against another woman's back. You let the other take the weight of your own back and allow yourself an experience of comfort and support. The role of carrying the other can, on the other hand, bring you in touch with feelings of having to carry too much responsibility without being able to ask for help.

Every healthy woman experiences muscular tensions that come and go with the stresses of daily life. We are all familiar with them and we all know the relief of changing a working position, like doing some physical exercise as an antidote to sitting down. We may also have a sauna or ask someone to massage our shoulders. But here we are dealing with muscular tension and slackness which cannot be controlled voluntarily. These pains, tensions and muscular deadnesses say a lot about both our shortcomings and our resources.

To give one last example: in the group a woman complains about fatigue and tension around her mouth. In letting the whole group tense the lips and clench the teeth we work out the problem. This woman was never allowed to answer her parents back. If she did she was ignored or humiliated. She learned to hold back any attack, rather like biting herself, rather than risk being heard and misinterpreted or ridiculed. In drawing attention to her mouth she gradually got a stronger sense of her own rights and could also let her lips become more sensuous.

When we ignore the fine impulses our bodies give in order to regulate our behaviour and emotions, we put ourselves in danger of permanent damage. Persistent neglect of physical impulses can lead to irritability, headaches and sleeplessness. Eventually a whole pattern of 'emptiness' is established, connected with feelings that something is wrong or that something important has been forgotten. It is easy to use cigarettes, too much food, alcohol or tranquillisers to dull the emotions so that you become out of touch with your feelings and your body.

## Relaxation and Movement Workshop

*Amelie:* The workshop usually begins with a breathing exercise. We sit down in a circle with closed eyes and let the breath flow naturally. That helps to calm down, to centre and to really 'arrive' in the group.

Then everyone answers the two questions: 'Why did you choose to come to this particular workshop?' and 'What do you expect?' I like to have this information to get a feeling of who is in the group and how everybody feels.

I normally have a structure outlined for the day, but I also like to work with whatever arises in the group, so I change the structure whenever it feels appropriate. The answers to my introductory questions range from: 'I don't expect anything in particular' or 'It's my birthday present to myself, I want to spend a nice day,' to 'I finished a long-term relationship last week, I feel desperate and want to sort myself out.' The answers given provide the basic individual material which will be around for the whole weekend.

After this we will have a game, learning each other's names, to get to know the women in the group and to make first contact with each other. With that the introductory part is at an end.

Everybody stands up now and we begin with loosening up. Exercising each part, we work slowly through the whole body upwards. A crucial point is the relaxation of the neck area. Some women begin to feel dizzy or light-headed and need to sit or lie down. We talk about it and find out that it is very difficult for them to let go. They feel that they need to keep their heads up and to be in control. The talking and the lying down I understand as grounding; it is necessary to counterbalance the fear of losing control.

Now I use some gentle but rhythmic music and ask people to move their bodies keeping the feet firmly rooted on the ground without moving them. Afterwards there is space for sharing the feelings about it, like feeling trapped or safe and so on.

Then every woman is asked to find a place in the room where she feels comfortable lying down. A deep relaxation exercise follows, 'The journey through the body'. It takes 20 minutes and focuses on every single part of the body one after the other. At this time a woman sometimes begins to cry silently. Feelings of sadness, connected perhaps with childhood experiences of loneliness and the relief of allowing herself to let go, find an expression in tears. It is important to watch and to support this process, if necessary perhaps by holding the woman's head. Talking is not necessary, only a sense of being there with the person. When the exercise is ended people are encouraged to take some deep breaths, to stretch and to yawn until all are ready to sit up again.

Without talking in between the next exercise is announced, a breathing exercise in a sitting position: the emphasis is put on secure contact between the bottom and ground and an upright spine. I introduce the image of a plume of feathers coming out of a point in the middle of the head and reaching towards the ceiling; there it will draw circles or other patterns. This is done for three to five minutes while breathing naturally.

Afterwards I ask every woman to find a symbol for how she is feeling at this moment; it can be an image, a word or a colour, and I encourage everyone to take seriously what comes up first. Everybody briefly describes what symbol they have chosen. Without interpreting or talking about them we break for lunch.

The afternoon begins with another lying-down relaxation exercise, something which helps to digest food and also gathers and collects energy again. With stretching and yawning everybody 'wakes up' refreshed for the afternoon's work.

We stand in a circle again and the women are asked to connect again with their symbol from the morning. To the sound of some gentle and soothing music, everyone together now puts their symbol into movement in a dance. It is a very personal dance, which allows each woman to express and explore her feelings about her symbol, and may open up an initial understanding of its meaning. Afterwards every woman draws on a big sheet of paper her symbol and her experience with it. Sitting down together now, every woman gets as much time as she wants and needs to talk about her drawing and her experience. The positive and negative aspects of relaxation are then talked about, fear of letting go being one of the main problems. Connections are made with everyday life, like lying down for five minutes when tired, and problems are related to their roots. This part of the day I see very much as psychotherapeutic work – not just talk or advice about the exercises but an attempt to raise formerly unconscious feelings (in the drawing or from the dance) into conscious awareness. Group members normally benefit a lot from it.

To close the first day of the workshop we stand in a circle, alternating between letting ourselves fall back into the circle to be carried by the whole group and coming back to stand on our own two feet.

I like to give the group something to work on till the next day, such as remembering what happened during the day and repeating the journey through the body before going to sleep.

The second day begins with the opportunity to share what has happened since the day before and to ask questions. This feedback is very important. It helps people to realise how much relaxation affects us in our everyday environment. Some women develop physical symptoms like headaches or sickness, especially women prone to migraine. Others respond with extreme tiredness. The first day of relaxation may have brought to the surface long-covered-up psychological conflicts and problems.

I am very aware that I will not be able to deal with all the material which is mentioned during the rest of the day. Nevertheless, it is important to listen to everybody carefully. It gives me the opportunity to point out particular issues to certain women. I might point out to a woman that she seems to have an unconscious tendency to depression. I might even suggest that she go into therapy if it feels appropriate. It also helps me to structure the day of the workshop which is still to come.

Sometimes this initial sharing and discussion leads to individual work. Once, one woman had developed a migraine during the first day of the workshop. She was willing to work with me individually, and through a gentle massage I tried to release the pressure at the base of her skull. Issues came up to do with being touched and letting her head drop connected with feelings of fear and utter sadness alternating with anger. We looked for connections in her present life and earlier experiences. The migraine didn't go, but the feeling of depression which she normally experienced alongside headaches was lifted. Both could be related to her suppressed, that means 'depressed', knowledge about things in her life that she was afraid to look at.

The feedback of other group members showed that they had got a lot out of this through observing what was happening. Interestingly enough, in this particular group there were four other women who also often suffered from headaches or migraine.

I like to use relaxation in a twofold and balanced way: both to open up and explore unconscious feelings, and as a quietening and calming method, to build a refuge and provide a resting-place in times of turmoil and upheaval. To achieve this I use relaxation exercises which focus on boundaries, bodywork and talking to strengthen the sense of self.

If there is no need or wish for individual work, the whole group gets on with bodywork after the feedback round, starting with the shaking off of tension. This time we begin with the hands and work downwards towards the feet. Afterwards each woman explores her 'personal space' through stretching. I introduce the concept of a space bubble surrounding each person; the boundaries of the bubble can be defined by the outermost limits of the outstretched arms. The exploration and experience of this individual space surrounding the body is for some people their first encounter with and definition of their psychological boundaries. The boundaries are not physical, but nevertheless they can be experienced and perceived – a realisation that often produces feelings of satisfaction and relief, though it can also be felt as isolation and abandonment.

The sense of containment is amplified through walking around the room while being aware of one's own space. Distance and closeness to other people are observed as well. Then we have some music with a clear beat, where everybody is encouraged to explore and use their personal space freely and creatively. In the movement it becomes apparent how helpful and relaxing the clear definition of boundaries can be for some women. Afterwards we share briefly our feelings about the exercises and relate needs for distance and closeness to personal history.

The afternoon of the second day begins with a breathing exercise in a big circle. After this we go on working in pairs; this is only possible on the second day, I believe – now we know each other a bit better and we have developed some trust.

One woman lies down and allows herself to be fully relaxed. The other begins to play with arms and legs, moving them gently about and relaxing every limb through stretching. She lifts the head just a tiny bit and holds it for a while. She does the same with the feet, pulling them gently. Then she puts her hands on particular parts of the body which her partner indicates: a relaxation which works through the warmth and the caring contact of another person. Without talking they swap roles. Finally, both women have time to share their experience with each other.

After a short break the final part of the workshop begins. We sit again in the big circle with closed eyes and centred inwards, breathing with awareness for a couple of minutes. Then I ask some questions: 'What have you experienced yesterday and today?', 'What have you gained?', 'What have you lost?' I ask the women to draw their answers, this time accompanied by a meditative piece of music. Afterwards we share what we have drawn with the group and, if appropriate, refer back to the first picture from the day before. This is the time on the second day when each individual woman can have as much time as she needs to express herself and to focus on the issues which have come up for her during the workshop. Sometimes a woman is only now able to relax, to let go, to show a tiny bit of her inner self and to share it with the others. One woman who had been quite angry with herself during the workshop, because she felt unable to cry, burst into tears when the meditation music began to play – and felt very happy about it.

We finish the day by standing in the big circle again. We say goodbye to each other silently. Then each of us takes one step backwards out of the circle, a step out of the group, back into her everyday life.

## Relaxation and Movement – an account by a group member, Maddy Paxman

Arriving at a group workshop is always an anxious moment. What sort of people are there? You shyly put out feelers to the other women – over the course of the weekend you are likely to reach a certain intimacy with them, sharing deep feelings and opening up parts of yourself that you usually keep hidden. You need to feel you can trust people and trust the workshop leader.

To begin with we went around the circle introducing ourselves and saying what we hoped to get out of the workshop, why we were there. Everyone was saying things about tense situations at home, at work, in relationships. Wanting to learn how to relax and cope. I said I had come because I tend to experience my body and my head as totally separate, and I want to try and integrate my feelings about them by doing bodywork. But I also identified with a lot of what the other women were saying, especially about being depressed and anxious, but covering it up with frenetic activity and setting goals for oneself all the time. Not really allowing yourself to feel things out. I felt as though we as a group were a huge mound of needs, appealing to the leader to soothe us and calm us.

We began with stretching exercises: working on individual parts of the body from the feet upwards, checking out how different they felt afterwards. One or two people started to feel a bit faint or sick – we were standing for a long time. I felt a bit queasy when we were given five minutes to roll our heads around in one direction. The leader dealt with this in an interesting way: she was caring, but pressed us to continue with the exercise and be very aware of *when* we felt bad and try to breathe deeply and relax into it. She talked about releasing the body's energy by moving parts we may have held tense for years! By the end we all felt lightheaded; we sat down and talked about our experiences. I liked having the space to say how I had felt.

I was still aware of some impatience in myself, the usual timetabling – 'If I get out of here at 4.00 I can do this and this . . .' – a sense that I was almost, though not quite, wasting time; being terribly self-indulgent, anyway.

The afternoon began with us lying on the floor and breathing, visualising energy flowing like heat through our bodies. The leader's calm voice led us through the exercises, and it was wonderful to lie there and be soothed by her voice. Often when I am tense or can't sleep, I try to do this kind of thing, but it is so much harder by myself. I get impatient and go too fast, or there is that constant stream of thoughts rattling away in one part of my mind. This time I almost drifted off to sleep several times, but when she said 'Come back to this room' we all became quite conscious again, and wondered if we had done the exercise wrong because we had relaxed so much! Then we did some breathing exercises standing up, to get the energy flowing.

Then something else began to happen. We lay down again and did an exercise which involved imagining a journey through the body from one foot to the other. For some reason I could only visualise a steel needle piercing through my leg; it was really uncomfortable. Concentrating on one side of myself made me feel totally unbalanced and disjointed. I found myself getting quite worked up, unable to listen to the leader's voice or to relax. I began to feel I was not achieving what I was supposed to, that the workshop was not helping me. Afterwards it took courage to say that it had made me feel bad and unhappy – everyone seemed content and calm. Then the leader put on music and asked us to put our feelings to the music, to dance. For me, music and dancing have to be happy. I felt immobile, and just hugged myself in a small ball. I was angry that people around me were happily swaying and moving in their own worlds, and relieved that one or two looked as uncomfortable as I felt. I was too self-conscious to get up.

The next thing was crayons and paper, which was great because I knew exactly what I wanted to draw – a big, red, jagged shape, like a star. I haven't felt before the need to put something down on paper like that, almost despite myself. Around the star I put an edge of icy blue and white, a cold front. We each talked about our drawings and the leader said mine looked like it had a frame around the star, to hold it in. I burst into tears and was finally able to talk about something that had been upsetting me for several days but which I had put aside for the purpose of relaxing. I wasn't sure if I was supposed to be letting out all this pain, but then a couple of other women also expressed their sadness and anger. There was a lot of empathy in the group, even from those who felt good.

I guess one thing I learned was that you can't relax when there are strong emotions that need dealing with. It's rather like trying to put a lid on a boiling stew – it'll just explode. Feeling calm and at peace has to do with more than learning the right breathing techniques; it has to do with giving yourself a bit of space to feel what's going on, taking care of yourself.

The second day was a calm and happier day for me. I knew I was still depressed, but the exercises we did made me feel warm and powerful. One I liked a lot was when we stood with our feet firmly on one spot and stretched our arms out all around to feel the boundaries of our space – as though we were in a bubble. Then we did this with music. When we lay down and did more of the journey through the body exercises, I experienced the same problem with the asymetrical ones, but this time it didn't make me sad, although at one point I had the sensation that I had totally dismantled one side of my body. I was able to deal with the discomfort and even learn from it.

The most powerful thing we did was on the Sunday afternoon. We got into pairs and we were quite shy because it was going to mean touching one another, which is always uncomfortable in our society. One person lay on the floor and the other lifted each limb and moved it around a little, lifted their head, their feet, as though they were a doll – then they sat for a while on the floor with their hands resting on the other person. It's hard to describe this in words – the sense of letting yourself go completely, not having to concentrate even on another's voice. Just being taken care of, manipulated and soothed by your partner. When it was my turn to do it to her I was amazed how pleasant it felt – not hard work. There was a tremendous flow of heat from her body to mine. It felt pretty sexual.

We finished off the weekend with another drawing. This time I drew a much softer, more swirly shape in pink and grey. Pink is a happy colour for me. I left the shape open-ended instead of closing it up. I really liked the drawing exercises, such a great way to express a mood.

I left feeling very relaxed – my body feeling rested and good. But it's amazing how tiring it is to relax for a whole weekend! Over the next couple of days I could feel the pain and stress reinvading me, and I tried to use the breathing patterns a little, although it was a lot harder outside the cosy group atmosphere. In actual fact I came to a couple of important decisions that weekend and had the sense that I had opened up ways of thinking in some part of myself, ways of listening to my needs. I hope I can at least hold on to that sense.

## Introduction to Bioenergetics Workshop

*Viqui:* Bioenergetics is a form of bodywork that lays particular stress on the release of energy blocks in the body. The weekend starts with a game to help learn everybody's name and then moves immediately into vigorous but unchallenging movements such as jumping or shaking, with the emphasis on loosening and allowing sound to come out. Talking about ourselves comes later, as this can be a threatening and anxiety-provoking situation for many women. The fact that it becomes easier to say who you are and what you want after the release of physical tension illustrates already some of the relevance of using bodywork in a therapeutic setting.

As the group comes back to sitting in a circle, there will be deeper breathing, some flushed faces and shared laughs. It is now time to focus on the individuals in order to create a personal commitment and an aim for the work in hand. The question to ask might be, 'What do you expect from this weekend?' The answers vary, of course, but for the majority they revolve around regaining contact with their bodies, stopping identifying only with their head, feeling their emotions. There is also a considerable list of aches and pains, tensions and numbnesses.

At the end of the round I answer questions about myself and the workshop. I also enquire whether anybody takes any medication or other drugs, whether there is any history of or recent breakdown (which I define as a prolonged inability to take care of oneself) and which group members are in ongoing therapy. All this information is of great importance when working with an open-enrolment type of group. The answers may mean changes in the general plan of the weekend in order to accommodate the needs of certain individuals.

I always suggest abstention from drugs such as alcohol, tranquillisers, sedatives and sleeping-pills during the weekend. Although I don't make this an imperative condition, all women so far have been willing and able to manage without them. And from later feedback I know that in at least two cases this was the beginning of giving up the drug. I have not had the same experience with cigarette smokers.

The rest of the morning is allocated to bodywork. I often start by asking people to walk around the room, and guide them through a detailed awareness of the way in which they place their weight on their feet, how they move their legs, how they tilt their pelvis, etc. This shows each individual woman as a constellation of tension and collapse. Awareness of the sensations triggered by their posture enables them to put into words the statements that their posture makes to themselves and others. Statements like, 'Don't look at me' or 'I can manage without you' seem to come spontaneously from the body, and these can be quickly understood by everybody. Very often these statements are of a defensive nature, and yet we live by them and shape our bodies to their command.

What follows is an exploration of how it feels to make an opposite statement about oneself; e.g. what it feels like to say 'Please look at me' or 'I can't manage without you', to find out more about what lies beneath tensions and contractions. The exercises aim to expand the breathing, release sound and facilitate emotional expression. Women are invited to find more words and new statements to make. These are often addressed to meaningful people in present life but eventually to important figures from the past, such as mother and father.

At this point we move into horizontal bodywork. This involves lying on the floor in order to contact a younger self and regress to a time in which legs were not for standing on. Lying down also allows people to cut off visually and forget the rest of the group in order to enter a more private world. Distress and anger usually surface during this period. My role here is to facilitate the expression of emotions that have been stored in a deaf-and-dumb fashion within the body. When allowed to unfold, they often give way to a less defined state in which it is possible to seek and find comfort and nourishment from another person and within oneself.

The afternoon is for sharing. Women are encouraged to talk about what they have experienced and how it relates to their present and past life. They are also invited to take things further with the undivided attention of the whole group. Not everybody wants this, and those who do are not always able to acknowledge it. This in itself raises issues for further work. But often two or three women will use the opportunity and, while working on themselves, they will also become a focus of identification and recognition for the rest of the group.

The day ends with the group dividing into pairs and giving each other a head massage or some other form of caring contact.

The second day follows a similar structure: the morning for vigorous and structured bodywork and the afternoon for individual therapeutic work. Activity is planned in relation to what has emerged so far. The work is either geared to feelings expressed during the previous day or will attempt to evoke what has been conspicuous by its absence – often anger and competitive feelings. Playing games can be a very useful way of starting the day. 'It', skipping or other games suggested by the group focus in a positive way a strength and power, something that so many women seem to have forgotten. I am always surprised by the physical skills that emerge when women recall their childhood. Running, jumping, pulling, balancing – all come naturally to many women who have otherwise allowed femininity or age to become a paralysing prison. Being physically spontaneous is associated with showing aggression and yet it should be noticed how often anger and laughter belong in the same wave of feeling. Yet the idea of being angry is usually connected with bleakness and destruction.

During the course of the morning more themes will come into focus to be developed in the afternoon. I organise this differently from the previous day by dividing people into groups of three or four and giving them the following instructions:

1   Each person has 40–60 minutes to themselves, according to the overall time available. She can do what she likes with the time, space and attention available. My suggestion is that she spend the first few minutes talking in order to define her present needs and that afterwards she remain quiet, just paying attention to her breathing and opening up to any spontaneous impulse within her.

2   The rest of the small group is there to facilitate. They are to watch, listen and feel before they become active. They are to support and to offer resistance, according to their sense of what is needed, avoiding words and trying to use their own bodies to communicate. However, talking should be used to check, request or halt any unhelpful situation.

3   I move around the small groups and can also be called for help and advice.

4   Everybody should remind each other to free their breathing.

5   Helpers should rely on their own feelings and intuition of what seems to be right.

Very deep and moving work is accomplished this way. Working in small groups offers a more intimate situation to women who may have found it too uncomfortable to be the centre of attention in the large group. This session also ensures that everybody will have had some individual space during the course of the weekend. In addition, many women discover their ability to empathise and to aid somebody else's therapeutic process.

The day ends with feedback from the small to the large group on what has been experienced and learned. One woman discovers that she can be angry and still be accepted by the group, another has dared to ask for contact as well as to state when she has had enough, another has become aware of how bad she needs to feel before she is able to do something about it.

The weekend draws to an end with an activity for the whole group which includes physical contact and a statement of what they have gained from the group.

## Mirror exercise

The large group is divided into small ones of three or four members. Everyone is asked to remain standing. After having decided who will work first, the group facilitator calls 'freeze'. While the person working (the subject) remains 'frozen', the rest of the small group observe her and eventually begin to mirror her posture. I suggest that this is done by starting with the feet and noticing how the weight is distributed on the legs. The mirrors gradually work their way up their own bodies, finishing with the facial expression. When everyone has got the image, the subject can relax and observe the mirrors for a while.

One by one the mirrors describe in detail what they are doing with each part of the body, what sensations they experience (including pain and pleasure as well as tension and collapse), what it is like for them to be in that position, what mood it produces, how it affects their breathing and their perception, and finally they look for a verbal statement that puts into words the physical attitude they are expressing. All this is done on the basis that the mirrors are not describing the subject, but merely how the body posture suggested by her makes *them* feel. It is hoped that some of their reflections will ring true for the subject.

Time is now given for discussion to assimilate what has emerged so far. It is particularly important for the subject to ask questions and to talk about herself and her attitude.

In the second part of the exercise, which follows after the talking, the whole of the small group returns to the original posture. Taking turns, each mirror explores movements that are inspired by the position. These often develop as counteractions to the tensions created by the original posture and indicate in a non-verbal way other aspects of the original posture. Sounds should be included as an integral part of each movement. Everybody in the group follows the person working and tries out what is being suggested. At the end of the round the subject can go through the movements that have been particularly useful, taking them further and sharing her thoughts about what has come up.

This whole structure is done once for each person. Given time for feedback from the small groups to the large group, a whole day should be allowed to take full advantage of the material that is likely to emerge.

## Conclusion

Body-awareness is something we all have. We develop it and achieve it through our senses. What we remember with our body we remember very well, positive experiences as well as negative ones. We are free either to recognise and use this knowledge or to hide and even deny it. Painful or frightening memories which had to be hidden from consciousness can be brought back safely by working with the body in a therapeutic way. In this chapter we have so far mainly talked about body-memories in connection with childhood. But other experiences such as our first menstruation and everything connected with puberty, adolescence and the menopause are equally important; as is how we experience our own sexuality, e.g. in relationships, which may include pregnancy and childbirth – our sexuality in all these fields is an expression of what we are.

It is particularly important for women to take their bodies seriously and to recognise their physical needs. In our society women's bodies are frequently used in an alienated and objectified way, e.g. in advertising. If *we* don't begin to see our bodies and ourselves in a different light, nobody else will do it! Bodywork offers women a different way of seeing their bodies; it helps us to come to terms with feelings of shame, resentment or awkwardness concerning our looks and the shape, smell and noises of our bodies.

We have learned to give and to care for others in our daily lives in such a way that this has become almost second nature to us. We often fail to notice when we are tired ourselves or when we need some exercise or friendly support.

Many of us are responsible for a job, a home and a family all at the same time. We exhaust our bodies, but at the same time feel the pressure not to show it. We may try not to get old or at least to hide any sign that we are ageing. Many of us have been taught to be quiet, passive and demure from very early on, but in all of us there is a voice that wants to be heard. Working with anger therapeutically can be a relieving experience, freeing us both physically and mentally, even if it is frightening at the start. If we discover our anger and learn to use it constructively, the restrictions put on us can be changed into boundaries against exploitation and objectification by others. We must learn not to regard our bodies as a system of bones and muscles that carry us around. The body is not a thing which I monitor for its shape and appearance, but my body is me and registers all my impulses. If we haven't learned to do so from early on, we have to learn later in life to act on the impulses that are truly felt in the body; then we cannot be manipulated against our own will. We can start to care for our own bodies and our own souls – at least as much as we do for others!

Body-centred therapies offer a method and a perspective to be acknowledged alongside other forms of therapy. They cater for similar needs as other therapies, but also have the very specific function of exploring the body in a structured and well-supervised way to counteract the fear and denial of the body and its expression in our Western culture.

Working with the body forces us to look at ourselves and our bodies; bodywork grounds what we are in physical reality and helps us to accept who we are, how we look and how we feel about ourselves. A woman's contact with her body we see as a basic requirement for being in touch with what she is herself.

Our sense of individuality is rooted in the body. And a woman's very personal view of her body is a symbolic expression for her sense of her own individuality.

# Part Five
# Running Groups

# 12
# Guidelines on Running Workshops
Sue Krzowski


## Why Workshops?

Before the women's liberation movement, most of us would have associated the word workshop with places where *men* worked, seriously practising their skills and crafts, usually in a very practical and material way, making and moulding in clay, wood, metal and stone the essentials of our day-to-day life.

As feminist therapists at the Women's Therapy Centre, we chose the word workshop to describe the work we were doing in another sphere, in the internal, psychological world. Therapy workshops are places where women work hard on themselves, finding out more about their emotional life, confronting aspects of themselves that they were unaware of or didn't like, learning new ways of dealing with their feelings and sharing this process in a group with other women (see Introduction).

As well as working with our bodies, the materials we work with are less tangible phenomena, such as thoughts, feelings, emotional patterns, defences, internal dynamics. We want this work to be taken just as seriously as work in the external economic world and, as a service, to be as accessible to as broad a range of women as possible. One of the most important conditions of the workshop programme is that women can refer themselves. They can choose and decide for themselves what they want to work on. The workshops offer a unique opportunity for women to get together to share their experiences about topics of deep concern to them, somewhere they can go to talk to other women about sexual jealousy, anger towards their children, menstruation, menopause, compulsive eating, self-image, where they won't be judged or labelled but where they can explore things at a deeper level than in consciousness-raising groups or by chatting with friends.

As we have said in the Introduction, workshops are different from discussion groups because they function at a feeling level and do not simply look at things intellectually. The purpose of the exercises is to help women get in touch with their emotional experience in a very immediate way. Workshops differ from ongoing therapy groups because they are short and time-limited, usually not more than eight weeks or sessions in all; the exercises promote or encourage feelings to be expressed rather than waiting for them to emerge more gradually as one might in an ongoing analytic group. The structure built into the workshops also contains and, to some extent, lessens the anxiety of a structureless analytic group.

Workshops have their limitations. You cannot change your life overnight, or in the space of a six-week group, but you can change a small aspect of yourself, or glimpse the possibility of doing things differently. A change in any part of a person's life will have an impact on the whole, like ripples on a pond. A process may be started that will carry on long after the workshop has finished. Structured groups are a very good way of doing short-term therapeutic work and can be applied in many different settings, including hospitals, residential homes and hostels, GP practices, community centres, educational institutions, women's centres, as well as in private practice.

## Leading a Workshop

It was when I first ran a training session for women wanting to lead experiential workshops that I actually sat down and thought about the process I go through when planning and running a workshop on any topic. This process has become even clearer in the subsequent Women's Therapy Centre training courses for workshop leaders that I have co-run with Vin Gomez. What I want to do in this chapter is to try and draw out some general guidelines for those workers who already have some basic group-work or counselling training and who have had some experience themselves of doing experiential group work or therapy. I think these two conditions are essential preparation for anyone wanting to do this work in a professional capacity. Although the focus of this chapter is on led groups, self-help groups may find some of the steps helpful.

### *Choosing a topic: what it means for you*
You may be approached as a worker by a group of women to run a workshop on a particular theme; you may work for an agency dealing

with a particular issue for women, such as abortion, which wants you to set up a group; or you may initiate a workshop on a topic that concerns you, knowing that other women will want to explore and work on that issue too.

When I think about the workshops that I have run, I know that it is my own interest and investment in that topic that has motivated me. That is when I work best. My richest source of knowledge and of insight has come from having struggled with an issue for myself. Once I have a sufficient understanding and grasp of its ramifications in my own life, I can feel free to listen to and work with other women's distress in connection with the subject. I remember running workshops for mothers and children when my own children were younger, and moving on to offer a workshop for mothers with adolescent children as they grew up and my own preoccupations changed. It is important for you to acknowledge to yourself your own investment in the topic you have chosen. What is in it for you? Look back and trace its history in your own life. Has it been a problem for you? How have you dealt with it? What is resolved? What do you still have difficulty with? Do you feel ready to help other women to focus on this topic? What do you hope to get out of the workshop?

## Brainstorming

Once you have located the topic in your own life, the next step is to locate it in a social, political and cultural context. What meaning does it have in women's lives? Where and how does it touch their lives? Is it important at a particular age? Does it affect a particular group of women? What difference do race, class, religion, sexual preference or physical disability make to the way in which women experience the issue? It is useful to do this exercise in a brainstorming session, i.e. write down as quickly and spontaneously as you can, off the top of your head, anything to do with the topic. Stereotypes, prejudices, common misinformation, media images and myths are all useful to consider as well as your more enlightened views, as it is the former that cause most distress when we inevitably internalise them. When you have finished your list, you can organise it and give it more thought. This is what other women will bring with them to the workshop.

## Your own skills and resources

The next step is to consider the relevant skills, knowledge and resources that you will bring to the workshop. Again, it may help you to make a list, as you probably know more than you think. We are so used, as women, to undervaluing ourselves! Resources can include your reflections on your own life experiences and development as a woman, your training in therapy, counselling or group-work skills, relevant reading and discussion around the topic. Consider what light your own theoretical perspective can shed on the topic and how it can help you to understand the issues. After the workshop, see how the material from the workshop informs your theoretical understanding. Does it confirm it, challenge it or enrich it? How can you use what you have learned as a resource for your next workshop?

## Co-leading

Another resource can be a co-leader who has more or different experience than you. A co-leader can give you support and confidence, and you can stimulate one another's thinking as you will have different skills, ideas and experiences to contribute, and different insights and perceptions about the group. To do this, you must be able to establish a good working relationship and be able to discuss openly any difficulties or conflicts that arise between you, whether they be your own personal feelings of competition, rivalry, differences of opinion, different ways of working or the projections of the group that you are picking up.

When I worked with a co-leader in a six-week group, we found that we worked at a very different pace. I ended up feeling that I was jumping in too quickly and cutting her out. I wished she would respond more quickly. She felt I was taking the words out of her mouth as she was about to say them and wished I would slow down. We both felt angry about it and after discussing whether I was jumping in out of anxiety and whether she could think more quickly, we adapted to a pace that suited us both. On another occasion, after a few attempts to work with a friend, we both agreed that some of the unresolved issues in our relationship were adversely affecting our work together. After a painful but constructive discussion, we maintained our friendship but decided not to co-lead groups.

There is an extended example of the process of co-leading in Jocelyn Chapman's and Amelie Noack's chapter on self-help groups. (See p. 210).

## Setting up the Workshop: Who is It For?

At the Centre it is our policy not to pre-select workshop members. This might seem risky to some, as they would be anxious about women attending the workshop for whom it is not appropriate because they are *so* distressed. We have not found it necessary to change this policy up to now, although some quite distressed women do attend. Perhaps the necessity of booking for the workshop in advance by filling out a simple booking-form and returning it selects out women who are not coping sufficiently with their lives to be able to do this. The women attend on a voluntary basis, although the workshop may have been recommended to them by their GP or social worker.

We aim to make the workshop programme as accessible to as many women as possible. Besides carrying out special advertising and outreach work in order to contact underprivileged groups, we have also begun a programme of awareness training for workshop leaders on various aspects of social oppression, such as sexism, heterosexism, racism and disability. These sessions are intended to increase the sensitivity and understanding of the workshop leaders to the needs of different women. For example, when talking about sexuality in a workshop it is important to acknowledge that the women's partner may be a man or a woman. A partner automatically and unconsciously assumed to be a he excludes the experience of any lesbians in the group and reinforces their social 'invisibility' and isolation. An exercise involving drawing will not be appropriate for a blind woman. The workshop leader would have to consider adapting the exercise, offering blind women an alternative medium, e.g. clay, or finding a completely different exercise which would serve the same function but which did not involve sight.

These are all issues that you need to consider when thinking about who will come to your group. How you advertise and publicise your workshop will largely determine who attends. You need to think about the group of women you want to reach and what their needs might be.

In order to include women who know nothing about therapy but who may benefit from attending the workshop, the language you use to describe it needs to be as simple and as accessible as possible Avoid using therapy jargon. Explain simply what you mean. Women with disabilities need information about disabled access. Where are the women you are trying to reach most likely to go for help or information on this topic? Various agencies and pressure groups have their own newsletters or information networks that you can use. Black women and women of colour have their own press and organisations. Health visitors, social workers, GPs and community workers have contact with women in different age-groups in the community and may be willing to refer women to your workshop.

If you wish to run a workshop in a hospital or residential setting, you may find yourself working with women who are not there on a voluntary basis. This is likely to be more difficult than working with a voluntary group. In a non-voluntary group it may take a lot of time to overcome mistrust, deal with resistance and help the group members find a reason of their own for working with you. Attendance may be poor and you may need support not to feel disheartened. On the other hand, it might be an opportunity to work with more distressed women who would feel too anxious, or be unable, to attend a workshop outside an institutional setting.

Leading workshops as part of your professional role in an institutional setting has its own complications. It may be difficult for leader and group members to switch from one mode to another inside and outside the group. Issues of confidentiality have another dimension if what happens in the workshop is to be written up in reports that others will have access to. Keeping the feelings that are expressed *in* the group from spilling over outside the group is much harder if the group remains in close contact after the workshop has finished, as they might in a residential home, for instance.

## The place
Again, when choosing the place to run your workshop, you must think of the needs of the women you want to work with. Does it have wheelchair access? Is it close to public transport? Is there a crèche? Ideally, the group needs a comfortable room, either with chairs or, if you prefer it, big cushions. Arrange the seating in a circle so that everyone can have eye contact and give one another attention. If you are going to do any exercises that involve movement or lying down, then make sure there is enough space for this. If the floor is not suitable, remember to ask the women to bring a blanket to lie on.

People will feel vulnerable in the group and will feel safer if you can ensure that the group is not interrupted by strangers, family, other staff members, etc. This may be more difficult in some organisations than others, but there is a good reason for it and it's worth trying to get other people's support and cooperation on this. This is where your own assertiveness skills come in! Ideally the room should be

soundproof enough for any noisy exercises or expression of feeling
not to disturb or distress others outside, and for group members to
feel that they cannot be overheard.

## Timing
You will need to consider what time of day will best suit your group:
day or evening, weekday or weekend, within school hours or after
school. Many women are afraid to go out alone after dark. Crèches
and nurseries are usually open in the daytime.

## What size group?
You will have to decide how many women you want to work with in
the group. We have found that around five is the minimum that works
well and that between seven and 12 is a good-sized group. Larger
groups can be worked with if there is more than one leader. If you start
with a very small group, then any absence is more of a threat to the
group. It also puts a different sort of pressure on the leader if, for
instance, only one or two women show up. It may feel more like an
individual counselling session.

## Working with mothers
When working with mothers, you need to consider childcare facilities.
As the workshop is a space for the mother to focus attention on
herself, having her children with her will usually be a distraction,
reinforcing what is already happening outside the workshop, where
she will probably be giving more attention to her family than to
herself.

On the other hand, the mother must not feel too anxious about
being separated from a very small child and may need to know that
she can be contacted if, e.g. the child is too distressed in the crèche. It
can be very useful to take this whole issue of separation and space for
oneself up in the group as a concrete example of the contradictions
mothers live with, and to use it to begin to focus on the mother herself.
Talking about the children may be a useful way of breaking the ice,
but it can quickly become a way of avoiding talking about oneself.
You may have to be very persistent on this point, gently but firmly
bringing the focus of attention back to the woman herself. Leave
plenty of time for settling children in the crèche and for picking them
up at the end of the session. A mother's day is organised very

differently from industrial time or an hourly work schedule. Small children's needs don't fit accommodatingly into hourly slots!

## Money

Working privately at home or for an organisation on a sessional basis raises the issue of your fee. Organisations may have a fixed rate or you may have to decide your own fee. If you are working privately at home, you will also have to decide how much to charge the women coming to the workshop. It is usually best, in any case, to decide how much you want to charge before you start negotiating, taking into account your preparation time, administrative hours, the cost of hiring a room, publicity, supervision, etc. Many women I have spoken to feel very anxious about valuing their skills in financial terms, especially as this kind of work has no concrete product to show, isn't easily measurable, feels like the 'invisible' work women are so used to not being paid for.

How much you charge for the workshop and where you publicise it will also influence who comes. If you want the workshop to be open to women on a low income, you could try to get funding. Alternatively, you could allow for some free or low-fee spaces for unwaged women when calculating the fee for your workshop.

## Supervision: Taking Care of Yourself and the Group

An integral part of your workshop planning should include provision for your own supervision and support. This is not a luxury but a necessity for running your workshop well. At the Centre, the workshop leaders have the chance to meet in a peer group to discuss their work. Individual supervision is also available.

Some topics arouse more anxiety and distress than others and you need to use your own judgment as to what you can confidently handle and contain. Supervision may cover any aspect of your workshop, from setting up the group, dealing with women who drop out, management issues and group dynamics to your own feelings and particular problems or crises that have arisen.

### Self-disclosure: talking about yourself in the workshop
This might be an issue for supervision. How much or how little is it

appropriate to talk about yourself in a workshop? There are a range of views on this, and you will see from these chapters that workshop leaders have dealt with the matter in different ways. Some would take the view that the workshop leader is in a very powerful position and that any revelations she makes about herself or feelings she expresses interfere with the other women's self-exploration. Women may feel that she has the 'right' way, or 'right' answers, and that they must be like her. Consequently, these leaders would say very little about themselves. On the other hand, some leaders would take the view that the leader should be willing to make herself as vulnerable as she is asking the group members to be. They would argue that it is important for her to model to the group members, for instance, that social taboos against speaking out about experiences of oppression can be broken, that difficult and painful feelings can be survived and that pride and joy are equally acceptable. Janet Hibbert's and Dorann van Heeswyk's Black Women's Workshop describes the importance of their acting as positive role-models, including within that modelling the taking of risks. Whatever the approach, it will arouse different feelings in different workshop members, and perhaps what is most important is to be able to acknowledge them and to explore the issues it raises for women, if necessary.

In any event, the workshop leader is maintaining an important balancing-act between keeping an open mind and the ability to respond spontaneously and, at the same time, hanging on to the capacity to think clearly in order not to over-identify and lose her usefulness. She must always keep in mind that as leader she has taken on the responsibility to provide a space for the women coming and that they may also be paying her. In most cases, it is inappropriate for the leader to take time for her own problems in a workshop, although it is essential that she does have some space, such as supervision, for her to explore her own feelings and reactions.

## Common group processes

Each group, however long or short, has a life of its own. This is the group process. Each group is different and unique. You can run 50 workshops on the same theme and the same issues will come up time and time again, but no two groups are ever alike.

Each woman brings to the group her own particular history and her own unconscious and conscious ways of being, and adds them to the collective pool.

As well as providing the structure as a way of focusing you also need to pay attention to the process, mood and needs of each particular group and to be flexible enough to respond to this in appropriate ways. Although the workshops are not analytic groups based on the use of transference interpretation, transference feelings will be aroused and projected on to the group and group leader, as Pat explains in the Introduction. Groups are fertile ground for re-creating family situations from our past. If these transference feelings become so strong that they start to paralyse the work of the group, then they need to be dealt with and understood in the group so that the group can unstick itself. As group leader you can use your supervision to understand what is going on in the group process that needs to be fed back into the group.

## Group process and group dynamics

As women work and share their feelings, they will recognise themselves in one another and realise their unity. At the same time their uniqueness and differences will in time become more strongly apparent. The differences are harder to expose and accept. Women are afraid to be different for fear of negative judgments and rejection. It is important for the workshop leader to support the recognition, acceptance and respect for these differences, especially where they are also the target of social oppression, as in the case of lesbianism, cultural origin, class, religion, etc. It is each woman's right to be treated with respect for whom she is in the workshop. In Chapter 5 Janet and Dorann give an example of one way of working with differences in the group between heterosexual women and lesbians when they noticed that oppressive attitudes needed challenging in the workshop.

## Dealing with criticisms or complaints

Dealing with criticisms or complaints about yourself as a workshop leader is a delicate issue. Most of us find it difficult or painful to be criticised. It may make us feel angry or defensive. It is important to listen carefully to the criticism and to hear it and to allow yourself the space to think about it and how you want to respond in your role as leader. If you feel the criticism is justified and that you have made a genuine mistake or handled something badly, acknowledge it. You are not perfect; you will make mistakes from time to time and one of the most constructive things you can do is to acknowledge them, learn from them, then explore what was going on for you in supervision.

If you feel that the criticism is not valid and seems like a destructive attack, it is useful to hold on to the possibility that it is coming from a place of distress in the woman. It may be that some transference feelings from the past have got stirred up and are being projected on to you in the present. It is important to acknowledge what the woman is feeling towards you. If there is time and it seems appropriate you could explore the woman's critical feelings further until you both understand what is going on. For instance, you may have come to represent a bad parent-figure who is perceived as cruel or withholding. If a resolution can't be reached or time doesn't allow any more than an airing and acknowledgment of the criticism, you may decide to leave things like that, acknowledging that the issue is unresolved. If this is not satisfactory, as a very last resort, it could be taken up after the workshop is finished. This is not a desirable solution because it takes the issue out of the group, where it comes from, and breaks the group boundaries, but it may, in an extreme instance, be necessary. This is just the sort of issue to take to supervision.

## Crises

I think a prevalent anxiety at the back of every workshop leader's mind, when faced with a new group of women about whom she knows nothing, is what to do if someone really breaks down in the workshop. Occasionally a woman enrols for a workshop who patently needs much more than the limited help and support that a workshop can offer. If this is obvious even before the workshop starts, you could gently but firmly suggest that the workshop is not appropriate and try to offer an alternative. Sometimes the extent of a woman's distress and inability to cope may only emerge after the group has started. In an extreme case you may have to take some time in the group to deal with the crisis. This will be frustrating and upsetting for the rest of the group but it is a reality that has to be dealt with. The main aim is to contain the situation and try to help the woman to talk about what is happening and what help she would like from you. Find out whether she has any family, friends, a therapist or a GP whom you could contact to ask for help. If you are working with a co-leader, one of you could take the woman out of the room to talk with her and see what is needed while the other leader stays with the group and deals with their feelings about what is happening. In the most extreme situation, if the woman is unable to communicate coherently at all and has completely lost touch with reality, you will have to take more drastic steps. Facilities for women in emotional crises vary enormously from one geographical area to another, and on the whole are insufficient and unsatisfactory. If all other avenues fail, you may suggest to the woman that voluntary admission to the nearest hospital is her only viable alternative.

For your own peace of mind, it is useful to make a list of local facilities, crisis centres, hospitals, sympathetic GPs or psychiatrists, etc. to be used in a real emergency.

I do not want to be alarmist. In 11 years of running workshops at the Centre such drastic steps have never been necessary. The few occasions when a woman has lost control have been dealt with within the workshop. If you have confronted your fantasy of 'the worst possible thing that could happen' and know what you would do in such an eventuality, you will probably feel more confident. When working with women who appear to be very fragile, respect their defences and do not push them. They will usually indicate very clearly what they can and cannot cope with. We all have our defences, and not without reason. I would not push or strongly challenge someone unless I had evidence that they had enough ego-strength to deal with it. Be sensitive to the cues and signals the woman gives out and trust your own intuition. Ultimately you must make your own judgments, bearing in mind that even workshop leaders are human and can make mistakes! Again, I would stress the need for supervision to deal with just such issues as these.

## Planning the Structure and Content of the Workshop

### Creating a structure

Once you have thought about the setting-up of the group and put your topic into context, you can begin to create a structure for the workshop which will enable the group to focus on the topic. You will get some idea of what I mean by structure from the accounts in previous chapters of how a session or day was planned. Having a structure gives you a map and a direction to go in, especially in the beginning when you are running your first workshops. As you become more confident, you will be able to adapt your plan as you go along according to the needs of the group. It is surprising how different each group is.

## Boundaries: space

The aim of the structure is to provide a safe space for women to come together to explore a topic in a therapeutic way. As leader, you have taken on the responsibility for providing this space, within which you are offering the group the use of your therapeutic skills, insight and knowledge. It is an emotional space for each woman to look inside herself, a space notably different from day-to-day social interactions and discussions. The boundary that marks the transition into and out of this space is the beginning and ending of each session and of the whole workshop, all of which have a special psychological significance and arouse different sorts of feelings in different people, both consciously and unconsciously. The room itself provides a physical and symbolic boundary and it is important that people stay in the room during the workshop, if possible, and do not run in and out. If it is a long workshop, have timed breaks for making coffee, eating, smoking, going to the loo, etc.

## Boundaries: time

The timing of the workshop provides another boundary. You will need to decide how long the workshop is going to be. Workshops at the Centre last from two hours in the evening to an eight-hour day at the weekend. Some workshops run for one session, some for 10 weeks, others take place over an intensive weekend. It very much depends on the topic how long you will need. Very painful or difficult topics are probably best given several weeks so that the group can build up safety and trust over a period of time. Different topics arouse different levels of anxiety. When you have decided on a time, it is important to keep to it. Starting late or running over time may engender a feeling in the group of anxiety or lack of safety. The group may feel out of control. Boundaries provide a sense of containment within the group, so that whatever happens in the workshop does not spill over uncontrollably on to the outside. It provides a model for handling difficult, painful or negative feelings, conveying that they can be safely contained and handled, rather than being either overwhelming or denied.

## The content of the workshop

Having decided the length of time and number of sessions of your workshop, you will then need to plan and time the exercises you will use to help the group to focus. You will find lots of examples of workshop structures and plans in this book, as well as specific exercises. Below I describe very briefly how to set up some basic exercises that workshop leaders have consistently used in this book. You will find lots more in *In Our Own Hands* by Sheila Ernst and Lucy Goodison (The Women's Press, London, 1981), along with information about different techniques.

## Beginning a workshop

Most workshop leaders begin their workshop by introducing themselves and then proceeding round the circle, giving each woman a chance to introduce herself to the group and to say why she has come and what she hopes to get from the workshop. You could ask women to say whether they have any special needs that they want the group to be aware of, e.g. a blind woman may need people to say their names when they speak so that she can put names to voices. You may invite women to say whether they have been in a workshop or a therapy group before, whether they are in therapy at the moment and whether they are taking medication. These introductions are the first steps for a group of strangers to get to know one another and for the leader to begin to assess the needs and texture of this particular group. Each group has its own character. It is a time for each woman to establish contact, begin to build trust and find her place in the group.

## Groundrules

Having opened the group, you may want to establish some groundrules. These are in no way meant to be punitive but are to help the group nurture and care for itself. The following are a list of rules or guidelines that we have used:

1   Emphasise the importance of coming on time and attending all sessions so that each woman gets the maximum benefit from the group and doesn't disrupt the work of others. Ask women to let you or a group member know if they cannot avoid being late or absent so that you don't waste time waiting for them and can let the group know what has happened.

2   Emphasise the importance of confidentiality. Each woman is entitled to talk about her own experience of the group outside it but should not reveal what other women have said. This is important for trust and safety.

3    Ask women to try to take responsibility for their own needs in the group, to ask for what they need and not to do anything they feel strongly they don't want to do.

4    Smoking has increasingly become an issue in workshops. I ask women not to smoke in the workshop because it is usually a way of avoiding feelings, as well as being a health hazard. Let women know when there is a break and where they can smoke or let the group decide what it wants to do about smoking.

## Warm-up

Warm-up exercises are very short, simple exercises that can be used at the beginning of a session to break the ice or raise the energy level of the group. They can be fun or silly to relieve tension and create laughter. They can be used to learn names. They should be used to create the appropriate mood for whatever is going to come next. The following are some examples. You can make up many more yourself.

*Exercise 1:* Throw a soft ball or cushion randomly to any woman in the group, saying her name. She then throws it to another woman and says her name, and so on.

*Exercise 2:* Go quickly round the group, each woman saying one word to describe how she is feeling right then.

*Exercise 3:* Play 'Follow the leader'. The woman who is leader makes a sound or gesture that expresses how she's feeling as she moves around the room. The other women follow, imitating her until she touches another woman, who then leads the group with her own sound or gesture.

*Exercise 4:* Do a 'shake out'. Ask women to stand at ease, knees slightly bent, noticing how their bodies feel. Shake out the tension from each part of the body in turn by relaxing and then shaking it vigorously. Start with the foot from the ankle down, then the lower leg from the knee down, and finally the whole leg from the hip down. Start with the left leg and then do the same with the right. Move to the hands. Relax and shake the hand from the wrist down, the forearm from the elbow down, the whole arm from the shoulder, first the left arm and then the right. Then slowly flop forward from the waist down, allowing the head, arms and trunk to swing loosely from the waist. Slowly shake the top half of the body and the head from side to side. Relax a few moments in that position, then very slowly come up, straightening the back from the spine to the shoulders. Finally, lift the neck and head back into the upright position. Notice how your body feels now.

## Going round the circle, or Go-round

This means literally going round the group giving each woman a set amount of time to talk, during which she has the attention of the whole group. When her time is up the leader moves the attention to the next woman. This can be difficult to do if someone gets upset or in touch with very strong feelings. If necessary, you can let the woman know that you will come back to her at the end of the go-round to see if she needs more time. She may just need to know that it's all right for her to carry on crying or to have someone hold her hand, or whatever feels appropriate for her while you carry on round the group. Any problems you have with this as a workshop leader will probably be to do with boundaries. It's okay to be flexible, but if you are too flexible you will run out of time. You must check out what is going on for you: are you having difficulty saying 'No' or stopping? Giving each woman an equal amount of time has the advantage of helping those women who find it difficult to have attention for themselves and those who over-talk. Every woman gets something without having to compete. She must take responsibility for what she does with her time.

A go-round is often useful as an opening exercise, but can be used at different times during a session, e.g. for feedback after an exercise. You will find many examples in these chapters.

## Talking in pairs

This exercise is borrowed from co-counselling. Ask the women to find a partner and sit facing one another. The women then take turns to be the worker and the listener. The woman who is working has the full attention of the listener for a specified amount of time (three, five, 10, 15 minutes). She will talk about whatever comes into her mind on the topic or question the workshop leader has asked her to focus on, noticing the feelings that are aroused in her. She can say what she likes. In the listening role, the woman gives her full attention and eye contact to the woman working. She does not interrupt or ask questions to satisfy her own curiosity or make judgments or comments on what the worker is saying. If she does make any comments, they must only be to prompt the worker or to help her to focus. At the end of the given time the women swop roles and repeat the exercise. Again, this exercise gives women an equal chance to give and receive from one another. Women who feel less comfortable sharing in the larger group have a chance to share in a one-to-one situation.

## Small group work

Women can also be given topics to discuss or tasks to do in small groups of three, four or five. Again, some women feel safer in smaller groups and more women can work at the same time. Allow time for coming back to the large group. Gill uses small groups in Leaving a Relationship and Viqui in the Bioenergetics workshops.

## Guided fantasy, cushion work and role-play

Do not underestimate the intensity of feeling that the following techniques can arouse. Don't use them until you have done some of this sort of work on yourself and have an appreciation of what it feels like. After working in this way, it is important to know how to close the exercise and bring attention back to the present.

*Setting up a guided fantasy*: A guided fantasy is a fantasy journey taken in the imagination with the workshop leader guiding the way. Fantasy work can be useful in getting through to the unconscious or pre-conscious level very quickly, by passing a more conscious and rational level. Used at the beginning of a session, it can draw out a lot of material to be worked on and is an exercise that the whole group can share in. Unlike dreaming, which it resembles, it involves the active use of our powers of visualisation.

We project on to the fantasy our own meaning and qualities, perhaps ones we didn't realise we had. We then work on the projections to reintegrate those aspects back into ourselves. Re-owning these qualities makes us stronger and more whole.

You could start by doing some physical exercise to get people out of their heads, before asking them to sit or lie down in a comfortable position. Spend a little time helping them to relax. Suggest they close their eyes if they feel comfortable doing so.

Before beginning the fantasy, make it very clear that there is no right or wrong way to do this exercise; whatever happens or comes up for each woman during the fantasy is all right. What you are asking them to do is to be aware of their experience *whatever* it is. They may get stuck or go off in another direction to the one you are suggesting.

Whatever happens, let it happen, and be aware. These instructions are important, so give them gently and clearly.

Describe the fantasy journey slowly and clearly to let the fantasy develop and take shape. Allow pauses between your instructions and ask the women to fill in the details of their fantasy, emphasising attention to qualities such as shape, size, colour, smell, texture, mood, feeling, light, etc. At the end of the exercise, allow plenty of time to guide the women back to the present moment and ask them when they are ready to come back into the room and open their eyes.

These exercises are very powerful and you must allow plenty of time for each woman to feedback and explore the feelings, memories and associations, either in pairs or in the whole group. Let each woman find her own meaning in the fantasy: don't judge or interpret. The images and symbols, in fact any part of the fantasy, can then be explored further using other techniques, such as cushion work, role-play, drawing, movement, etc.

Guided fantasy can be used in many ways, as you can see in these chapters. In the Mothers and Daughters and Fathers and Daughters workshops, Tricia and Stef use guided fantasy to go back in time to an earlier age and explore early relationships with our mothers and fathers and then help the women to own qualities they attributed to their mothers or fathers as qualities they have within themselves in the present. In the Lesbian workshop, Pam and Jo use it to explore past and possible future situations, using the fantasy to rehearse a situation, such as coming out as a lesbian, and explore the feelings it arouses. It can also be used to explore blocks by imagining a desired situation and uncovering what it is that you would have to deal with if you got what you wanted or where you wanted to be.

*Cushion work:* Cushion work is borrowed from Gestalt therapy and could, for instance, be used to work on the material or images that come from guided fantasies, drawings or dreams. Once again, these exercises, like the guided fantasy, can be very powerful and must be set up and followed through sensitively and carefully.

The idea is for the woman who is working to have a dialogue with a part of her fantasy, drawing or dream. Take some time to set up the dialogue. Ask the woman to choose a cushion or a chair to represent the thing or person she wants to talk to. Ask her to find one that feels the right size or height (assuming, of course, that there is a choice). Ask her then to put the cushion at a distance that feels right for her and to notice how close or how far away she wants the cushion to be. Then suggest that she put the person or thing that she is visualising in her mind's eye on to the cushion. Ask her to describe in the present what she sees. Invite her to talk to the person or object on the cushion. Allow her time to find what she wants to say. When she has talked from her position, as herself, ask her to reply to herself from the position of the person or object on the cushion. Slowly, allow a dialogue to develop between the two, the woman speaking first as herself, then as the object or person. The theory behind this work is that whatever the cushion represents is an aspect of, or projection of, a part of the woman herself, and in the moving to and fro in the dialogue, she will discover and take back into herself this aspect.

Initially, women may feel embarrassed or silly talking to the cushion, but very quickly it becomes an 'as though' situation, as though the fantasy figure were really on the cushion. The cushion or chair is just a concrete tool to focus the emotional work. It won't get hurt, feel rejected or hit back if you say outrageous or angry things to it. It can't run away either. So it is a safe representation that the woman can feel in control of.

When the woman feels that the dialogue has come to a natural close, ask her to put the cushion away wherever it feels appropriate. She may want to keep the cushion close to her or to put it far away. Then get her attention back into the present. Suggest she make eye contact with the other group members to get back into the room. Tricia gives an example of cushion work in Chapter 1.

*Role-play:* Role-play is the acting out of an imaginary situation. It could be the re-enactment of a scene from the past or an imaginary situation in the future. You could also re-enact a dream or a part of a guided fantasy. Whereas in real life one often only gets one chance at something, by using role-play one can replay a situation in as many different ways as one wants. For instance, a woman could choose a situation from her life that she finds difficult, such as expressing anger to someone close to her or someone she works with. Help her to set the scene and to choose a group member to play each part. She can play herself or ask another group member to play her role while she observes. Ask the rest of the group to pay attention to the interactions and to offer feedback. They may, for instance, point out to the woman that the message she is giving with her body posture or facial expressions contradicts what she is saying verbally, or they might point out that her voice is trailing off to an inaudible whisper when she is really very angry. The woman working can rehearse the scene again in the light of the feedback from the group. The group leader will help her to explore her feelings as she tries out new ways of behaving in this safe environment, before trying it out in the real world if she wishes. Stef uses role-play in the Fathers and Daughters workshop.

## Winding down and ending exercises

As a session draws to an end, you need to give the women a chance to close what has been opened up in the group until the next session, to help them to prepare to leave the group and go back to their day-to-day lives. The following are some examples of ending exercises:

*Exercise 1:* Ask the women to close their eyes and just let their minds scan over the session, thinking of one good thing from the session to take home with them. It could be a feeling, a new thought, a sensation, a gesture, anything they feel good about.

*Exercise 2:* Do some relaxation. For example, make yourself comfortable and take some deep breaths. Relax and go inside. Notice what you are feeling. Notice how your body is feeling, notice your breathing. Just stay with your awareness of yourself for a few minutes. Now open your eyes.

*Exercise 3:* Hold hands in a circle and look around the group, making eye contact with the other women. Notice who you have been with before you each take a step back out of the circle and say goodbye.

## Follow-up

Very often at the end of a workshop the wish is expressed to go on for longer, for one or several more sessions. This wish is very real, but you should think carefully about how to respond to it. The group may ask for a follow-up, but in my experience, follow-ups can be disappointing, with very few people turning up. It's worth considering whether this is a way of avoiding the feelings of sadness and loss about the ending of the group. At the end of each workshop at the Centre we give every member a form to fill in and return to us, giving positive and negative feedback and criticism to help us to evaluate our work. In reading the feedback, almost every one includes a phrase like 'We needed longer', 'Not enough time', 'One extra session would have been better.' I am struck by the constant demand for more and longer, whatever the length of the group. I think this dynamic needs to be grasped in the workshop at the ending, if possible. I think it can be an expression of neediness, as well as a denial of feelings of frustration, disappointment and dissatisfaction. There is an underlying fantasy of a completely satisfying workshop that would make everything all right, or of a workshop that would never end. Bringing out the dissatisfactions and disappointments, as well as the achievements, at the end of the group gives a space for these feelings and fantasies.

As the workshop leader, you may get hooked into this powerful dynamic too, by feeling that you haven't given enough, that you should have given more. It may play into your fantasy of being the perfect mother who takes away all pain and disappointment. You don't want to be the withholding mother who begrudges an extra session. I have always been touched by the powerful bond that can grow among a group of women in such a short space of time, a strong feeling of solidarity, warmth and trust. It *is* sad and painful to lose it when the group finishes, and these feelings need to be acknowledged by the group members and the leader before deciding whether to arrange a follow-up session.

### Where to go next

The ending of the workshop is a time to talk about the future: where do the women want to go next? Some groups are committed to continuing as self-help groups. Some of the workshops at the Centre have carried on in this way, particularly the compulsive-eating groups, which are intentionally set up to follow a self-help model. You may want to offer to be available to the group from time to time to help them if they get into difficulties, or to suggest other resources they could use (see Chapter 13 on Self-help). You can explore other ways of continuing the work that has begun and help the women to draw up a plan of action for themselves.

## Conclusion

Finally, having prepared yourself as far as you can, there is no substitute for jumping in at the deep end and learning from experience, just as the workshop leaders in this book have done. This was only possible with the help of all those women who trusted us enough to allow us to share with them their own experience of being a woman struggling to grow.

# 13
# Leadership and Self-help Groups
Jocelyn Chaplin and Amelie Noack

Issues about leadership come up in all the workshops. We have therefore devoted a whole chapter to the subject. We also include self-help groups in the same chapter, as they raise particular questions about leadership – such as 'Do we need it at all?' and 'What do we mean by leadership?' – that are relevant for all kinds of groups.

Although self-help groups do not, by definition, have *official* leaders, they may have rotating chairs or other forms of leadership. We have been 'leaders' of workshops organised for women interested in self-help groups for over three years at the Women's Therapy Centre, and it is largely out of this experience that the ideas in this chapter have come. We also have experience of other kinds of therapy and consciousness-raising groups.

## Leadership as the 'Hidden Agenda'

In this connection we are talking about leadership in general in all kinds of workshops and groups, not only in ones concerned with self-help.

The feelings that group members have about the leaders are like the hidden agendas of each session. There are often unspoken assumptions about the leaders. We often think that she must be 'totally sorted out'! She is often seen unconsciously (or consciously) as a mother- or father-figure. This may arouse feelings of resentment, especially from women interested in self-help groups who have usually deliberately chosen not to have permanent leaders or parent-figures.

We also have feelings about being leaders. It can be hard to be detached, especially when women do seem to resent our leadership. At other times we feel that we alone are totally responsible for everything that happens in the group, forgetting that it is a two-way process. We sometimes feel that it is all our fault if women drop out or if they don't seem to be getting enough.

After a general movement of rejecting leadership altogether in the 1960s, many women involved in the women's movement are now looking for structures and styles of leadership that reflect our basic anti-hierarchical stand. Hierarchical relations can be seen as vertical – with one person or one side superior and in control of the other. It is not essential for leadership to be hierarchical. But we often get the two concepts of hierarchies and leadership mixed up.

## Hidden hierarchies.

Being anti-hierarchial has become one of the main themes of the women's movement. It affects the way women organise, e.g. at Greenham Common, where decisions are made collectively. It is also expressed in our suspicion of experts who so often try to take control of our lives. We are becoming increasingly aware that almost everything in our society is structured hierarchically. There are the subtle (and not so subtle) class hierarchies that permeate all aspects of our lives, but even among groups of women friends we find ourselves looking up to some women and down on others, because of the way they dress or because of the jargon they use or don't use. When we argue we often catch ourselves using the old hierarchical attitudes of 'one side must win and be on top while the other must lose.' It goes very deep.

After all, we have had thousands of years of hierarchical structures and ways of thinking: e.g. seeing mental work and the *mind* as superior to and needing to control inferior physical or emotional work and the body. This is a powerful unconscious attitude at the heart of Western civilisation. Our education system, for instance, still rewards academic achievement over all other abilities. So when we try consciously to develop cooperative organisation, non-directive learning or self-help groups, these unconsciousness hierarchies of thinking can still interfere with our 'right-on' intentions. In a local consciousness-raising group one woman seemed to have a much clearer feminist ideology than the others. She had read more books. She appeared to know more. The other women, who felt rather confused and inadequate, began treating her as the leader. They looked up to her as the more educated person. But at the same time it was supposed to be a self-help group with no leader, so the other women began to resent her bossing them about, using the hidden hierarchy that had developed. They started dropping out one by one.

## Wanting to be 'fed' but not 'led'

Unconscious feelings are very powerful in self-help groups. These often include our needs for parent-figures or simply for being taken care of. And unless these needs are acknowledged, understood and catered for by the whole group, problems can result. One woman may take on the role of parent all the time. The others expect her to look after them. Eventually she resents this role or starts to become an authoritarian parent, which the others resent. Or if there is no parenting at all, women end up feeling frustrated and uncared for.

In one leaderless self-help group we all sat down in silence for what seemed like hours – it was actually only five minutes. No one wanted to take the lead. Eventually, one woman demanded to know what the agenda was. Another younger woman began to explain patiently, but with rising irritation, that there wasn't an agenda – we had to decide together what we were going to talk about. Most of the time was used in an argument between two strong personalities who wanted the group for very different purposes. One wanted a campaigning group for childcare in the area; the other wanted it for sisterly support and consciousness-raising. Few of the other women got a chance to say what they wanted. After two hours of fruitless argument we emerged feeling angry, frustrated and extremely hungry. Most of us dived into the nearest chip shop and devoured food as though we hadn't eaten for years.

We hadn't wanted traditional leadership with one person telling us what to do, but we *had* wanted to be taken care of, to be nurtured or even, symbolically, to be fed. We didn't want an authoritarian leader, but we did want a mother, or rather some form of shared mothering. We wanted flexibility but also some kind of structure. It seems that these dilemmas are common to many kinds of groups. But it is in self-help groups that they are often most noticeable.

## Self-help Groups

Self-help groups of all kinds are becoming increasingly important in this stage of social change. Group after group of hospital patients, black people, working-class people, women, etc. are questioning models of leadership in which experts or people with 'higher' status tell others what to do (even in as nice a way as possible). Self-help is about taking control of our lives into our own hands. It is about recognising and developing our own abilities and skills and not relying on the professionals all the time.

We recognise that in our society control is generally in the hands of people or groups with more power than ordinary women – power given to them through class, education, colour, professional status or simply gender. In most mixed groups men still tend to assume and be given more power and control than women. But the same differences can arise in women's groups, where, e.g. one woman has a particular higher work status or comes from a higher-class background.

Self-help implies a non-dependence on traditional leadership by people or groups with special status. It rejects the idea of one person or group permanently controlling another. But it can also imply rejection of any kind of leadership at all. One of us became interested in self-help groups at first because she rejected any kind of leadership: 'My therapist told me that I was still rebelling against my father and reacting to all leadership as I reacted to him. I believed that I had a valid political stance . . . I now believe that *both* points of view are true.'

Our personal experiences have more recently led us to feel that within the basic self-help framework some kind of leadership is needed. This does not have to be one person all the time. Leadership can be rotated, with everyone taking turns. Or it can be an agreed leadership style shared by everyone. It doesn't have to fit into the old patterns of hierarchical leadership. However, without any leadership at all groups seem, all too often, to fall into what in the 1960s was called the 'tyranny of structurelessness'. That is, when there are no formal structures the people who are most confident or noisy take over and become like little tyrants. It is often more oppressive than when there are definite structures because the hierarchies are hidden and unacknowledged. Now, in the 1980s, we are much more aware of just how complex relationships in self-help groups actually are. We are beginning to recognise how much unconscious feeling and need there is under the surface, e.g. our needs for safety and nurturing and our desire for structure and boundaries. We need to be mothered and nurtured, but we also need to focus and get on with business. It does not have to be one or the other. We need both 'mothering' and 'fathering' – both being parents, leading, and being children, following.

## Power and leadership

We have found it necessary to distinguish between hierarchical forms of power relationships and the kind of power that comes from consciously attending to our needs for nurturing and focusing. We need to develop forms of leadership that develop the power within everyone. But as women we often find it difficult to recognise the positive aspects of our own power. Issues of power and leadership are always around in groups. But they are often ignored. It can be difficult for women to confront them, for various reasons. We may want to hold on to the belief that because we are sisters there shouldn't be any power struggles. Sometimes we feel safer in stressing our sameness as women rather than our differences. We don't want to separate ourselves from the others. Girls are brought up to feel that if we show our power we won't be liked. We might be labelled bossy. So a powerful woman in a group might deny her role, even if it is pointed out to her, for fear of being labelled aggressive when being assertive. Some of us have never learned to handle power, leadership or even differences and disagreements. So when they arise we sometimes overreact and act in line with ideas of traditional male power.

In this chapter we hope to share some of our experiences of power and leadership, especially in relation to self-help groups. We will describe some models of leadership in groups that we have found useful and show how we have used them in workshops we ran for women interested in self-help groups.

## Contradictions in leading self-help workshops

It is almost a contradiction in terms to lead a self-help workshop. But it is a familiar contradiction. Anyone working in the helping professions, while trying to move away from the traditional hierarchies, is faced with a similar contradiction. It can feel as though we are saying, 'We are all equal but some are more equal than others.' We might try to resolve the contradiction by saying instead, 'We are all equal and everyone has valuable skills and experiences to offer, but today I am responsible (being paid, say) for organising this particular event or group.' That is perhaps more honest than pretending that we are all the same. Even in a self-help group it seems to work better if there is a rotating leadership in which each week one or two women take on a leading role. If everyone is seen as equally responsible, it often results in no one actually being responsible for the structures, e.g. time-keeping. But the question then arises as to how we actually perform this role. We don't want to be authoritarian, but how can we lead? How can we be powerful without it being the kind of power that dominates or oppresses? How can we use our power to bring out the powerfulness in everyone rather than simply enhance our own power?

Power doesn't have to be a dirty word. It can mean the power to *act*, the power to *express* ourselves, the power to *be*.

## A Personal History

*Jocelyn*: My first role in therapy/educational groups was that of the rebel. I was usually the one who disagreed with the leader, questioned her role, even secretly thought I could do it better and sometimes suggested that we could perfectly well do without her, thank you! Inside me was, and still is, a deep rage against the white, male, middle-class-dominated hierarchies of society. Some of this anger comes from my personal childhood experience in a particularly patriarchal family. But it also came from what I rationally perceived as injustice, even as a child growing up in Africa. It was a rage that often left me feeling powerless. Sometimes it would come out against people who were not actually being oppressive. Any hierarchical situation, even between women, would anger me, and often still does. But I found it easier to attack clearly defined, especially male, authority-figures than women in groups whose 'status' was less clearly defined or hidden altogether.

Over the years I realised that I was often giving these authority-figures a lot of my *own* power. I put them on pedestals, saying to myself, '*they* are *very powerful* and I am *totally powerless.*' This realisation did not change my awareness of real economic, social and political power hierarchies, but it helped me to get in touch with some of my own powerfulness. And I didn't need to spend so much of my energy inappropriately rebelling against individual authority-figures. I began to put some energy into helping create alternative ways of working in groups. This led me to an interest in self-help.

In 1981 a group of us living in West London came together through an ad in *Spare Rib* to form a self-help therapy group. We were mostly in some kind of therapy training or were social workers with therapy experience, so we were all fairly similar in terms of experience. This helped enormously in creating an atmosphere of equality. Even so, we still had our problems of unequal commitment to the group, lateness, etc. However, the connections we made then still exist. And I am still working with most of those women. Three of us, who now work in private therapy practice, meet as a 'peer supervision' group. We are able to talk about the hidden hierarchies that arise and try to explore any envious or competitive feelings that develop.

I also began co-leading self-help therapy days at the Women's Therapy Centre. The first one was on a warm summer's day. There were only six women and we had a lot of fun together, painting, dancing in the garden and working with two women's personal problems. But already it was clear that some women looked on us as the 'experts' who would 'teach' them skills. And we didn't want that role. Each time we held a day of self-help, this request for us to teach or be therapists became more pronounced. Sometimes, especially in big groups of 20-plus, it didn't feel safe enough. The women wanted structure, wanted to be fed. They seemed to be asking for parenting, for the safety and feeding of mother-figures and for the focused structuring of father-figures. We responded to these generally unspoken requests by giving more structure to the days.

Yet much of this time I felt uncomfortable. There was a glaring contradiction in being a leader in a self-help group session. Many of the women who came had chosen to be in self-help groups because they rejected the hierarchical relationships of experts, professionals, even of leaders or authority-figures who were trying not to be oppressive. Sometimes they rebelled against us even while at the same time asking for more 'feeding'. The contradictions were in them too, Yet there is no change or movement without contradiction. And eventually it was through the tension of the contradiction that Amelie and I began to create a new approach.

## A Personal History in Self-help

*Amelie:* It is now ten years since a woman friend of mine took me with her one evening to meet other women to set up a self-help therapy group. I didn't know at the time what self-help therapy meant, and my main feeling at meeting other women was fear. I enjoyed the gentleness and kindness with which we treated each other that evening. And when my friend dropped out of the group a couple of weeks later, I stayed.

We had themes for each session, and there was no shortage of material. We were actually more concerned with how much we were able to cope with in the group. Those of us who were in therapy or had some kind of experience of it didn't feel so threatened by some of the very traumatic experiences we shared and listened to. Others got so involved that they couldn't go to sleep after the group. It was a long process of defining our personal limits and what we felt we were able to carry for each other.

I was very shy, frightened of not being accepted by the others, and also had some fear of being affected or influenced by them, so I remained in the background for quite a while. I slowly learned to assert myself in the group. That also had some effect on my life: I decided to leave a long-term relationship I didn't feel happy in.

I was a member of the group for three years, then we decided to finish. Some of us met for another year to discuss women's issues more theoretically. Besides that, a very close and warm friendship between some of us had been developed: two women from this group are still my best friends today.

There was a gap in my experience of self-help after this that lasted a couple of years. I was training and working in different study groups. Here I felt much more confident from the beginning. I actually saw myself here in a leader's role very often. I was also running my first group, leading movement sessions for a working-class women's group. The days of self-help seemed to be over.

Having moved from Germany to England, I found myself in a foreign country looking around for contact. This time I initiated a self-help group myself. In this group I was the only woman working in the therapeutic field. Somehow it felt very difficult from the beginning. After a while I realised that this group was a non-starter, since the personal differences in experience were too great. It made me aware that a self-help therapy group works best when members share a roughly equal level of experience concerning insight and self-awareness. Differences in age or life-experience in a group can be a challenge, but will definitely create a lot of difficulties.

Around the same time I got the offer to be the self-help therapy contact person for the Women's Therapy Centre and to run workshops for self-help therapy groups. Now I saw that there was another side to self-help as well. It was not only a matter of being in a group; there was also the side of teaching other people how to work in self-help groups.

My first Self-help Skill-sharing Day, a one-day workshop for women who were or wanted to be in self-help groups, I ran jointly with Jocelyn, who had done it before. We had planned the day roughly, according to what we thought might come up, like issues of power and leadership. We also were prepared to adjust the structure to the needs of the women coming. During the day we became aware that the group was trying to split the two of us, to polarise us into the good and the bad mother. We were puzzled, and the 'bad mother' felt hurt. We talked about our observations and feelings during the break and decided what to do about it. We decided to reverse the roles the group wanted us to play in the second part of the workshop, to counter-balance the dynamic of the morning session.

I liked working with Jocelyn. She seemed to be noticing things in the group which I wasn't aware of. I also felt it was a relief to work with a co-leader: the stress of feeling responsible was shared. We decided to run the next workshop together and were very dis-appointed when it was cancelled. We used the time to discuss our understanding of self-help, and the idea came up to write something about it. We began discussing our ideas and they gradually developed into a model, which is described later in this chapter.

Coming back one day from a self-help workshop I had run outside London, I was sitting in the train and contemplating the day. Thinking about what had happened and what I had observed, an idea began to take form. I had been working with two kinds of subgroup that day. One of them functioned very well and the women were eager for help and advice about how to go deeper into their work. The other didn't work well at all and had actually finished meeting some months before; these women had wanted to look at their difficulties at not being able to get started. I felt it had been a great gift for me to watch the dynamics of these two groups surfacing during the day. It gave me an insight into the different needs at different stages of self-help, and the patterns which are active behind the scenes.

I was already aware that there is a great need for security in any therapeutic situation. This particular day showed me clearly that this need is connected with what we later described as the need for mothering. The experience of the two groups seemed to me to express good and bad mothering. Mothering, the basic fundamental pattern for trust and security, is always around in situations where people want to support and help each other. It seemed only logical that it would be even more obvious and emphasised in women-only groups.

Nevertheless, when the next day of self-help came, we planned it like the one before. This time, using mainly the same exercises as before, we didn't experience a good/bad mother split. But something else happened: we realised that we were again performing different roles. One of us was acting as mother, offering care, support and nourishment. The other was acting as father, providing theory, focus and confrontation. We were quite surprised, laughing at ourselves for acting in this way, and accepted this experience gratefully as another stepping-stone to more understanding concerning self-help. In addition to mother, father was obviously also active in self-help, which at the time seemed to be a revelation.

This particular group was much more aggressive. Members

demanded our attention in a quite dismissive way, and we felt a lot of competitiveness from a particular woman who obviously had a lot of problems with authority and leadership. How do you lead somebody, we asked ourselves, who doesn't want to be led? It feels so paradoxical anyway to *lead* self-help groups; how do you do it properly? We tried to be there and very wide awake this day, leading without being dominating, using our authority as leaders without being authoritarian. Responding to the need of this particular workshop, we gained further insight into the part that 'father-energy' plays in self-help groups.

At this stage the idea for the workshop leader book was put forward. Jocelyn and I felt very excited; this was the opportunity we had been waiting for. We began to put our ideas on to paper. The process of writing a first, very short outline felt incredibly valuable. Our ideas began to take form. Out of our experience we began to develop a new model for self-help groups.

The next one-day workshop at the Centre we planned according to this model. And on that day we felt for the first time that the group was supportive towards us, keen to listen and to take in what we could offer. This may well have been because of the particular individuals, but we also believe that it was an outcome of our discussions and our own need to understand and define the process of self-help. In further workshops the new structure again worked so well to everybody's benefit, that our model seems to have been vindicated.

## A Model for the Group Process in Self-help Therapy

This model describes the group process in four main stages: (1) getting started, (2) the stage of the mother, (3) the stage of the father, and (4) the stage of interrelatedness.

It took us a long time to agree on names for the stages. The names we have chosen are an attempt to describe the main characteristics and qualities of each stage, and we are aware that they could be misunderstood, so we would like to say a bit more about them.

The names and the descriptions which follow are not concerned with the experience of the personal mother or father of an individual, which might have been similar or very different indeed. Quite the contrary; the stages try to describe general and basic principles of human experience necessary for development in a symbolic language. The words mother and father are therefore always used here in a symbolic way.

The four stages provide different kinds of experience and each stage has its own specific values. For the sake of clarity, we like to point out that a group can experience a fluctuation of stages, oscillating from one to the other. However, we see this model as a guide for the journey of a group and the different stages that we feel a healthy group seems to need to go through to integrate these values.

To make it easier to find your way through our model we used the following structure. First, a *general description* for each stage. Then *guidelines* which can act like a thread to hold on to for the group moving through a particular stage. Then we mention the specific *problems* of the respective stages, and finally suggest *exercises* and techniques to help in dealing with these problems.

Some of the exercises are described in the workshop account which follows. Other exercises are given in other sections of this book. A detailed description for the rest of the exercises and also for the techniques that we mention can be found in *In Our Own Hands* by Sheila Ernst and Lucy Goodison (The Woman's Press, London 1981), which is very helpful for self-help therapy groups and offers a lot of useful ideas and information. You will also find that some of the techniques we mention have to be adapted to your particular group's needs.

## 1 Getting Started

We see the first stage of getting started very much as a preparatory stage, especially concerned with practical issues.

Somebody needs to have the idea and the will to initiate a self-help group. All the details of purpose, structure, number of people, etc. have to be worked out. You will need patience to find the right people to be in the group. One person at least must be willing to take some kind of responsibility for asking other people whether they are interested in joining and for organising a meeting. Initiative and enthusiasm are very important at this stage.

The *guidelines* for this stage are centred around practical arrangements concerning premises, times and days to meet, and structure. The reason why people come to a particular group is very much connected with its objectives or aims and what people need or want from the group. Therefore, the basic *problems* will concern issues of structure, commitment and defining a common aim. If the group can't agree on basic common rules, it can't get started, like one group which was described by its members as follows: 'We had no idea how to start off. There were always problems with people not turning up. We didn't have a common aim.' Therefore, the *exercises* connected with Stage 1 are concerned with practical issues.

The most useful thing to do is to talk and try to clarify the situation. The questions which arise and need to be looked at are: 'Do you want to be in this group and why?', 'Is there anything you don't like about the group/structure?', 'Do you really want to meet on an equal basis to work with each other?' Have go-rounds on these questions. Listening to other people's ideas and thoughts often helps to make up your own mind. And it will help to ask the group members to make a commitment to the group – or to ask them to leave, even if it is difficult. Otherwise you will be stuck already in Stage 1.

## 2 The stage of the mother

Once the group has got started it is important to develop a feeling of trust and security in it. These are qualities of the good mother. The good mother is able to provide a safe environment for the group and the individuals in it. This is one of the most important preconditions for any group, since personal growth can only take place in a safe space. This emotional containment is like mothering to the child. Without this mothering a person or a group cannot begin to unfold and grow on a psychological level. In practical terms this means providing a place for every meeting and a fixed time for it in a regular rhythm. Every single member should be given some attention at the beginning of each session in a go-round. Then everyone can feel they are being well taken care of, can relax and begin to develop trust. It is the task of the whole group to provide this secure space, but it might be a good exercise to have a rota system for the chairwoman, so that each member is able to experience being responsible for it.

How long the focus has to be on providing good mother-energy depends very much on the group: anything from one month to one year or even longer. When a group succeeds in providing a secure feeling for every member in it, a lot has been achieved. In one group a woman said: 'The group is my mother . . . I never had a mother and in the group I can feel for the first time in my life what "mother" means.'

The *guidelines* for this stage are basically concerned with emotional conditions like acceptance, understanding, mutual support and nurturing. This stage is about grounding, which means a feeling of groundedness in reality and a basic trust in life, and this is developed through a secure and reliable link with mother, the earth and reality. Thus confidentiality is essential. It may need some conscious effort to achieve this whole atmosphere of security.

If the group is not able to create good mother-energy, it will not be able to function. People will start to complain about *problems* of lack of safety. Individuals will feel too vulnerable to be able to open up, as in one group, whose members said: 'It felt so superficial, we didn't know how to deal with personal issues and had problems to express what one wants ...' Another woman in the same group also said: 'We were just beginning to build a safe place to open up', indicating that the first stage had been completed; but the second stage had just been touched on, although this particular group had been meeting for six months. The responsibility for the group not functioning can very easily be projected on to one particular member. If no one in the group is aware of what is happening, this woman may become the scapegoat for the whole group. In this stage it means she is taking on the role of the bad mother, acting unconsciously for everybody else. This situation may require asking somebody from outside to help the group to find a way out of being stuck.

We want to stress again that the good mother is not the one who allows everything and is just 'nice' to everybody. The good mother is the one who sets limits in order to provide secure boundaries for growth. She sets 'dos' and don'ts', not to suppress but to protect and avoid hurt and damage. If these limits are not set, anger, frustration and disappointment will be the only outcome.

There are a lot of *exercises* which are helpful in attaining and exploring the stage of the mother. Any introductory exercise, like going round in a circle on a particular theme or question, works well. Trust exercises are very often connected with touch, like being held by one other person or being handed around by the whole group in a circle. Physical grounding exercises can help people to get a sense of trusting their bodies and the ground they are standing on.

We believe that good mother-energy is essential to build trust and security. But we also find that a lot of women's groups get stuck in this stage. It feels so nice and warm that we may lose a sense of our individuality. We notice that mothering then changes into smothering, and protection into overprotectiveness.

We have to make a conscious choice to take us further in the process; the decision to get on our own feet, to use our own personal sense of groundedness for the new experience of walking, like the child who leaves mother to explore the world. It is the step from Stage 2 to Stage 3. It means leaving mother and approaching father.

## 3 The stage of the father

As we explained before, our model is a description of group processes on a symbolic level. It involves basic patterns of experience which we have found active in the different stages of a group. The stage of the father is therefore not primarily about our personal fathers. It describes fathering as a symbolic notion in the same way as the stage of the mother describes symbolic mothering. Nevertheless just as the second stage may have involved talking about our mothers, so the third stage may evoke a lot of talking about our fathers.

The stage of the father first of all means leaving mother. So this stage is about separating and separation; it means standing on our own two feet. We now feel safe enough to confront another person without losing friendship. We want honest and direct feedback in the group.

Approaching father also means realising that he is different from mother; he is also different from us. Does that lead to the conclusion that we are different from each other? Confronting father goes along with the recognition of boundaries between people, between the individuals in the group. Having learned in the mother-stage that we are equal, we can now begin to be different. We can begin to become real individuals, which means to be ourselves and to be able to use our personal strength and power.

The *guidelines* are therefore connected with the development of strength and power. We have to analyse, to differentiate and to separate. Analysing a situation enables us to focus on one aspect at a time, so that we gain greater clarity. Father is much more abstract than mother – always remembering that we are here referring to different ways of being, not men or women. He is not so much concerned with feeling but with thinking, trying to define the meaning and give an understanding of things. Sorting things out and placing them in some kind of order helps to direct energy effectively towards a goal. Good father-energy helps you to find your goals and to approach them through the ability to focus.

The women in one group, who felt very loving towards each other, experienced the *problems* which can occur at the beginning of this stage. They complained about 'No clarity, what is going on in the group?', 'Not using one's power', 'Not dealing with power issues' and about the fact that 'No personal differences are allowed.' This group had completed the stage of the mother. It was approaching father but, we felt, was afraid to make the connection.

*Exercises* which help to reach the stage of the father and to explore it are life-planning exercises, concerned with: 'What do I want?' and

'How do I achieve it?' Assertion exercises and Gestalt techniques can also be used here very well. The model of transactional analysis is helpful too, since it looks at the different aspects, like the child, the parent and the adult, all active in one person.

The fear we felt in the group mentioned above turned out to be connected with not being able to use personal power properly and appropriately. This is one of the dangers of the third stage. Domination, arrogance and hierarchical power relationships are aspects of negatively used father-energy. Since we all know these days that father is not at all always right, the 'you can't teach me anything' or 'knowing it all' attitude should make you suspicious. (So please, treat this model with the same caution; it's just a model, not the truth!)

In the same way as mothering can become smothering, fathering can become patronising and turn into oppression. Not being flexible about leadership roles or cutting oneself off from one's own feelings or from other people can lead to being stuck in this stage.

## 4 The stage of interrelatedness

It takes time to realise what the stage of interrelatedness actually means. It's neither only fatherly nor only motherly any more, but includes all the qualities of the other stages. Each individual in the group is able to lead *and* be led, something a self-help therapy group is aiming for from the beginning. It means overall shared leadership between equals. Decisions about what the group will do, and how, are made by everyone. It can also be decided who will lead and when. A leadership role can be played more comfortably by each member, in their own style at different times. But no one is a permanent leader.

The group works as a whole but the different strengths and skills of individual members are recognised and used. Each person develops a sense of her own self and her own value but still feels part of the group.

The so-called motherly and fatherly modes are also consciously used alternately, and the group can choose to move from one mode to the other according to the needs of the situation. It means being supportive and receptive one moment, and assertive and directive the next. It also involves everyone noticing, from their conscious 'centre', which mode seems to be needed and when it feels right to switch from one to the other. This conscious movement from mothering to fathering and back again sometimes needs to be directed by whoever is acting as leader for the day.

The *guidelines* in this stage are to acknowledge our strengths as much as our weaknesses; to allow ourselves both to lead and to be led;

to let ourselves feel our dependency needs as well as our need for independence.

This may all sound paradoxical at first. How can we be *both* dependent *and* independent, leaders *and* followers? But these opposites are actually just two sides of the same coin. And we can be both at different times, through alternation, through the process of constant rhythmic change.

The theory of the stage of interrelatedness may sound ideal, but putting it into practice can create *problems*. When we are in a group, most of us tend to give up parts of our identity. For example, in a feminist consciousness-raising group we might not want to admit deep love for a husband. Being a loving wife may not be felt to be an acceptable identity for that group. Or we may be so aware of our individuality, of being different, that we don't seem to fit in to the group. We feel like the odd one out. An understanding of our separateness and difference as well as of our togetherness and sameness can help solve this problem. In a group one of us co-led recently a woman said she felt different because she thought she was the only one who was single. We told her how we appreciated her courage in admitting this feeling and stressed how we all feel different in one way or another. Then we explored the reality of the group in which there were actually a number of other single women. It also brought the group even closer together as other members talked about their feelings of difference.

Another difficulty is that when we are in a particular mood, e.g. feeling angry, we forget that there is always the opposite too. We might feel one day that we totally hate a particular woman in our group, forgetting that at other times we have felt love for her. When we rebel against the woman leading on a particular day, we forget how we felt when we were in a leadership role. It doesn't mean that we should stop having strong feelings, but that a part of us can at the same time watch ourselves having the feelings and know that the opposite is also there, i.e. 'Aha! Now I am feeling angry with Sue but I know that yesterday I loved her.'

Dependence and independence are two other opposites that we often find hard to cope with. In one group a woman was talking about the need to leave her husband. 'I want to be independent and live *my* life. So I can't go on being married.' Another woman in the group then asked her, 'Why not?' The question shocked her at first. She had assumed that marriage meant total dependence and leaving it meant total independence. Eventually she realised that it was possible to stay in the marriage and have *both* independence *and* dependence. As it had been a good marriage, this realisation came as a great relief.

There are many *exercises* that help us gain this new perspective of the interrelatedness of opposites. A very popular introductory listening-exercise involves the opposites of listening and being listened to in a structured way. The group is asked to divide into pairs and then for five minutes or so one person talks about themselves, perhaps on a given topic, and the other person just listens. Sometimes the listener is asked to encourage the speaker with questions, but she is there essentially to focus on the other person. Then they are asked to change around: the speaker becomes the listener and the listener becomes the speaker. By separating out the opposites (listening and speaking) both people are able to experience them – but at different times.

Another exercise we use is for experiencing the opposites of giving and receiving. One partner is asked to give something precious to the other without speaking. The other person has to receive it without speaking. The roles are then swopped. Some people find it easier to give than to receive, others find it harder to give. Exercises involving both sides of ourselves help us to get more in touch with the side that we have difficulty in expressing. Many of these exercises are described in *In Our Own Hands*.

Another way of exploring opposites is to divide the room into two halves. One side is described as the powerful or independent side and the other as the powerless or dependent side. Group members are asked to place themselves in whatever part of the room they feel comfortable in right now and to explore their feelings there. Then they are asked to move to the opposite side of the room. They then express t eir feelings about being in the less comfortable side. Doing this exercise often shows a group that a woman labelled as the powerful, leader type also has a dependent, vulnerable side that can be a surprise even to the individual concerned. Conversely a timid member of a group may reveal that she has a very powerful side. One woman who first sat on the powerless side ended up standing on a table on the other side pretending to boss everyone about. By getting into opposites, women can learn to accept both sides and then realise that they can move from one to the other when they choose. It tends to result in our being less extreme in our opposites, e.g. our fears about being too bossy decrease when we have a chance to act them out in a game, and next time we can feel more comfortable about being powerful without going to the extreme of authoritarianism.

Many group rituals are actually ways of bringing the opposites closer together. For example, in most groups everyone has a turn to get some individual attention as she talks about herself. There is often an opening session in which we go round the circle giving everyone a turn to say how she feels or to introduce herself. This is a way of acknowledging the differences between us. At the same time, it creates a good group feeling and a safe atmosphere. A ritual closing circle does the opposite. It starts by emphasising the group identity and our togetherness before we separate and leave to go our different ways.

There are many different styles of therapy that involve bringing opposites closer together or creating a dialogue between them. These styles are described in greater depth in *In Our Own Hands*. They include Gestalt therapy, which gets us acting out opposite sides of ourselves and 'talking to ourselves'; transactional analysis, which uses the idea that we have an internal parent *and* an internal child; and psychosynthesis, which helps us through fantasy, etc. to get to know our hidden opposites.

## Conclusions

In describing a group's development, we have also touched on one of the biggest collective problems of our time – the polarisation of masculine and feminine values in purely male and female roles that is becoming less and less useful in modern society. Father-energy, directed outwards towards the world assertively, analysing it through separating out ideas and concepts, doesn't need to be cut off from mother-energy, which is more receptive, weaves connections between ideas and uses feeling values more. Both can enrich each other. They belong to and can be used by both men and woman equally.

In groups we need both the nurturing and safety of mother-values and the focusing and assertiveness of father-values. Problems always arise if only one side is used. Most of us have had the experience of attending meetings where no one was introduced, no common objectives were shared and where there was no sense of safety and belonging. Such groups lack mothering. They get on with father business, without first attending to our needs for mothering. And then at the next meeting the leaders wonder why no one has turned up. Mothering is not a waste of time, as people often think. It is vital for a group's very existence.

On the other hand, a group can be smothered with mothering. One self-help therapy group felt so comfortable chatting with cups of tea each week that they forgot to get down to work and explore themselves more deeply. They forgot the task. They needed some fathering collectively or from one of the women. This involves focusing, being clear about the tasks and the priorities. It may even mean leaving some things out, e.g. choosing one person's interest over another. It requires decision-making. This group was stuck in the mother-stage and needed to move on to the father-stage.

But this stage too can have its dangers if taken to extremes. We believe that present society has taken the father-stage too far and now there is a vital need for mother-values to be brought back into the forefront of our lives. Without mother-values this stage creates intense competition and power struggles. It often results in splitting, with one side cutting themselves off completely from the other. It happens both on a small scale in groups and on an international scale when nations or even the whole world are stuck in the father-stage.

Moving on to interrelatedness requires thinking in terms of 'both/and' rather than 'either/or'. Finding ways of working through our often contradictory needs for mothering *and* fathering in small groups may help us in wider contexts. As one woman put it to us recently: 'What I want from a group is unconditional acceptance, but I couldn't· be in a group with women who were not feminists.' We explored with her the possibility of getting the acceptance within her group, which we relate symbolically to mothering, but also making a decision to separate herself from others who don't share her ideology. Separating and acknowledging differences we associate symbolically with fathering. We need mothering *and* fathering, but at different times.

We also need to be parents and children at different times, to lead and to follow, to depend and to be depended upon. Everyone has the potential for both sides, but we often lack the confidence or skill for the parenting, leading side to be expressed. But these can be developed.

Still, we all have different leadership styles. Some find mothering easier and others fathering. As in everything else, it is important to get to know our own opposite style of leadership as well as the one we feel most comfortable with.

And also every group is different. A group can be in one of the stages, in all four or any two or three at a given time. The problems only come when a group is stuck in Stage 1, 2 or 3.

We hope that this simplified model will help groups to clarify some of their hidden conflicts and to manage them. We also hope that it will help in looking at the hidden agenda of leadership, that it may enable us to replace authoritarian relationships with genuine interrelatedness.

# Workshop Description: Introduction to Self-help

This workshop, Introduction to Self-help, is designed for newcomers in the field of self-help concerned with problems of the early stages of working together and also gives an idea of the process a group will have to go through. The follow-up workshop that we do, Problem-solving for Self-help Groups, is designed for groups who have already been working together for some time and want to look at particular issues in depth. Here we offer a broader variety of techniques and teach how to reach more unconscious issues. This also includes looking at and working on problems between individuals in the group, which can create a lot of difficulties.

The one-day workshop normally begins with a lot of action: registering, getting cushions down into the playhall to sit on and making cups of tea. We finally start, when everybody has found her place, with a go-round in a big circle, introducing this also as a basic technique. Every woman is asked to say her name and to answer three questions: 'Are you a member of a self-help group?', 'Why did you choose this workshop?' and 'What do you expect?'

Some women either came to the group as their first contact with any kind of therapy or are actually looking for a self-help group. Other women may have had individual therapy and be looking for a different way of working on themselves. What they say about themselves normally comes across as quite matter-of-fact and unemotional, unlike the atmosphere in other workshops. Self-help is concerned with working with each other on an equal basis, where everybody is offering their very personal skills and faculties, so the women normally come across as quite confident. Women for whom this day is the first experience of the therapy world may often be much less nervous in this workshop than they would if they were coming to one not labelled self-help.

We introduce at this time the general idea of self-help, pointing out the different kinds of self-help groups which exist in the medical field (e.g. for cancer and tranquilliser patients) or in the area of general health (e.g. menopause or compulsive-eating groups). And we describe our understanding of self-help therapy groups as, on the one hand, being part of the field of mental health and, on the other, having derived from the women's movement.

We also distinguish between self-help therapy and professional psychotherapy; this is very important information, since it defines the limits of self-help therapy. Self-help is very often seen as a substitute for psychotherapy, but we would like to say it is not. It is a very valuable tool and produces a lot of positive results as long as we avoid seeing it as a solution to all our problems. In one group a woman said she was so disappointed by the fact that her therapist wasn't able to treat her and be friends with her at the same time that she left therapy; now she wanted to be in a self-help therapy group, since here she could get both. That's throwing out the baby with the bath water. We believe professional therapy has its own value. It could have helped this particular woman to look at her negative feelings, like disappointment, and come to terms with them.

We also indicate problems that arise from issues of power and leadership that are normally kept hidden in self-help groups. So we put into the open that, e.g. the woman who prepared the tea for the whole group at the beginning had taken a kind of leadership in a very subtle way.

We then introduce very briefly our model with its four stages as a means of facilitating the process of the self-help group and avoiding the major pitfalls.

Now we suggest an exercise for exploring the first stage of the model, getting started. The big group, which comprises up to 20 women, is split up in small groups of four or five, and the groups are to discuss: what is necessary to get started? After 10 to 15 minutes we ask the small groups to choose a spokeswoman to present the outcome of their discussion to the big group. We give only two minutes for each report. Everybody listens, the main issues are written down on a board and are discussed. A lot of practical issues come up: you need to know who is going to be in the group; you have to find like-minded people; the number of people has to be defined; a place must be found to meet; objectives of the group must be discussed, and so on. Some women report from their own experience: 'You need enthusiasm to start a group', 'You have to talk with each other about why you want the group and what you want it for.'

We relate what has been said to the first stage of getting started, point out problems which haven't been mentioned and ways of working on them. Then we talk about the process of electing the spokeswoman: 'Why was a particular woman chosen?', 'How did it happen?' We also discuss what it feels like to move from the big main group into a smaller one.

Now we ask the women to get up for another exercise. Standing up, half of the women close their eyes. All of the other women will lead one 'blind' woman through the room in a caring way. Then we swop, giving each person five to 10 minutes to explore being led as well as leading. Afterwards we share in the big group how everybody felt about it. The women realise how difficult it can be to trust – or how easy. The need to feel safe and secure is related to the ability to give up control and let yourself be led. It can be very enjoyable to feel the care, acceptance and understanding of the leading partner, but it can make you feel vulnerable too. When leading, the women say, you have to be aware and take the responsibility to do it properly, so that the other woman can feel comfortable.

We relate all these feelings to the second stage of the group process, the stage of the mother, writing the issues which come up on a second list on the board. We talk about resentment or pleasure when being led or leading, and point out the general connection between trust and issues of leadership.

That's the morning's work and we then break for lunch.

The afternoon begins with a relaxation exercise. We find that relaxation is a very valuable tool to develop trust and a sense of safety. It emphasises contact with the ground and the earth, both symbols for mother.

Normally it takes some effort to get the group going again after lunch, especially after the relaxation. We do stretching and yawning exercises to help people wake up and feel refreshed, and we point out that just as it needed a conscious effort to get going again after lunch, so it needs a conscious effort to go on to the next stage.

We introduce an exercise which supports this process. Every woman is to write down individually what she wants from self-help. We ask for physical, emotional and mental wants separately and give five minutes for each category. We encourage people to write down whatever comes up. Then each woman has to choose three priorities from the whole list. The three issues can be from one category only. After this we split up in pairs for a co-counselling exercise. We explain co-counselling, introducing it as a very valuable technique for self-help, and give each person five minutes to talk. Each woman is to talk about her three most important wants.

Afterwards we share information about what the women want from self-help in the big group. Again we write things on the board, arranging what is said according to the categories of physical, emotional and mental wants. It helps to differentiate and to focus on one aspect at a time; this analysing we explain as an attribute of father-energy.

Then we have a little game: we go back into the same pairs as before. Without talking, first one and then the other woman has to decide what the most important want of her partner might have been. Then she has to present this to her partner in a symbolic way, using gestures and movement only. Normally there is a lot of laughter during this exercise. How do you express yourself without words? This 'giving and taking' we see as an *exercise* for Stage 4, the stage of interrelatedness. The laughter seems to indicate that this stage can include quite a bit of fun.

After a short tea-break we talk about the giving and taking in small groups of four or five women. Now everyone says what it is they were giving and puts into words what they felt about it. We have noticed that there is always a lively atmosphere at this time.

We come back together as a whole group to conclude the day with a go-round in the big circle. There is time for questions and feedback, and we ask everybody for criticism, regrets and appreciations concerning the workshop.

We finish the group with some words of encouragement, indicating that self-help is something which goes on outside this workshop. Afterwards there is always some time for people to exchange addresses or to get information about existing groups that we know of.

Looking back on the workshops we have run on self-help, we would like to say that each of them has given us a lot of valuable experience and information. It is from this information that we have been able to describe the process of self-help, as we understand it, and we would like to thank everybody who contributed to it.

# Resources

What if you have read through this book and want to attend a workshop, or indeed obtain training and help to run such workshops yourself? If you live within reach of London, the Women's Therapy Centre itself is a good place to start. You can obtain a list of current workshops by sending a large stamped addressed envelope to:

The Women's Therapy Centre
6 Manor Gardens
London N7 6LA

The workshop programme also includes details of training courses available at the Centre, including a workshop leader's training course.

Elsewhere the route may be less obvious and we have tried to offer guidance on how to track down the kind of help you need. There are books that various contributors to this volume have found useful and a selection of these is given at the end of this chapter. The first section is about finding a workshop, or other kinds of counselling or therapy. After that we make some suggestions for women seeking training for running workshops themselves.

## Finding a Workshop

As far as we know there are few places outside London offering a regular workshop programme; we hope that this book will encourage the setting-up of many more. However, women's therapy centres are gradually appearing in other parts of the country. If you live within reach, the nearest one would be a good place to enquire about workshops.

Womankind
Bristol Settlement
43 Ducie Road
Barton Hill
Bristol BS5 OAX
(A women and mental health self-help project)

Women's Counselling and Therapy Service
Oxford Chambers
Oxford Place
Leeds LS1 3AX

Birmingham Women's Counselling and Therapy Centre
43 Ladywood Middleway
Birmingham B16 8HA

Manchester Feminist Therapists Group
27 Victoria Park Road
Whalley Range
Manchester 16

Southampton Women's Centre
1a Bevois Hill
Portswood
Southampton SO2 OSJ

Taking account of the difficulty, referred to in the introduction, that many people from different cultural backgrounds have in finding therapy, Nafsiyat has been set up as an intercultural therapy centre in London, offering free counselling and therapy services to women and men.

Nafsiyat
278 Seven Sisters Road
London N4 2HY

Your local Women's Centre will have information about resources for women in your area and may also be open to arranging a workshop – perhaps by employing a workshop leader on a sessional basis – if they receive a request. The address of your nearest women's centre should be available from your local library or social services department. Alternatively,

A Woman's Place
Hungerford House
Victoria Embankment
London WC2N 6PA

is a good source of information, as are the back pages of magazines like *Spare Rib*.

Another possibility is to join up with other women with an interest in the same topic and set up a workshop together. You may be able find a leader or facilitator locally. You could try the social services department, or the clinical psychology department in your local hospital, as many social workers and psychologists have some training and interest in groupwork and are glad to be approached – though unless you are a group of their clients, you will have to discuss payment for what would be private work. The worker will know whether under the terms of her particular contract she is allowed to take on such work outside her paid hours.

If there is no one you feel confident of approaching locally, try the Women's Therapy Centre. They may know of someone reasonably local, or may be able to suggest a London workshop leader for your topic. Of course, it will add to your costs if you have to pay travel expenses as well as a fee.

## Other Kinds of Help

We are aware that there are many women who feel isolated with their difficulties and unsure about how to find the help they need. We also know that resources for therapy and counselling are very unevenly distributed, and that you have a better chance of finding a professional to talk to in or near London. Unfortunately, it is particularly non-fee-paying or low-cost facilities that are in short supply. Unless you can find sympathetic help on the NHS or from the social services, you will almost certainly have to pay. However, don't despair. Your GP should know what help is available on the NHS locally, and may also be well informed as to alternative resources (which may, however, cost money). If for some reason you find her/him difficult to approach, try asking for guidance from the social services department. Different councils have different priorities, so that unless you are a troubled parent you may find that the social services department cannot offer you a counselling relationship with a social worker. However, a social worker can be a valuable source of help and support in finding what you need elsewhere.

If you live in an area with a branch of the Family Welfare Association, you could ask whether they would offer you help as an individual. If you have children under 16 and your problems involve them too, your GP may suggest a Child Guidance Clinic. These are also known in some areas as Child and Family Centres. Family Service Units have branches throughout the country and may be able to help you. The Westminster Pastoral Foundation has affiliated branches in various parts of the country.

The central addresses for these organisations are as follows:

Family Service Units
201 Old Marylebone Road
London NW1 5QP

Family Welfare Association
501–505 Kingsland Road
London E8 4AU

Westminster Pastoral Foundation
23 Kensington Square
London W8 5HQ

Open Door
Association for Agoraphobics
446 Pensby Road
Heswall
Wirrell
Cheshire L61 9PQ

Some voluntary organisations in some areas offer support in groups or on a one-to-one basis. You can, if you wish, approach them directly.

If you feel your difficulties are connected with a bereavement, CRUSE is the group to approach. The address of the central office is:

CRUSE House
126 Sheen Road
Richmond
Surrey TW9 1UR

For people who have already had contact with psychiatric services,

MIND (National Association for Mental Health)
22 Harley Street
London WIN 2ED

has some local support groups.

The Phobics Society have information on national self-help groups for agoraphobics:

The Phobics Society
4 Cheltenham Road
Chorlton-cum-Hardy
Manchester M21 1QN

The Samaritans, with branches all around the country, offer a crisis telephone service, as do Rape Crisis Centres. The latter usually offer various forms of support, practical as well as emotional, for women who have been raped.

London Gay Switchboard has a 24-hour, 365-day telephone service on 01-837 7324 (covers the UK).

If you can wait and are able to consider paying for therapy, either the local Marriage Guidance Council or your nearest Child Guidance Clinic (also known as Child and Family Centres in some areas) may be able to help you find a counsellor or therapist by suggesting workers known to them whom you could approach.

If all else fails, the following directory should be available at your local library:

British Association of Counselling
Resources Directory
37a Sheep Street
Rugby
Warwickshire CV21 3BX

And there are two useful books on finding therapy: Lindsay Knight, *Talking to a Stranger, A Consumer's Guide to Therapy,* Fontana, London, 1986, and Windy Dryden, *Individual Therapy in Britain*, Harper & Row, London, 1984.

## Self-help

Partly because of the difficulty of finding appropriate help where and when they need it, some women may want to consider setting up a self-help group. To start, you could read Chapter 13 in this book, along with Sheila Ernst and Lucy Goodison, *In Our Own Hands*, The Women's Press, London, 1981, a valuable practical guide to self-help therapy.

The Women's Therapy Centre workshop programme also offers workshops in London for women wanting to set up self-help groups. Send a large stamped addressed envelope to: The Women's Therapy Centre (see p. 233 for address).

## Training Resources

The workshop leaders represented in this book come from a wide range of backgrounds, with numerous strands of training and experience. A professional qualification in one of the careers that are likely to include counselling and groupwork among the necessary skills – social work, psychology, psychiatric nursing – is helpful but not essential. Whatever your working background, there are training courses that will consider you on the basis of your personal strengths and interests.

The following organisations have lists or directories of training courses:

British Association of Counselling
Training Directory
37a Sheep Street
Rugby
Warwickshire CV21 3BX

MIND (National Association for Mental Health)
22 Harley Street
London WIN 2ED

CCETSW
(Central Council for Education and Training in Social Work)
Derbyshire House
St Chad's St
London WC1H 8AD

Institute of Group Analysis
1 Daleham Gardens
London NW3 5BY

Tavistock Clinic (Training Office)
120 Belsize Lane
London NW3 5BA

Irish Association for Counselling
The Mews, Eblana Avenue,
Dun Laoghaire, Co-Dublin
(information only)

The following reference books contain useful information: Francesca Inskipp, *Counselling: The Trainer's Handbook*, published by National Extension College, 18 Brooklands Avenue, Cambridge CB2 2HN, 1986, and Windy Dryden, *Individual Therapy in Britain*, Harper & Row, 1984.

## Useful Reading

More booksellers these days are becoming aware of women's interest in their own lives, and it is always worth enquiring whether your local bookshop has, or would order, the titles suggested.

New books are published almost daily, and you may wish to write to publishers for their women's booklist. Four publishers that concentrate specifically on women's issues are The Women's Press, Virago, Pandora and Sheba and Attic Press.

The Women's Press
34 Great Sutton Street
London EC1V ODX

Attic Press
44 East Essex Street
Dublin 2

Virago
Centro House
20–23 Mandela Street
London NW1 0HQ

Pandora
15–17 Broadwick Street
London W1V 1FP

Sheba Feminist Publishers
10a Bradbury Street
London N16 8JN

A comprehensive range of books of interest to women can be obtained from:

Silver Moon
68 Charing Cross Road
London WC2H 0BB

Sisterwrite
190 Upper Street
London N1 1RQ

Two big London bookshops will also supply books by mail:

Compendium
234 Camden High Street
London NW1 8QT

Karnac Books
118 Finchley Road
London NW3 5HJ

Compendium is an excellent source of imported and British books on psychology, sociology and women's issues in general. They are strong on the 'humanistic' psychology side. Karnac Books has a comprehensive range of books on psychology, etc. from a psychoanalytic perspective and also a selection of books from a humanistic viewpoint. Both shops also sell good-quality novels, poetry, etc.

If your local library does not have the book you want in stock, you can always ask them to buy or borrow it from a library elsewhere.


## Background Reading

Erik H. Erikson, *Childhood and Society*, Penguin, Harmondsworth, 1963.
A much-loved book that explores patterns of child-rearing and relates them to adult personality features.

Neville Symington, *The Analytic Experience: Lectures from the Tavistock*, Free Association Books, London, 1986.
A very helpful and readable historical and theoretical survey of psychoanalysis.

D. W. Winnicott, *The Child, the Family and the Outside World*, Penguin, Harmondsworth, 1964.
A famous paediatrician and psychoanalyst, Winnicott's book is based on radio talks for mothers and gives a valuable informal guide to object-relations theory.

## Women's Psychology

Jean Baker Miller, *Toward a New Psychology of Women*, Penguin, Harmondsworth, 1976.

Nancy Chodorow, *The Reproduction of Mothering, Psychoanalysis and the Sociology of Gender,* University of California Press, Berkeley, Calif., 1978.

Luise Eichenbaum and Susie Orbach, *Understanding Women*, Penguin, Harmondsworth, 1983.

Sheila Ernst and Marie Maguire, *Living with the Sphinx*, The Women's Press, London, 1987.

Nancy Friday, *My Mother, Myself*, Fontana, London, 1979.

Marilyn Lawrence, *Fed Up and Hungry*, The Women's Press, 1987.

Juliet Mitchell, *Psychoanalysis and Feminism*, Penguin, Harmondsworth, 1975.

Robert Stoller, *Sex and Gender: The Development of Masculinity and Femininity*, vol 1., Maresfield Library, H. Karnac, London, 1984.

## Relationships

Sue Cartledge and Joanna Ryan (eds), *Sex and Love*, The Women's Press, 1983.

Anja Meulenbelt, *For Ourselves*, Sheba, London, 1981.

Alice Miller, *The Drama of the Gifted Child*, Faber & Faber, London, 1983.

— *For Your Own Good*, Virago, London, 1983.

— *Thou Shalt Not Be Aware*, Pluto, London, 1985.

David Scharf, *The Sexual Relationship, An Object Relations View of Sex and the Family*, Routledge & Kegan Paul, London, 1982. A book about sexual therapy, mainly directed at professionals in the field but accessible to the general reader.

## Outer World

Bell Hooks, *Ain't I a Woman,* Pluto, 1983.

Audre Lorde, *Sister Outsider*, Crossing Press, New York, 1984.

Various black re-evaluation counsellors, *Black Re-emergence*, 1, 2, and 3, published by Rational Island, P.O. Box 2081, Main Office Stn, Seattle, Washington 98111, USA, 1982.

Various students at South London College and The Book Place, *So This is England*, Peckham Book Publishing Project, London, 1984.

Claire Weekes, *Agoraphobia*, Angus & Robertson, London, 1984.

Alice Walker, *In Search of Our Mothers' Gardens*, The Women's Press, London, 1984.

## Inner World

George Brown and Tirril Harris, *The Social Origins of Depression*, Tavistock Publications, London, 1978.

P. Ferruci, *What We May Be*, Tavistock Press, London, 1982.

Dorothy Row, *Depression*, Routledge & Kegan Paul, London, 1983

## Bodywork

Arthur Balaskas, *Bodylife*, Sidgwick & Jackson, London, 1977.

David Bodella (ed.), *In the Wake of Reich*, Coverture Ltd, 1976.

Leon Chaitow, *Relaxation and Meditation Techniques*, Thorsons, Wellingborough, 1984.

Ken Dychtwald, *Bodymind*, Pantheon Books, 1977.

The Federation of Feminist Women's Health Centers, *How to Stay Out of the Gynaecologist's Office*, Peace Press Inc., USA 1981
— *A New View of Woman's Body*, Simon & Schuster, New York, 1981.

Bruno Hans Geba, *Breathe Away Your Tension*, Random House Inc., New York, 1973.

Richard Jackson, *Massage Therapy*, Biddles Ltd., 1977.

Alexander Lowen, *Bioenergetics*, Penguin, Harmondsworth, 1975.

Allan Pease, *Body Language*, Sheldon Press, London, 1981.

Marianne Wex, *Lets Take Back Our Space*, Frauenliteratur Verlag, Frankfurt, Germany, 1984.

## Running Groups

Wilfred Bion, *Experiences in Groups*, Tavistock Press, London, 1961.

Anne Dickson, *A Woman in Your Own Right*, Quartet Books, London, 1982.

Sheila Ernst and Lucy Goodison, *In Our Own Hands*, The Women's Press, London, 1981.

Francesca Inskipp, *Counselling: The Trainer's Handbook*, published by National Extension College, 18 Brooklands Avenue, Cambridge CB2 2HN, 1986.

Frederick S. Perls, *Gestalt Therapy Verbatim*, Real People Press, ?1969.

Anne Kent Rush, *Getting Clear*, Random House Inc., New York, 1979.

John O. Stevens, *Awareness*, Bantam Books, London, 1973.

# Notes on Contributors

**Tricia Bickerton**, 40, a Londoner, trained as an actress and teacher at the New College of Speech and Drama and worked in education and the theatre for many years. She became involved in the Women's Movement and subsequently trained as an analytic psychotherapist. Now in private practice, she lives in Hackney with her partner and 12-year-old son. She has led a number of groups at the Women's Therapy Centre and contributed a chapter entitled 'Women Alone' to *Sex and Love* (The Womens Press, 1983).

**Jocelyn Chaplin** grew up in West Africa and was educated at Achimota School (Ghana) and Durham University. She now lives in Shepherds Bush, London.

She trained in counselling at the Westminster Pastoral Foundation in London, and now has a private practice as a counsellor and teaches psychology and social anthropology. At present she is especially interested in exploring the 'female principle' of interconnected opposites and rhythm, and its application to social and psychological change in the world today. She has written a book on this theme called *Feminist Counselling in Action* (Sage, 1988); she also paints and is developing ways of expressing the 'female principle' in 'goddess' imagery.

**Vin Gomez** is 38, and lives in London with her partner, daughter and son. After switching from music to social sciences at Cambridge University, she took up community work with children and families in North Kensington. As a result, she set up a small educational centre for local children. Since the birth of her own children she and her partner have been struggling with sharing childcare, paid work and training. She has trained in traditional and humanistic psychotherapy with the Minster Centre, and in analytic psychotherapy with the Association for Psychotherapy within the NHS. Apart from her private practice, she is involved in training and group work in the areas of integrating different perspectives, women's psychology, depression, and parenting.

**Janet Hibbert**, mother of Junior, aged seven, was born and still lives in Clapham, South London. She was educated at Kingsdale Secondary School. She has trained with Redwood Women's Training Association, is a Re-evaluation Co-counsellor and also holds an Intermediate Training Management Diploma. She is currently working as a Senior Training Officer for a North London Borough and is trying to live her life well.

**Inge Hudson** was born in Berlin in 1939. She went to live in Australia at the age of ten and studied psychology at the University of Sydney. She spent four years living and working in New Zealand. She has lived in England since 1965, where she completed her training as a Clinical Psychologist in Cambridge. She is currently working as a Clinical Psychologist within the NHS in West Essex, she has a particular interest in psychotherapy, the psychology of groups and systems and in the connection between personal, social and political issues.

**Birgitta Johansson** was born in Sweden in 1945. She trained as a body therapist and psychotherapist in Copenhagen, Denmark. She has lived in North London since 1981 and has run numerous workshops and seminars at the Women's Therapy Centre, including bodywork, workshops for lesbians, and assertiveness training. The major part of her work is as an individual therapist in private practice. Her special areas of interest are eating problems and assertiveness training.

**Gill Martin** is 44 and grew up in Yorkshire. She has lived in London for 21 years, originally working as a community worker in Stepney and Islington. For the last seven years she has practised as a psychotherapist. She is also currently doing research work into disability for the NHS. She trained at the Minster Centre in analytic and humanistic psychotherapy and has also had some basic training in psychosynthesis and family therapy. She is about to move to

York where she will continue her work as a psychotherapist. She has married for the second time and has two daughters and a stepson.

**Gabriela Muller** is an artist and an art psychotherapist working in a therapeutic community; she also lectures at City University. She was born and went to school in Mannheim, Germany and later continued her education in Gambia and in England. She now lives in North London with her 15-year-old son. She has contributed to *Women's Work: Two Years in the Life of a Women Artists Group* (Women's Work, 1985) and *Glancing Fires* (ed. Lesley Saunders, The Women's Press, 1987).

**Amelie Noack** was born in Lubeck in Germany and lived in Berlin until 1982, when she moved to London. She is a psychologist and psychotherapist in private practice. She also runs therapy and training groups for the Westminster Pastoral Foundation and the Women's Therapy Centre. She is currently training as a Jungian analyst.

**Steph Pixner** was born in London in 1945. She was educated at Leeds University and the London School of Economics. She still lives in London, where in addition to running groups and workshops she has a private practice.

**Viqui Rosenberg** was born in Buenos Aires, Argentina, in 1945 and came to England in 1968. After working as a drama teacher and qualifying as a social worker she trained in Reichian therapy and has led bioenergetic workshops at the Women's Therapy Centre, the Institute for the Development of Human Potential, the Minster Centre and other centres. She has a private practice as a psychoanalytic psychotherapist in London.

**Joanna Ryan,** born 1942, lives in London and works as a psychotherapist at Open Door in Haringey, and privately. With Sue Cartledge she co-edited *Sex and Love* (The Women's Press, 1982) and with Frank Thomas has written *The Politics of Mental Handicap* (Free Association Books, 1987).

**Pam Trevithick** was born in Lancashire in 1947 and now lives in Bristol with Jill Brown and their two children, Tom and Bridget. She has been actively involved in the Women's Liberation Movement since 1972 and currently works as a development worker for Womankind, a self-help project concerned with women and mental health. She is also a singer/songwriter.

**Dorann van Heeswyk** was born in Georgetown, Guyana, and emigrated to England with her family when she was 13 years old. She lives in London, has two children, is married and works as a freelance trainer. She teaches re-evaluation co-counselling.

# Index